2 95/TBG

The Sociology of Survival
SOCIAL PROBLEMS OF GROWTH

D1569238

THE DORSEY SERIES IN SOCIOLOGY

Editor   ROBIN M. WILLIAMS, JR.   *Cornell University*

The sociology of survival

SOCIAL PROBLEMS OF GROWTH

CHARLES H. ANDERSON

1976

The Dorsey Press Homewood, Illinois 60430
Irwin-Dorsey International Arundel, Sussex BN18 9AB
Irwin-Dorsey Limited Georgetown, Ontario L7G 4B3

First Printing, March 1976

ISBN 0-256-01752-2
Library of Congress Catalog Card No. 75–43162
Printed in the United States of America

TO MY
MOTHER

Preface

No course on the sociology of survival has, so far as I am aware, yet been introduced in any academic curriculum. Yet, it is a subject that must be studied if we are to succeed in making our way in today's world. Its several components, if taught at all, are incorporated into a variety of departments, including sociology, economics, biology, agriculture, food science, and perhaps others. In this textbook, several topics including political economy, economics, technology, work and leisure, ecology, resources, population, food, and social change are included. They are brought together so that a better understanding of their interrelationships can be achieved.

Today's greatest social problem is survival and this volume is an attempt, using the above integrated approach, to study the problems of growth and survival. Each component of the complex is critical to the study of the sociology of survival, to the study of the forces at work undermining the viability of human society and its natural support systems. At the same time that survivalism seeks an understanding of the challenges confronting human existence and the quality of that existence, it also points the way towards viability. This is done not in terms of detailed blueprints or an operator's manual, but in relatively broad theoretical terms. The actual practice of survivalism, of social viability, is the challenge which all of us as individuals must work out in ongoing group contexts. The problems to be met are described herein.

The concept of growth is central to this study. Growth, the expansion of economy and technology, underlies the necessity of a sociology of survival and the development of a survivalist society. The nature and problems of growth can only be clarified upon careful study of the entire book, so there is little to be gained by entering here into a comprehensive definition of growth. It should be noted, however, that growth has economic and technological references unless otherwise indicated, as in connection with population growth. Both types of growth, economic and population, pose survival challenges, but the two should be held analytically separate at all times.

The organization of the book is as follows: An Introduction makes a preliminary overview of problems to be treated in the text. Chapters 1, 2, and 3 take up the issue of growth directly—its significance, meaning, and necessity. Chapter 4 examines the internal problems of the growth economy and details the system's own logical difficulties. Technology and economy are placed in juxtaposition in Chapter 5, while Chapter 6 reviews the relationship of work to growth. Chapter 7 discusses the impact of growth upon the environment. The linkages between growth and resources are the subject of Chapter 8, with energy as the main focus. Population growth occupies attention in Chapter 9, while the closely related problem of food supply is dealt with in Chapter 10. Chapters 11 and 12 analyze the relationship of socialism and underdevelopment to growth. The brief final chapter explores the question of alternative directions for a survivalist society.

The Sociology of Survival is intended to provide the framework for an understanding of the dangers and threats posed by growth to the existence of human and biological life and to the quality of that life. The details of that framework must be filled in by the individual within his or her particular life situation. Survivalism is far too large a problem today, and growing larger day by day, for any single survivalist to provide anything more than a general portrait of the challenges at hand. Its scope extends from economy to population and from environment to food; the field is immensely diverse in between. The challenge to the reader only begins with the study of this book. The larger challenge begins when the reader recognizes survivalism as a real issue and decides to orient thought and action—and society—on its behalf.

I would like to thank Jeffry Royle Gibson for a thoroughly done critique and review of the manuscript. Thanks are also due to Robin Williams and Don Shamblin for helpful criticisms and suggestions.

Spearfish, South Dakota   CHARLES H. ANDERSON
February 1976

Contents

1

The dangers of growth

The problem stated

The past ten years have not been at all like what most people had anticipated. Seven years of war. Four years of serious inflation. No gains in real income over an eight-year period and a 10 percent decline in real purchasing power of earnings between 1972 and 1975. Individual net financial worth declines of 35 percent since 1967, setting average financial well-being back to only 10 percent higher than it was at the end of World War II. Recent official unemployment rates at post-Depression highs of 8.5 percent and unofficial rates much higher. An entire presidential administration forced out of office for corruption and scandal. Two devaluations of the dollar and growing instability in the world monetary system. The flow of over $80 billion annually to a few Arab governments. The comprehension of limits to conventional energy supplies and an energy crisis. Dwindling, exhaustible resources critical to production. The threat of ecological catastrophes. The elimination of long standing American grain surpluses, famines, and the shrinkage of world food reserves to less than one month's supply. The insolvency of the world's financial center, New York City. It is thus understandable how a recent poll could find that only 17 percent of Americans favor the present economic system and 41 percent want *major* changes.[1]

---

[1] *Wall Street Journal*, Friday, August 22, 1975, p. 1.

These are only a few of the highlights of the past decade which would have seemed highly unlikely to most observers ten years ago. Yet the makings of all of these events have been in the mill for much longer than this, just as the makings of tomorrow's events are in the mill today. The globe's exploding population has been among the few critical developments which was well plotted in advance, though there were scattered understandings of many of the others such as the food shortfalls and growing economic instabilities. The point is that we must make a much greater effort to decipher the future from the present and make every effort to circumvent the dangers and threats which current trends portend.

The number of other problems which cannot be easily phrased in a sentence are numerous. They have all combined to produce a steady lowering in the quality of life for the large majority of Americans as well as for a great many other peoples around the world. As much as possible, many of these regressing circumstances will be examined during the course of the book. Suffice it to remark here that the optimism of unlimited progress of the early 60s has drastically faded in the mid-70s. The good life has largely eluded so many people who thought it was within their grasp only a decade ago, while so many starting out today have little room for optimism about their futures. Pensioners' savings are being systematically wiped out. Careers are being disrupted in mid-term by unemployment. The prospect of home ownership for young couples becomes more of a dream than before. The college graduate starts out, if at all, at a job level much lower than had been anticipated when college plans were being mapped out in high school. Women's incomes have gained nothing on men's after years of "women's liberation." Young working people have less purchasing power than did those ten years ago. Blacks *have* made a 24 percent gain relative to whites, but during a time when whites were standing still or treading backwards.

These hard economic conditions are only the surface of the stagnation. Many qualitative declines have occurred during the same time. Environmental degradation and pollution have detracted from and interfered greatly with life enjoyment and general livability. Population pressures have placed restrictions and limitations on freedom of movement and recreational accessibility. The volume of motorized traffic is literally consuming urban areas. The quality of durable goods has declined. Food products contain more and more chemicals and poisons of unknown long-term impact, while their nutritional content and natural taste qualities have been markedly reduced. The rich take more luxurious vacations, while the wage workers skimp or stay home. Entering college students find it increasingly difficult to pass standard exams in math and English.

All of the time the quality of life has been eroding, the economy has been getting bigger and bigger and technology has been getting more and more sophisticated. Should not economic and technological growth lead to a better life? The answer this study gives to this central question is no, at least not within the requisites of capitalism at its present stage of development. On the contrary, economic and technological growth have been the prime forces in the deterioration of life quality, except for those affluent who measure life quality by the size of their investments. More growth can only exacerbate the problems such growth purportedly is designed to correct. This is growth within the guidelines of capitalism, and not growth based directly on existing human needs and desires. Such growth, growth in quantity and quality of mass housing, medicine, education, transportation, work milieu, leisure time, consumer product safety, environmental preservation and improvement, public civility and safety, recreational facilities, and much more, is what we might call social growth based upon economic development. It is growth with a specific human content and purpose, not growth for its own sake and for the sake of those with stakes in the preservation of the existing growth system. Social growth is also growth of social equality, participatory democracy, cultural productivity, and personal development. It is the growth of trust and confidence in one's social surroundings and society.

In reading this book it should be kept in mind that growth has different implications for societies at different levels of economic development. Underdeveloped societies require growth in concrete economic and technological ways which advanced societies do not. The latter have become growth societies per se and as a result have become overdeveloped societies. Also, by growth society is meant not only those advanced economies operating on explicit capitalist principles, but any economy which places quantitative growth above social growth as a matter of policy. Thus, a state-planned economy could also be a growth society, and we shall regard the Soviet Union and other advanced economies patterned after it as approximating growth societies. We say *approximating* a growth society, for as we shall point out, the state-planned economy is not bound to the same principles of growth as a privately incorporated capitalist one. It has greater latitude to abandon growth as a principle and switch over to an entirely social purpose in development. The paragon of the growth society is the United States, although the entire capitalist world is subsumed under the rubric of growth society. Finally, a stationary-state society shall be regarded as a society without economic growth per se as a way of life, but rather promoting stability in economic affairs and development in social and cultural ones. The stationary-state society has considerable affinity, though not identity, to a socialist or social growth society. The relationship between growth and socialism receives extended consideration in Chapter 11 as well as on briefer occasions elsewhere in the book. All these distinctions receive considerable attention in the text and have been noted here for only preliminary definitional purposes.

Unless otherwise specified, the term growth refers to economic and technological growth within the capitalist system or state-planned system dedicated to such quantitative growth as an overriding policy principle. Population growth is always indicated as such and is not necessarily a component of the growth society, although up to now it has been. Population growth is actually more rapid and problematic in the underdeveloped societies of the world. The underdeveloped societies have to a large extent been taken into the orbit of the advanced growth societies and have become an important part of growth plans for these societies. The underdeveloped societies could hardly be termed growth societies themselves, although in some ways countries such as Brazil, South Korea, and Taiwan display many of the same characteristics of the mature growth systems. However, as we shall argue, these and other Third World (Asia, Africa, and Latin America) countries, with the exception of those which have experienced nationalist-socialist revolutions like China, Vietnam, and Cuba, will in all likelihood fail to make the transition to full growth societies and will remain as underdeveloped societies. Underdevelopment has a specific content and meaning which shall be discussed in Chapter 12.

With this condensed initiation to the problems of growth and survival, we turn directly to an analysis of the nature and impact of growth.

Threats to survival

In its full scope, this book is concerned with the survival of humanity. It is equally concerned with the quality of that survival. The stakes involved in this crisis of survival are in the extreme sense nothing less than the physical continuation of human beings on this planet. The possibility of an end to human life, or at least a large segment of it, is difficult to conceive. Yet Homo sapiens has no special guarantee of survival. Quite to the contrary, the species may be highly vulnerable to various environmental catastrophes, or even genetic or viral threats, engendered by its own inept actions or by natural processes in reaction to such human interventions.

In the less than ultimate sense, the survival stakes for advanced societies are a decline and regression of the human condition, even to levels of living which seem quite unthinkable today. For the world's poor, the stakes concern the worsening of an already desperate existence. A central contention of this book is that, for the large majority of the globe's people, including those in the developed countries, decline is already well underway. The extent of deterioration or danger is not even known and may announce itself in terms of quite unanticipated breakdowns and disasters. To some extent, however, the decline is both known and acknowledged, albeit to an extent insufficient to generate the required social changes. Unfortunately, one of the major weaknesses of humanity is the failure to exercise the necessary foresight to change before the costs of change become extremely high or before the possibility of constructive change is completely removed. Yet human beings are endowed with the crucial capacity to think and act purposively and in advance of dangers. The presently emerging crisis of survival puts to serious test the human capacity for collective rational action.

The crisis of survival is not a single or unitary one. The challenge to survival extends from the ultimate environmental threat to all or part of earthly life to less severe but nevertheless marked declines and regressive changes in the manner in which life itself is lived. The challenge to survival encompasses a complex of dynamically interacting factors which include the environment, economic production, science and technology, resources and energy, population and food, conflict and war, the human mind, and above all human social and political organization. For example, the rapid developments occurring within science and technology and the increasing scale of economic growth are far from being an unmixed blessing. With increasing regularity we learn of the real and potential dangers accruing to human life as a result of expanding technological and economic impacts upon the natural world. Such knowledge of danger is but the tip of the iceberg which lurks out of range of present understanding. By the time the threats of large scale technological intervention and economic growth upon the natural world become more fully known, it may well be too late to reverse a fatal decline of the human habitat, or at least large portions of that habitat. Technology is moving with blinding speed and with scant attention to biological and environmental impacts. Greatly magnifying the technological impact is extensive economic growth and resource consumption. On another front, world nuclear holocaust is at any time but minutes away, and with the proliferation of nuclear power the danger constantly grows. The press of burgeoning global population also threatens to greatly reverse the fortunes of humanity. The environment, and in particular the land, may be overtaxed in the support of the additional billions of people making demands upon it.

While the present study addresses itself in various degrees to all of these factors, it considers social and political organization as the most crucial link in survival. The capacity to successfully respond to the survival challenges hinges to a large extent upon the form of social organization which people are working within. More precisely, it is the manner in which social organization interacts with the other challenges to survival which shall determine the outcome of the human experiment. Another argument of this book is that advanced capitalism as a form of social organization is incompatible with human viability upon the earth. A new social order must be created which has the capacity to live in technological and economic harmony with nature.

The chief reason why capitalism is incompatible with survival is that as an economic system it possesses a built-in growth drive. The internal logic of capitalism has always been and shall remain to be growth. Growth is not a matter of choice to capitalism; it is a matter of life and death. Growth within capitalism is first and foremost the growth of capital, of profit-producing wealth. Such economic growth both fuels and is fueled by technological growth and development. This is technological growth which has as its primary purpose that of preserving and expanding profit. The consequences of profit-minded technological growth are rapidly approaching disastrous proportions, but little can be done to deter such developments so long as technology must serve the vital survival needs of growth within capitalism. An end to economic growth in capitalism means the eventual end of this system; but the continued growth of capitalism means the end of the environmental milieu within which it functions. We shall elaborate upon the growth mechanisms within capitalism in Chapters 3 and 4.

It is important to distinguish here between capitalism and industrialism. Capitalism preceded industrialization by over a century. The capitalist drive for profit and expansion provided strong impetus for technological revolution, and this drive has persisted as the fundamental force behind technological change throughout the capitalist world. Even after enormous increases in productive power, capitalism cannot cease pushing industrial development further and further. Technological change is crucial to economic growth, and growth is necessary to capitalist survival. Stagnating capitalism is a doomed system, and everything must be directed toward restoring growth, including industrial and technological innovation and change, regardless of need or impact.

By the same token, industrialization and technological development can take place outside the confines of capitalist social and economic logic. Growth of productive powers can be oriented directly toward people's needs and the needs of the natural world. Western society's precedent of technology in the service of capital growth is not an unalterable one. The Soviet Union has followed the precedent rather closely, whereas China has chosen an alternative road in which political and cultural ends dictate heavily the kinds of industrial and technological forms developed. The latter point suggests that socialism, but not as currently practiced in the Soviet Union, is the kind of new social order which must be created if humanity is to survive. The nature of socialism, as a cooperative and rational society, shall be discussed in Chapter 11. Suffice it to stress here that, while socialism has economic growth on the agenda as well, it is growth consciously and democratically directed to the needs of all the people instead of to capital and economic growth per se. More importantly, socialism in its higher stages need not entertain economic growth at all, as is the case with capitalism. Socialism may become a "stationary-state" society from an economic standpoint. A socialist society can eventually turn from building up a material existence to that of social, cultural, and spiritual cultivation. It may become a growth society in the individual and human sense, rather than being a growth society based upon economic expansion after the fashion of capitalism. By so doing, socialism can come to terms with the challenges to survival facing capitalism and those underdeveloped societies now enmeshed in the world capitalist system. ("System" is here used very generally insofar as world capitalism is not so much an integrated socioeconomic order as it is a congeries of precariously articulated, often warring, disparate national and corporate entities.)

The threats to survival take on different dimensions in different situations. Advanced capitalism is besieged by superfluous economic growth and resource consumption which threatens to engulf it; underdeveloped countries face surplus population and food deficit. Both advanced and underdeveloped countries are confronted with mounting environmental problems and technological distortion. International and national inequalities of wealth and power threaten to undermine the entire sociopolitical foundations of world capitalism. Wherever possible throughout our discussion, we shall distinguish the special relevance of the particular survival challenges. In the end, however, *all* challenges are relevant to *all* parts of the world, for all challenges apply in some degree to every region of the globe, if not by dint of local origin then of overflow from elsewhere. This may be most readily grasped through environmental pollution, but technology, resources, food, population, economy, and inequality also apply.

The challenge to survival, whatever the scope and application, should take on greater clarity and definition as this study progresses. To write of a sociology of survival does not mean our society is destined to destroy itself, even though it could if present trends are not sharply altered.[2] Survivalism stresses the danger inherent in existing economic, technological, environmental, resource, population, and agricultural conditions. But it also points toward the kind of social reconstruction required to surmount the survival challenges. While we shall variously touch upon the nature of such required changes during the course of our descriptive and critical discussions, we shall reserve a more detailed elaboration until the final chapters.

The necessity of achieving an end to economic growth and the realization of a balanced economic system is taken as self-evident in a finite world, though we shall take steps to substantiate this necessity. The necessity of turning technology toward human need rather than toward more economic growth is also clear. That the environment must be carefully preserved rather than carelessly destroyed requires no great logic or documentation, though we take pains to demonstrate why this is so. Resources cannot be increasingly consumed and yet last

---

[2] Emile Benoit, "A Survivalist Manifesto," *Society*, March–April 1975, p. 16.

as a means of survival in the future. Population growth cannot continue without greatly increasing the pressures of humanity upon scarce resources and upon the environment. And we recognize the urgency of increasing food production in an era of malnutrition and starvation. What must be done in these areas is not hard to envision. The difficulty arises in connection with the kind of social order which will permit the attainment of positive ends. Neither this book nor any combination of books can be expected to delineate such a society. We shall attempt to draw some broad guidelines in our discussions of socialism.

However, socialism is by definition a system of democratic change, not to be outlined in advance by intellectuals. Karl Marx, the person most commonly associated with the concept of socialism as propounded in this book, himself had very little to say about the nature of the future society. What is more evident is the decline of the existing order and arrangement of things, and it is important that we come to an understanding of how and why this decline is taking place. Problems must be described and understood before they can be permanently solved. And solution, a socialist solution, is the work of everyone. The nature of socialism as an idea can be set forth in broad terms; the terms themselves must be filled in by the people struggling for survival and the genuine social growth which lies beyond. In effect, a sociology of survival is to a large extent both a critique of the present growth system and an inquiry into the nature and prospects of a socially and environmentally rational society.

Survival literature

The concern over the direction of contemporary events, and the prospects for the survival of humanity in part or in total which these events imply, has been expressed by a variety of scholars. One of the modern period's most influential economic philosophers, Robert Heilbroner, argues that "the outlook for man is painful, difficult, perhaps desperate, and the hope that can be held out for his future prospect seems to be very slim indeed."[3] He writes of "a deterioration of things, even an impending catastrophe of fearful dimensions." At bottom, the

---

[3] Robert L. Heilbroner, *An Inquiry Into The Human Prospect* (New York: W. W. Norton & Company, Inc., 1974), pp. 22, 13.

survival threats as Heilbroner sees them involve passing the thresholds of global toleration in population, war, environment, and technology and science. Heilbroner's concern is as much if not more with the capacity of human society to *respond* to these external challenges as with the challenges to survival themselves. In this connection, we shall hold that it is not human beings or human society in general which will or will not be able to deal with the survival challenges, but specific types of societies or forms of social organization which both have the capacity to create the external survival dangers and to deal successfully with these dangers. The form of organization we know as capitalism, and its international counterpart of imperialism, has elevated an historic survival crisis to critical and new levels. This system responds in earnest only to prospects of capital growth. It is thus a growth society, and growth itself lies at the center of the survival crisis. Therefore, capitalism can hardly be expected to respond effectively to external challenges themselves products or by-products of this system. This does not condemn humanity to destruction, since capitalism is a humanly contrived system and can be changed by humans as well.

The threats to survival are expressed in different ways by different scholars. An Italian mathematician and electronics engineer, Roberto Vacca, sees the convergence of the population explosion, increasing industrial production, environmental pollution, and the exhaustion of natural resources as pushing large parts of the globe toward a new dark age. Vacca's primary concern, however, is with the initial breakdown of the complex technological systems upon which a large part of the world's population has grown dependent: "My thesis is that our great technological systems of human organization and association are continuously outgrowing ordered control: they are now reaching critical dimensions of instability."[4] A major breakdown in communication, transportation, energy, and industrial production in conjunction with the aforesaid pressures would lead to total congestion and soon after, a sharp diminution of population followed by a piecemeal breakup of large systems into numerous smaller and much more primitive ones— indeed very uncivilized and even barbarous ones. One may not find it difficult to conceive of such a course of events actually taking place in

---

[4] Roberto Vacca, *The Coming of the Dark Age* (New York: Anchor Books, 1974), p. 3.

the absence of any basic change in the overall organization of contemporary society.

From another tack, Michigan State agricultural scientist Georg Borgstrom warns that "nothing less than a war for human survival needs to be invoked." Borgstrom focuses upon the race between population growth and food production. He is impatient: "These issues will reach overwhelming proportions in the seventies, this being the last decade when we still have a chance, although slim, of saving mankind and civilization. In many ways it is already five minutes past twelve."[5]

From an ecological point of view, we may consider the evaluation of the highly respected biologist Barry Commoner: "My own judgment, based on the evidence now at hand, is that the present course of environmental degradation, at least in industrialized countries, represents a challenge to essential ecological systems that is so serious that, if continued, it will destroy the capability of the environment to support a reasonably civilized human society."[6]

Taking an evolutionary perspective of the survival crisis, Harrison Brown and Edward Hutchings observe that "the divergence between the conditions the human body is built for and the conditions under which it lives is rapidly becoming wider." The increasingly artificial and altered environment within which advanced technological society finds itself allows genetic changes to occur which must be understood as possibly fatal deterioration in relation to bacterial and viral enemies: "however, although the changing envelope keeps ahead of the genetic erosion that it leaves, the erosion is there nonetheless, and turning back becomes increasingly difficult."[7] Yet the prospect of catastrophic reversal is precisely what critics such as Heilbroner, Vacca, Borgstrom, and Commoner foresee in current trends. Such a deterioration in living conditions would lay bare any newly acquired genetic weaknesses. In a related evolutionary vein, anarchist and ecologist Murray Bookchin of Goddard College warns that man's crudely applied technological activities are disassembling the delicate biotic pyramid and reversing com-

---

[5] Georg Borgstrom, *Focal Points: A Global Food Strategy* (New York: Macmillan Publishing Company, Inc., 1973), p. 10.

[6] Barry Commoner, *The Closing Circle* (New York: Alfred A. Knopf, 1971), pp. 217–18.

[7] Harrison Brown and Edward Hutchings, Jr., eds., *Are Our Descendants Doomed? Technological Change and Population Growth* (New York: The Viking Press, 1972), p. 15.

plex evolutionary processes which have supported humanity for mil-
lenia; such an undermining of the organic world threatens to reduce
the biosphere to a stage capable of supporting only simple forms of
life.[8]

The construction of the biotic pyramid is not the only unrepeatable
creation. The entire industrial civilization which rests upon this biosphere, and which is in deep and mortal conflict with it, is itself an unrepeatable creation. It, too, has been built up from the simple to the
complex, with each stage having in large measure used up or lost the
building blocks of the immediately previous stage so that each step in
a forward transition requires the existence of the human and physical
resources of the preceding one. Thus, with regard to resources and energy, there could be no saving leap to some highly sophisticated use of
nature's elements following catastrophe or marked deterioration within
the existing industrial order. With the old building blocks gone, only
return to more primitive means of existence would be possible.

The problems surrounding survival are especially dangerous owing
to their *exponential* nature of growth. Exponential growth feeds upon
itself in such a way as to start slowly and unimpressively, but after
taking into itself all that it produces and then proceeding again at the
same rate, it assumes very large proportions within a very short period
of time. What appeared to have been only a harmless speck on yesterday's horizon has blotted out today's noonday sun. Thus it is with
world population growth, the base of which is now teaching us a hard
lesson in exponential growth; each new billion arrives ever closer together. Thus it has also been with capital accumulation or economic
growth, scientific knowledge and technology, resource and energy consumption, and the impact of all of these upon the environment.

That the growth of such external challenges is of an exponential nature renders all the more problematic and menacing the fact that so
little is really known about the long-range consequences of such growth
upon the environment or about the limits of environmental toleration
to such growth. With ever increasing speed and force, humanity presses
forward upon the unknown limits of its own life-support systems. The
breaking point, or a point of irreversible "no return," approaches in
such major life-giving systems as the atmosphere, hydrology, nitrogen

---

[8] Murray Bookchin, *Post-Scarcity Anarchism* (Berkeley: The Ramparts Press,
1971), pp. 67–68.

cycles, and photosynthesis.[9] It is the nature of living systems to have threshold levels, meaning that things may appear to be going quite all right until virtually all of a sudden the system is in a state of irreversible decline. Add to the fact of the unknown thresholds of the major life-support systems the fact of accelerating, exponential growth of environmental impacts and we can understand why Paul Ehrlich and his colleagues warn that "the time between the appearance of unmistakable symptoms and real disaster is likely to be but an instant in human history."[10]

It would be easy to dismiss the survival literature as a mere extension of perennial doomsaying. Indeed, such is the most common response among both lay people and professionals. The evidence which follows throughout this book would contradict making this easy assertion. In all matters concerned, whether they be economic, technological, demographic, agricultural, or environmental, we are confronted with differences both in quantity and quality from previous history. Where in previous history can we find an economic machine to compare with that of the United States? Modern technology takes new turns almost daily and grows to previously unimaginable proportions and power. Today's global population and its rate of absolute increase dwarfs that of a mere century ago. Accordingly, food yields must live up to wholly unprecedented increases in demand. And when before has the environment been subjected to such total and extensive assault emanating from these economic, technological, demographic, and agricultural magnitudes and qualities as it is today? To assert that nothing is really new, that every current development is simply a repeat or extension of the old, is a dangerous assumption. It breeds passivity and fatalism, ignorance and neglect. We *do* happen to be living at an extremely critical juncture in human history. The fact bombards us daily from every direction. Blindness will not make it go away.

The discussion thus far has been conducted at a very general level. It has been intended to provide only the broad outlines of the kinds of questions and issues with which the sociology of survival must deal. The remainder of the book examines the major problems of survival at

---

[9] Barbara Ward and René Dubois, *Only One Earth* (London: Andre Deutsch Limited, 1972), p. 84; and Barry Weisberg, *Beyond Repair: The Ecology of Capitalism* (Boston: Beacon Press, 1971), p. 6.

[10] Paul R. Ehrlich, Anne H. Ehrlich, and John P. Holdren, *Human Ecology, Problems and Solutions* (San Francisco: W. H. Freeman and Company, 1973), p. 10.

close range. The linkages between the several challenges are as of much concern as the separate problems themselves; indeed, a full understanding of the crisis of survival may be had only by way of a comprehensive sociology of survival which is attuned to the entire complex of social, economic, political, technological, demographic, and ecological forces at work.

The false dichotomy

The sociology of survival, as we shall conceive of it here, embraces all issues which bear upon the social quality of human existence as well as those which relate to physical survival. The two aspects of social quality and physical survival are inseparably interwoven in a myriad of ways, and they imperceptibly shade off into one another. Social quality, if such quality is to be stable and secure, requires a viable physical and material foundation. A feeling of social and psychological well-being and of cultural involvement necessitates a reliably self-sufficient and consistently reproducible life-support system. This life-support system may be conceived of as both the necessary material creations of man and the gifts of nature—from which all human material products obviously come in the first place.

To dichotomize between social quality and physical foundation is a false dichotomy. It is precisely such a forced dichotomy which within the present social order has produced the major survival challenges, ranging from moral to material breakdown. *The manner in which people organize their materially productive activities is the crucial linkage between the social quality of life people experience and the reproductive viability of the physical life-support system.* An organization of production which ties society's members together in relations of cooperation and equality, and directs their efforts toward the production of socially useful things in an environmentally rational manner, not only assures the maximum long-term viability of the material life-support system, but establishes the conditions for the attainment of sociocultural well-being and growth. In this way, then, the organization of production can integrate—and *must* integrate if the society is to survive—the spiritual and the material, the mental and the manual, the social and the physical. A society which in its organization of production alienates these spheres of life from one another cannot be a viable society in either the sociocultural, social quality sense, or in the sense of its material foundations. The linkages between them are simply too interdependent to be severed.

Yet, it is just such severance which characterizes our society and thus underlies the emergence of the survival crises. Our organization of production fails to tie society's members together in relations of co-operation and equality, and it fails to direct their efforts toward the production of socially useful things in an environmentally rational manner. By its very internal prerequisites, the prevailing system objectively sets people against one another, produces a flood of socially unnecessary and harmful things, and makes disastrous inroads into life's natural foundations. In an attempt to justify the necessity of the productive organization's own internal logic of growth, the system's promoters and ideologists have propounded an ethic of infinite material consumption and defined a "high standard of living" as the attainment of such an ethic. The insoluble contradictions generated by the logic of the organization of production and the associated failures of its ethic grow painfully more obvious.

Early symptoms

One need not hold up as a standard of comparison a socialist utopia to begin to draw out the beginnings of mounting awareness of decline and deterioration in the quality of life (even as defined by the capitalist ethic itself) and its material foundations. British economist E. J. Mishan's book *Technology and Growth: The Price We Pay* puts into critical focus the rising volume of problems accumulating within contemporary society.[11] Traffic, pollution, omnipresent noise, loss of privacy, hucksterism, physical threat, dangerous products, loss of open space, and numerous other encroachments upon a person's mind and body have made just plain living more costly in both psychological and financial terms. Mishan is no romantic who has produced a collection of nostalgic reminiscences. He only documented in 1967 what Vance Packard predicted in 1960. At that time Packard wrote in *The Waste-makers* (which has turned out to be the most significant and far-sighted

---

[11] Originally published as E. J. Mishan, *The Costs of Economic Growth* (London: Staples Press, 1967).

of his many books) that "the outpouring of goods and people which marketeers are counting upon will change the style of life in the United States. Even though consumption continues to churn upward, it seems inevitable that the United States will see a real decline in the amenities of life."[12] Not that Packard in 1960 marked the first realization that existing social and economic trends augured ill for the future. Right near the beginning of what C. Wright Mills has called The Great American Celebration—"the affluent society" that emerged after World War II—K. William Kapp took note in 1950 of certain incipient postwar trends in *The Social Costs of Private Enterprise*.[13] Nor need we start with Kapp's book; the whole corpus of Thorstein Veblen's writings in the early part of the century provided ample warning of things to come.

Now the trickle of complaint has turned into a veritable flood. Quantitative argument has been made that the "golden age" is passing and the quality of life is likely to decline,[14] while it becomes increasingly common to note the rapidly deteriorating living standards of the vast majority of the population of the United States.[15] Paul and Anne Ehrlich write that "overpopulation right now is lowering the quality of life dramatically in these [developed] countries as their struggle to maintain affluence and grow more food leads to environmental deterioration."[16] Swedish economist Staffan Linder (the Swedes being among the most undaunted believers in contemporary-type progress) complains that "it seems that a process of economic development involves both an increase in the quantity of service and decline in quality."[17] (Fifty-six percent of the respondents in a recent Harris poll would agree with Linder inasmuch as they felt the quality of products and services are worse now than ten years ago.[18]) *Newsweek*, a magazine not known to take an unduly critical view of things, sums up some extensive probing into American life by saying that "at the bottom, the

---

[12] Vance Packard, *The Wastemakers* (New York: Pocket Books, Inc., 1960), pp. 164–65.

[13] K. William Kapp, *The Social Costs of Private Enterprise* (Cambridge: Harvard University Press, 1950).

[14] Jay Forrester, *World Dynamics* (London: Wright-Allen, 1971).

[15] Jacob Morris, "Stagflation," *Monthly Review* 26(December 1974):8.

[16] Paul R. Ehrlich and Anne H. Ehrlich, *Population Resources Environment* (San Francisco: W. H. Freeman and Company, 1972), p. 3.

[17] Staffan Linder, *The Harried Leisure Class* (New York: Columbia University Press, 1970), p. 46.

[18] Louis Harris, *The Anguish of Change* (New York: W. W. Norton & Company, Inc., 1973), p. 3.

mood adds up to a nagging sense that life is going sour—that, whatever is wrong, the whole society has somehow lost its way."[19]

Poll data indicate that the proportion of respondents reporting to be "very happy" drifted upward between 1946 and 1957, but then began to fall so that by the late 1960s all income categories evinced declines in happiness. In France, half of the respondents polled felt that the quality of life had deteriorated in the past five years.[20] As late as 1966, three fourths of respondents to a Harris poll credited business with bringing them better quality products than before; then attitudes began to sour and by 1973 a substantial majority distrusted a wide range of products and were negative toward many businesses and services.[21] An awakening was taking place during this period, an awakening which seems to have moved fast enough to remain abreast with the current deterioration of amenities as well as to make up for some earlier years of unwarranted celebration.

The general erosion of attitude toward life quality is paralleled by a number of "social disorganization" indicators which might be taken as reflections of much broader processes of disintegration within the present society (Table 1). That is to say, behind the increases in each of these "extreme" indicators lie rates of breakdown many times larger but in lesser degrees of severity. The violent crime and murder is but a small portion of the total amount of bitterness and hatred which rends the society. The treated mentally ill are only a small fraction of the depressed, disoriented, or deranged. The divorced are but a small sample of disintegrated family relationships. The cirrhosis deaths are only a small guide to the extent of alcoholism. And police reported narcotic addicts mirror a vastly greater extent of drug dependency of all sorts. That these trends are paralleled by significant increases in the so-called standard of living as indicated by per capita income, per capita consumption expenditures, per capita energy consumption, and invention patents is a manifestation of the false dichotomy and severance of sociocultural life from its material foundations by an alienating organization of production.

Not only do the social disorganization indicators display parallel in-

---

[19] Cited in Richard Parker, *The Myth of the Middle Class* (New York: Harper & Row, Publishers, 1972), p. 138.

[20] Edward S. Herman and Richard B. Du Boff, "How Not to Eliminate Poverty," *Monthly Review* 25(February 1974):51–62.

[21] Harris, *Anguish of Change*, pp. 101–03.

TABLE 1
Economic growth and social disorganization

	Percentage increase 1960–65	Percentage increase 1965–72
Per capita income constant dollars	13	48
Per capita energy consumption, Btu	12	25
Invention patents issued	34	19
Violent crime per 100,000 inhabitants	24	101
Homicide per 100,000 15 years old and over	14	56
Mentally ill, all treatment facilities, per 100,000 inhabitants	33	44
Divorce per 1,000 women 15 years old and over	11	59
Cirrhosis of the liver deaths per 100,000 inhabitants	13	23
Newly reported narcotic addicts	n.d.	310

Source: *U.S. Fact Book*, New York: Grosset & Dunlap, for 1975, pp. 326, 517, 541, 147, 150, 82, 66, 62, and 87.

creases with the economic "well-being" indicators in each time period, the rate of increase for *both* is greater in the more recent period than the earlier period. As the pace in the rise of the "standard of living" accelerates, so does the pace in the rates of social breakdown. (The two-year longer time span for the second period does not appreciably alter the picture. Invention patents don't fit this pattern, but inventions typically involve a time lapse of some years prior to widespread use.) The more actively the severance of life quality from its required material and natural foundations is pushed, the greater the harvest of alienated relationships and lives.

A correlate of rising crime has been rising fear, certainly no ingredient of a high standard of living. Louis Harris observes that "fear grew in waves throughout the 1960s."[22] Virtually no one mentioned concern about crime and violence as an important issue in the early 60s, and

[22] Ibid., pp. 168–69.

even as late as 1964 only 8 percent mentioned it. By 1968, however, 65 percent did so. The majority of people reportedly live in some fear even in their own homes. Other Harris data indicate that 62 percent of women in the big cities are afraid to walk the streets; 81 percent of the general population felt that law and order had broken down in America. (Population growth and larger numbers of youth only go part way, perhaps no more than half, in accounting for the increase in crime—as if there were any inherent reason why youth should be disposed to criminality in the first place.) How justifiable such fear actually is is not the essential issue; the *presence* of fear is the reality. Fear and a related sense of insecurity is admittedly one of the major factors influencing thousands of Americans every week to seek information from Canadian consulates about emigration to that country, not yet so marked by the fear and distrust south of its borders.

The decline in the quality of life may take place in ways unseen, even unexperienced, as well as directly. The growing flood of chemicals has upset the balance of both the environment and the human body. Substantial documentation of the motivations, extent, and consequences of chemical proliferation is available.[23] The profusion of chemicals in production and consumption has in all likelihood much to do with a 3 percent increase in the rate of deaths due to malignancies during the 1960 to 1965 period and a 9 percent increase from 1965 to 1972.[24]

At work the quality of life is as bad as ever despite much recent fanfare about improvements and safety. Work-related accidents claim almost 15,000 lives a year, 90,000 permanent impairments, and 2 million temporarily total disabilities. In 1969, exposures to industrial pollutants at the workplace caused 1 million new cases of occupational disease, including 3,600 dead and 800,000 cases of burn, lung and eye damage, dermatitis, and brain damage.[25] Work-related accidents and illnesses in 1973 accounted for twice as many man-days lost as strikes and lockouts even in labor-restive Canada.

Any general critique of life quality would not be complete (this is not intended by any means to be complete) without mention of what

---

[23] See James S. Turner, *The Chemical Feast* (New York: Grossman Publishers, 1970) and John G. Fuller, *200,000,000 Guinea Pigs* (New York: G. P. Putnam's Sons, 1972).

[24] *The U.S. Fact Book* (New York: Grosset & Dunlap, Publishers, for 1975), p. 62.

[25] *Work In America* (Cambridge, Mass.: MIT Press, 1973), p. 26.

Mishan calls "society's greatest nightmare"—motorized traffic. In 1973 Americans registered 125 million cars, trucks, and buses; they junked 8 million and turned out 12.6 million new ones.[26] They drove their cars over 1,000 billion miles over 3.8 million miles of roads, drove trucks 260 billion miles, and buses (only) 5 billion miles. In the meantime, the number of railroad locomotives in service shrank from 42,000 in 1950 to 29,000 in 1972, passenger train cars from 38,000 to 8,000, the number of freight cars dwindled by 300,000, the number of passenger-miles declined from 31.8 billion miles to 8.6 billion miles, and freight tonnage remained virtually the same but dropped from carrying 57 percent of total freight volume in 1950 to 38 percent in 1972. Operated track mileage was reduced by 40,000 miles, while highways were growing by 500,000 miles.

Mishan's nightmare leaves in its wake from over 25 million annual crashes, some 5 million Americans injured and 55,000 dead. The motor vehicle is the leading cause of death for people between 15 and 34 years of age. As a check on the American population, the motor vehicle's claim of 1.7 million deaths easily outperforms war's 1 million since 1775. What percent of cardiovascular disease, lung cancer, and respiratory disease is attributable to auto pollution is not ascertainable, though with roughly one half of air pollution caused by motor vehicles the percentage may be significant.

The cost of the motor vehicle is, of course, not only physical. Its cost in terms of resources that could be applied or conserved elsewhere is practically incalculable. The production, distribution, and care of the auto consumes approximately 16 percent of the labor force and 13 percent of the gross national product.[27] This does not include the hospitals, police, courts, and a myriad of other agencies and institutions in its service. Americans spent $94 billion on personally operated transportation in 1972, $10 billion more than they spent to clothe and care for themselves and only about $10 billion less than they spent on all housing costs. Eighteen billion was spent on insurance premiums alone in an effort to partially protect themselves from the carnage. For years government has let some $6.5 billion in highway contracts. When in an unemployment and recession squeeze, one of the first things to come

---

[26] U.S. Fact Book, pp. 555–56, 549. The subsequent statistics are from the same source on pages 568, 547, 562, 376, and 548, respectively.

[27] Weisberg, Beyond Repair, p. 102.

to mind for the President is to release $2.5 billion of impounded funds for highway construction.

These are only a partial accounting of the financial costs. There are other costs to be reckoned as well, which include social, cultural, and aesthetic losses. The impact of automobilization upon the appearance and contours of urban areas is, of course, legend. Cities and their sprawling environments have become so ugly over the past 25 years that a sense of public aesthetics has been greatly destroyed. Freeways slice through neighborhoods (usually working-class or poor ones), open areas become drive-ins and parking lots, and highways and interchanges gobble up some of the nation's most fertile and increasingly necessary acreage. Billions of man-hours are spent crawling through traffic, billions of youth-hours are spent dreaming of horsepower, billions of woman-hours are spent chauffering children. The car is driven for the shortest distances and most whimsical reasons. What the auto has done to family, neighborhood, and primary group sociality in general would require a book in itself.

"Considered by some to be one of the greatest inventions of American science and technology," writes Barry Weisberg, "in reality the automobile has been responsible for more death and human misery than any other single factor in American life."[28] From our partial list of costs and investments in the auto, it should not be hard to agree with those who suggest that any significant transformation in the use of the automobile would require nothing less than the reconstruction of the present American economy. To reconstruct transportation so as to create a balance between people and their social and natural environments demands not only economic restructuring, but restructuring of our entire mode of living. The auto is the paragon of consumer society and a pillar of economic growth; but consumerism and economic growth must give way to creativity and social growth in a viable society.

Searching for explanations

What has produced such a decline in the quality of life and living conditions in the world's richest land? Why has the Great American Celebration ended with such astonishing abruptness? Is the current cri-

---

[28] Ibid., p. 118.

sis only a momentary turndown to be followed in time by a second great celebration? Or have recent years marked the beginning of the end of ascendancy for the American Way of Life around the world? Answers to such major historical and societal questions cannot be made with any certainty, even though it is the central task of the social scientist to struggle with them. The pursuit of these and similar queries make up the task which here lies before us, and only after a careful perusal of the remaining pages will our answers begin to take shape.

We might note that Heilbroner traces the current pessimism to three broad areas:

1. Topical causes, foremost the Vietnam war, but also violence as exemplified by street crime, race riots, bombing, hijackings, and a failure of traditional values in the new generations.

2. Attitudinal causes which underlie and reinforce the topical causes, including a loss of assurance with respect to the course of events as found in seemingly unmanageable inflation, racial hatred, world poverty, deteriorating environment, resource limitations, and costs of growth.

3. Civilizational malaise arising from the failure of materialistic civilization. About the latter Heilbroner writes that "civilizational malaise, in a word, reflects the inability of a civilization directed to material improvement—higher incomes, better diets, miracles of medicine, triumphs of applied physics and chemistry—to satisfy the human spirit."[29]

Such a shotgun approach is bound to hit something right, at least on the surface. Certainly the Vietnam war had a highly destructive affect upon American society. No one yet has even attempted to a complete accounting, perhaps because the task would be overwhelming. Domestic violence, value disorientation, inflation, racial conflict, world poverty, environmental problems, resource shortages, waste excesses, and spiritual poverty are also evident enough and may in various combinations be taken as "causes" of the new pessimism. However, in this catchall bag of explanations we have no way of distinguishing cause and effect, no way of knowing where to start in an attempt at constructive change. Rather we are provided with a list of *symptoms* of something which is wrong in a sense much larger than any of Heilbroner's explanations either taken alone or in their entirety.

---

[29] Heilbroner, *Inquiry Into The Human Prospect*, p. 21.

Heilbroner fails to decipher the larger problem for the same reason that he would set up Western industrialism as a kind of universal system from which there is no escape and as a determinant of the kind of society in which it is found. Civilizational malaise is real enough, and it does indeed arise from the failure of material growth, science, and technology to satisfy the human spirit. However, Heilbroner is either unable or unwilling to see that the material growth, science, and technology of which he speaks is the work of a very distinctive organization of production known as capitalism. For example, why should we be satisfied with the results of a science and technology which has for 35 years concentrated chiefly upon perfecting the arts of destruction at the expense of meeting urgent human wants and social needs? Is there no possibility of a materialism designed to directly meet needs, a science and technology aimed at liberation instead of personal gain and enslavement? If not, then we shall all go down to defeat with Professor Heilbroner. However, many people are both able and willing to see things differently. The world cannot so easily be consigned to an ignominious fate by pessimistic and ethnocentric intellectuals. "The theoretical basis for pessimism," observes Stanley Aronowitz, "turns out to be nothing but the assumption that the structure of the present is the only possible society."[30] This is a fatal assumption. The dangerous and destructive traps of the present growth society can be averted and overcome if the social visions and political willpower to do so are in sufficient supply. A society which can remain permanently stable without economic growth is both possible and necessary to survival. Growth of a different kind, social and cultural growth, will then be the recipient of human developmental powers.

---

[30] Stanley Aronowitz, "Is the Enemy Really Us?" *Social Policy*, November–December 1974, p. 59.

2

Growth and social progress

Growth

At the center of the survival crisis there is emerging a crucial question which is the concern of growing numbers of people: what does growth have to do with the various survival challenges which have come to confront humanity? In the context of this emerging debate, "growth" refers chiefly to economic growth in the sense of an increase in the production of goods and services. The growth issue also encompasses the closely related phenomenon of technological development, which shall be dealt with in Chapters 5 and 6. The debate over growth generally subsumes population as well, and we shall deal directly with population in Chapter 9. Any attempt at a clarification of the nature and impact of growth must give ample consideration to each of these three manifestations of the growth society, and especially the relationships between them. What might be considered as a fourth aspect of the growth society, bureaucratic or organizational growth, shall in the present context be considered as primarily a response to the needs of economic growth and of technological growth as it has developed within capitalism. Bureaucratic growth is discussed in Chapter 6.

Growth as thus conceived is nevertheless an incomplete accounting, since it does not include growth in social relationships, cultural participation, and personal development. These forms of growth should be the chief goals of a viable society. Indeed, our position here shall be that these extraeconomic forms of growth *must* become the ends of human action if the survival challenges are to be overcome.

Growth within the present social order, however, means a very narrow kind of economic expansion and technological development. In subsequent discussion, therefore, growth will refer to expansion and development in this sense.

Growth and human welfare

In his *Principles of Political Economy*, J. S. Mill posed a question which today is more nagging than ever before:

> In contemplating any progressive movement, not in its nature unlimited, the mind is not satisfied with merely tracing the laws of the movement; it cannot but ask the further question, to what goal? Towards what ultimate point is society tending by its industrial progress? When the progress ceases, in what condition are we to expect that it will leave mankind?[1]

Mill was sharply critical of political economists for equating human progress and well-being with economic growth.

More than a century's intervention has not altered the dedication of growth proponents. Top-ranking economist and former presidential advisor Walter Heller argues that "growth is a necessary condition for social advance, for improving the quality of the total environment." Heller believes that "it is still demonstrably true that growth in per capita gross national product has been associated with rising levels of human well-being."[2] The University of Wisconsin's Robert Lampman concurs: "The pattern of growth in the United States in the postwar years yielded benefits to individuals far in excess of the costs it required of them. To that extent our material progress has had humane content."[3]

Among the benefits of growth are, according to its proponents, an

[1] J. S. Mill, *Principles of Political Economy*, vol. 2 (New York: D. Appleton & Company, 1908), p. 334.

[2] "Coming to Terms with Growth and the Environment," in Sam H. Schurr, ed., *Energy, Economic Growth, and the Environment* (Baltimore: Johns Hopkins University Press, 1972), pp. 11, 29.

[3] Robert Lampman, "Recent U.S. Economic Growth and the Gain in Human Welfare," in Walter W. Heller, ed., *Perspectives on Economic Growth* (New York: Random House, Inc., 1968), p. 162.

increased range of choices, greater control over the environment, more services and goods, improved status of women, a release from the drudgery of hard work, greater humanitarianism, and the reduction of social tensions.[4]

The growth enthusiasts have been especially emphatic on the relationship between growth and creativity. Veteran economist Louis Hacker puts this view as follows:

> A society that is growing (again, assuming it is free) has a greater elan, a higher spirit, a sparkle and a derring-do about it. Creativity is encouraged and supported. For the venturesome, doors to opportunity are opened, there exists a vertical social mobility, there is room at the top. Innovators, risk-takers, adventurers emerge, are welcomed rather than rebuffed and are given the recognition (possibly fortunes, too) that is their due.[5]

It is argued that in a society without growth people might feel they had less "adventure," less hope of discovering some larger purpose in life, less hope of something better ahead.[6]

The growth proponents are thus able to avoid Mill's question regarding purpose by equating growth with the good society itself, by taking growth as an end in itself. Growth is never viewed as a means of gaining access to some other kind of life. Human well-being is best served by going ahead with the pursuit of more growth on into the indefinite future; the belief is that an end to growth would mean an end to creative change and a diminution of human well-being. As shall be clarified, the growth enthusiasts view historical development entirely within the capitalist framework, and to so view history is to commit oneself to the *necessity* of growth. Given a capitalist organization of production a society without growth *is* a stagnating one and could indeed experience a diminution of overall well-being—at least in narrow material terms. As to the status of cultural creativity and social innovation within stagnating capitalism, this is a moot point. It would depend upon what kind of "creativity" and "innovation" one had in mind. Under the best of growth conditions, the social and cultural achievements

---

[4] Louis Hacker, *The Course of American Economic Growth and Development* (New York: John Wiley & Sons, Inc., 1970), pp. 353–54.

[5] Ibid.

[6] Roland N. McKean, "Growth vs. No Growth: An Evaluation," *Daedalus* 102 (Fall 1973):22. The entire issue, entitled "The No-Growth Society," is devoted to a discussion of the pros and cons of growth—the pros being given a substantially larger portion of the debate.

of contemporary America leave, at the very least, something to be desired. It would be all too easy to paint a very depressing picture of contemporary cultural standards and social innovation—and this after 30 years of almost uninterrupted economic expansion and a surfeit of resources.

Opposing the growth proponents, the critics of growth are in most instances the same people who are most concerned with the mounting survival challenges. One such critic contends that the health and welfare of the American people decline proportionately to the soaring GNP. Barry Commoner observes that to a considerable extent growth "reflects ecologically faulty, socially wasteful types of production rather than the actual welfare of individual human beings."[7] E. J. Mishan also sees a negative relationship between growth and well-being, stating, "That an increase in social-welfare—an increase in the range of effective choice—may be brought about by negative economic growth may appear paradoxical, if not infuriating, to some growthmen." Those who hold that growth expands the range of choices for the individual "have failed to observe that as the carpet of 'increased choice' is being unrolled before us by the foot, it is simultaneously being rolled up behind us by the yard."[8] Whereas growth proponents stress the need for continued economic expansion as a requirement to eliminate social problems, growth opponents counter to the effect that if economic growth to the present American level has been unable to get rid of public squalor, or possibly has even increased it, how could it be expected that further growth would mitigate or remove it?[9] Given a trillion dollar output of goods and services, how many additional trillions are required to solve our major problems? To the critics the plea for increased growth is a hollow solution to our problems. Instead of a panacea, growth itself lies at our problems' roots.[10]

Given the discussion in Chapter 1 of the decline in the quality of life, the critics of growth are on much firmer ground than the growth pro-

---

[7] Barry Weisberg, *Beyond Repair: The Ecology of Capitalism* (Boston: Beacon Press, 1971), p. 150; and Barry Commoner, *The Closing Circle* (New York: Alfred A. Knopf, 1971), p. 295.

[8] E. J. Mishan, *The Costs of Economic Growth* (London: Staples Press, 1967), pp. 116, 85.

[9] E. F. Schumacher, *Small is Beautiful: Economics as if People Mattered* (New York: Harper & Row, Publishers, 1973), p. 256.

[10] Paul M. Sweezy and Harry Magdoff, "Notes on Watergate One Year Later," *Monthly Review* 26(May 1974):9.

ponents. The scope of post-war growth in America has been unprecedented. If growth could even begin to deliver a society from its social
problems, it should have been taking place during the past 30 years.
The resources to make major strides toward the elimination of social
problems have never in human history been present in such great magnitude as in America. A richly endowed natural environment, a highly
trained work force, superior technological know-how, and the highest
per capita income in the world—such are the resources which have long
been available. Yet the sociologist of social problems and social disorganization has never had more to occupy research time. Economists
are doing frantic juggling acts in an effort to keep afloat a sinking ship
of state, all in an attempt to rekindle the flames of growth. If another
boom is on the horizon, so is another bust. For 150 years this has been
the story of capitalism. Most everyone during this long period has
come to associate good times with growth and bad times with stagnation. Whatever "good times" there actually are in this erratic system
would apparently come with growth. Yet many now concur with the
critics that an end to growth would improve well-being and alleviate
many social problems.

Growth and equality

One of the arguments frequently set forth by the advocates of
growth is that growth alleviates poverty, and that those who would
establish a no-growth society are elitists ready to sacrifice the interests
of the poor on behalf of the privileged. One view suggests that no-
growth is being promoted by the upper echelons of the society,[11] a
curious belief inasmuch as the very power and privilege of the capitalist class depends upon the continuation of economic growth (see Chapters 3 and 4).

The notion that an absence of growth is associated with poverty is
a gross oversimplification. By reversing this logic we have the implication that a growth society will *not* work against the interests of the
poorer members of society. While this certainly could and should be
the case, it rarely has been. In the great American growth period of the
1950s and 1960s, the real income gap between the top and bottom fifths

---

[11] Richard Zeckhauser, "The Risks of Growth," *Daedalus* 102(Fall 1973):109.

of the society increased from $10,565 to $19,071.[12] From 1947 to 1972 the real income gap between the top 5 percent of families and the bottom 20 percent widened from $13,279 to $22,224.[13] For unrelated individuals the gap almost doubled from $6,790 to $12,004. Even growth enthusiasts may admit that growth is dependent upon and leads to inequality of income.[14]

Since the end of World War II, one fifth of the population has remained below 50 percent of the median income, being quite impervious to the fabulous intervening growth. Considering inflation and tax increases, critics point out that the proportion of the population under the 1969 federal poverty level was virtually unchanged from that of ten years earlier.[15] One may also observe that after five years of economic expansion following the Watts riot in 1965, unemployment in that area was 60 percent higher than in the riot year.

Looking back into the record further, we see that the economically roaring 1920s substantially widened the gulf between rich and poor. In all likelihood, 19th century industrial expansion itself pauperized and degraded as many people as it elevated to positions of well-being. Karl Marx posited as a general law of capitalist development that "the greater the social wealth, the functioning capital, the extent and energy of its growth, and therefore, also the absolute mass of the proletariat and the productiveness of its labour, the greater is the industrial reserve army [the unemployed]. The more extensive, finally, the lazarus layers of the working class, and the industrial reserve army, the greater is official pauperism."[16] In checking this proposition, it has been found that 4.6 percent of the population of England and Wales in 1865 were officially listed as paupers, whereas 7 percent of the 1973 United States population were on public welfare.[17]

What the growth advocates are really saying is that, given the as-

---

[12] James H. Weaver, "Economic Growth, Inequality, Hierarchy, Alienation: The Impact of Socialization Processes in Capitalist Society," *The American Economist* 17(Fall 1973):9–16.

[13] *The U.S. Fact Book* (New York: Grosset & Dunlap, Publishers, for 1975), p. 384.

[14] Hacker, *Course of American Economic Growth and Development*, p. 354.

[15] Richard Parker, *The Myth of the Middle Class* (New York: Harper & Row, Publishers, 1972), pp. 98–99.

[16] Cited in Harry Braverman, "Labor and Monopoly Capital: The Degradation of Work in the Twentieth Century," *Monthly Review* 26(July–August 1974):121.

[17] Ibid., p. 133.

sumption of a capitalist organization of production (and this tends always to be assumed), we had *better* have growth or the poor and the great mass of people in general will have to go without the trickle-down which growth affords them. (Trickle-down may be illustrated by any used goods, including those as large as housing, being discarded by those with new financial means and then being picked up for second-hand use by those poorer. New but cheap goods may also be a part of trickle-down, as any advances in quality go first to the rich. Or a small increase in workers' income may come on the heels of a far larger one for the bosses.) And without trickle-down the illusion of upward social mobility will be shattered. The dire result of this would be heightened discontent and revolutionary potential. What the growth advocates are really up to becomes plainly evident when Heller warns, "Imagine the tensions between rich and poor, between black and white, between blue-collar and white-collar workers, between old and young, if we had been forced to finance even the minimal demands of the disadvantaged out of a no-growth national income instead of a one-third increase in that income [during the 1960s]." [18] In a growth society, the poor can become a little richer while the rich can become much richer.[19] The crux of the matter is that growth is a substitute for equality of income, and growth provides the hope which makes continuing large income differentials tolerable.[20]

The social and political turmoil of the 1960s and 1970s would suggest, however, that the trickle-down strategy of conflict deterrence is not working so well. Two things have gone wrong with the pacification through growth strategy: the trickle-down is being relatively dwarfed by the flood of wealth upward, and what is trickling down is no longer interpreted as upward social mobility by the populace. Since growth-accompanying inflation set in with earnest in the late 60s, large strata of the population have been sliding backward even by the crudest of measures. Far from being a guarantee against conflict, growth may just as well generate it, owing to the subsequent increased inequality. Nor are the inevitable periods of stagnation any more conducive to social tranquility.

A point which requires emphasis in a discussion of growth and equality is that the unpaid costs of pollution and environmental degradation

---

[18] Schurr, ed., "Coming to Terms with Growth and the Environment," p. 10.

[19] Kenneth E. Boulding, "The Shadow of the Stationary State," *Daedalus* 102 (Fall 1973):95.

[20] "Zero Growth," *Newsweek*, January 24, 1972, p. 62.

stemming from growth are borne most heavily by the working class and poor and the most lightly by the affluent. Ecology is class issue of great significance.[21] Whether on or off the job, the worker and the impoverished suffer most from the erosion of resources and environment. On the other hand, environmental exploitation frequently accrues to the benefit of the rich. Further, the price on "purifying" one's living environment is going out of reach for more and more people, leaving only those with financial means able to mitigate or avoid environmental declines in the quality of life. The privacy, beauty, safety, freedom, and purity which was previously taken for granted by most people now comes at a cost higher than most people can afford.

Even if social conflict is dampened by economic expansion, this expansion cannot go on much longer. Environmental limitations clearly exist. To the extent that economic growth does resolve social conflict, such resolution will increasingly encounter these environmental limitations.[22]

Class conflict dampening through economic growth is not so much a conscious strategy as it is an incidental but appreciated by-product of a far more basic "strategy"—the entire logic and necessity of capitalist expansion. Growth is a matter of survival to the capitalist class, whereas the capacity of the earth to endure growth impacts, and the degree of class conflict, are of concern to this class only as limiting parameters of growth-oriented action. It may be granted that the capitalist class seeks to push back the limits of the earth and restrain the forces of class conflict, but such actions are only supportive of the main pursuit of growth. Neither environmental conflict nor class conflict, or even the imminent threat of environment collapse and class revolution, can deter the pursuit of growth. To give up growth is to give up everything that really matters to the capitalist class *qua* class. One should never be in doubt about the priorities of the society in which we live. It would matter relatively little to the calculations of the capitalist class whether an estimate of an economy five times the size of the present one could be environmentally tolerated or whether the environmental limits were being approached within the next few years. No cost can be unacceptably large when growth is at stake, because growth is the

---

[21] Gus Hall, *Ecology: Can We Survive Under Capitalism* (New York: International Publishers, 1972), p. 18.

[22] Richard England and Barry Bluestone, "Ecology and Social Conflict," in Herman E. Daly, ed., *Toward a Steady-State Economy* (San Francisco: W. H. Freeman and Company, 1973), p. 207.

life sustenance of capitalism and the capitalist class. Rationality and rational action flows from one's premises, premises which may be ecologically insane but yet sound to capitalists. Of course, even they must ultimately face up to the limits of the earth to support their growth system. To wait so long for such a recognition would be as fatal as to continue to follow the premises of growthmanship.

In discussing growth and equality, we have focused largely on economic aspects of equality. A word may be injected on the impact of growth upon political equality. As might be expected, growth advocates hold that growth enhances political equality and democracy, whereas no-growth promotes the conditions for political oppression.[23] Again the assumption is made that the capitalist forms of production and distribution are universals. Even given this, there is no persuasive evidence that growth and political equality are positively associated. On the contrary, the history of growth in Western society has been marked by greatly increased concentrations of power in every major institutional sector. The powerless are as voiceless and dependent as ever, perhaps even more as the monolithic state and giant corporation engulf all. By the same token, those who administer and control the state and corporations today hold power over people and events the scope of which would be envied by their most power-hungry predecessors.

In other national contexts, we note there has been no great flowering of political equality and participatory democracy in the wake of rapid Soviet economic growth, although compared to prerevolutionary Russia the rights of the individual are incomparably better today. In the underdeveloped world, Brazil means an economic growth miracle to some people, but the worst kind of political oppression to others. Political democracy cannot be used in the case for growth. In most contexts with which we are familiar, growth has involved greater concentrations of power and powerlessness, a greater degree of hierarchical authority, and an increased need for state control. Such need not necessarily be the result of growth; it is the result, however, whenever the end of capital accumulation overrides all other social and political values.

A stagnating economy, as well as a growing one, may also create the

---

[23] For example, S. M. Lipset, *Political Man* (Garden City, N.Y.: Doubleday & Company, Inc., 1960).

conditions for increased repression.[24] Without economic trickle-down through growth, or with a shrinking volume of production, the pressures for redistribution of wealth could conceivably mount. To maintain the existing distribution of wealth would then require increasingly harsh measures by the state.

The crux of the growth and democracy issue is that political equality is variously threatened whether the economy is growing or stagnating. The capitalist system is inherently at odds with working democracy. Growth concentrates power and wealth. Stagnation is politically destabilizing and fosters a more repressive regime. Only when equality serves as the main goal and growth applied in its support can working democracy be achieved.

The conclusions to be drawn from the discussion of growth and equality up to this point have been very adequately summarized by Edward Herman and Richard Du Boff:

> A growing body of political economic analysis and empirical evidence, then, points to the conclusion that growth *per se* is an unreliable means for eliminating poverty (however defined), that it fails to reduce and may even increase relative deprivation, and that it poses a potentially catastrophic threat to our natural environment. Any study of the objective social effects of postwar economic growth in the West would show, we believe, that rapid growth in today's "free" market systems tends to consolidate the power of affluent classes and top business decision-makers, who benefit most from "consumerism" and find it advantageous to promote it—public sector decay, urban blight, environmental degradation, and human alienation notwithstanding.[25]

Growth, equality, and underdevelopment

If the impact of growth upon inequality and impoverishment in the United States has had slight ameliorative and possibly negative effects, what, then, might be said about growth and equality in the underdeveloped countries. In this connection, it should be made explicit at this point that economic *development* is held to be an absolute necessity by growth critics. The economic and technological development of the un-

---

[24] See Harvey Salgo, "The Obsolescence of Growth: Capitalism and the Environmental Crisis," *Review of Radical Political Economics* 5(Fall 1973):26–45.

[25] Edward Herman and Richard Du Boff, "How Not to Eliminate Poverty," *Monthly Review* 25(February 1974):60–61.

derdeveloped countries is a definite prerequisite to triumph over the present survival challenges. The classical growth critic J. S. Mill was careful to point out the importance of increased production in the backward countries of the world.[26] After more than a century the demand for such increased production is more urgent than ever before, since the gap between the needs of the exploding populations of Asia, Africa, and Latin America and the necessities of life available to them has widened greatly in the intervening period.

However, it must be stressed that growth has diverse manifestations and may take markedly different courses which have markedly different results for the populations implicated in growth. This proposition holds true for the underdeveloped areas of the world as well as the developed. Growth in China has very different meaning for its population than does growth in Brazil. Because of the persistent and extensive interventions of the developed countries into the affairs of the underdeveloped, and we shall see in Chapter 11 that such intervention (imperialism) *is* the underlying reason for underdevelopment, the kind of growth which has transpired in much of the Third World has been severely distorted and unbalanced. Such distortion in the organization and utilization of a country's human and natural resources makes the transition to a balanced and self-sustaining growth all the more difficult. Yet, the transition must be made to cope successfully with the survival challenges.

The difference between balanced and unbalanced growth, between growth that equips people to meet their own urgent needs and growth that sinks them into deepening poverty, may be readily observed in the contrast between China and India, Cuba and Puerto Rico, Vietnam and Thailand. Real growth means growth in nutritious diets for everyone, growth in health services and medical care for everyone, growth in literacy and education for everyone, growth in constructive employment and income for everyone, growth in adequate clothing and housing for everyone, and growth in community participation and decision-making for everyone. Distorted growth means luxury and power for the few at the expense of the many. It means the best the Western world has to offer for a miniscule elite and a deepening despair for the masses of people. It means luxurious jetports, highrise office buildings and hotels, new cars and expressways, exclusive villas and resort re-

---

[26] Mill, *Principles of Political Economy*, vol. 2, p. 338.

treats to the national bourgeoisie and foreign bigwigs and tourists. By contrast, writes Theodore Roszak, "their people wind up as bellhops and souvenir sellers, desk clerks and entertainers, and their proudest traditions soon degenerate into crude caricatures."[27] This is if they are "lucky" enough to get such jobs. All too often prostitution stands between someone's child and starvation in the "growth" economies of the Third World.

A symposium on Third World problems states that "in many countries high growth rates have been accompanied by increasing unemployment, rising disparities in incomes both between groups and between regions, and the deterioration of social and cultural conditions."[28] Among the glaring illustrations of growth distortion is Brazil. In recent years Brazil's "growth rate" has been, to the thinking of bourgeois economists, nothing short of phenomenal, that is, around 10 percent per annum. It has taken over Japan's role as the capitalist world's wonder country of growth, and Japan itself is funneling large amounts of capital into the country. Growth in Brazil, as growth in any underdeveloped country, is attributable not so much to the indigenous development of Brazil as a sovereign state as to the activities of foreign corporate and financial interests. The most profitable concerns are foreign-owned and controlled, especially by Americans.

As with growth in other underdeveloped countries, growth in Brazil is geared to the power and privilege of the few. The Ministry of Public Health received 1 percent of the government budget in 1970 at a time when rural inhabitants may have had only one doctor for as many as 14,727 people (for the rich of Rio de Janeiro, there is one of the highest concentration of doctors in the world).[29] By contrast, the armed forces and internal security police dominate the government budget. Infant mortality is on the increase in the burgeoning slums of São Paulo. University education is increasing for the affluent, while over 25 million people are officially classified as illiterate. Catering to the export market and the national bourgeoisie, the consumer durable goods industry has been growing at over 25 percent annually, but the food industry at only 1.8 percent and textiles 0.1 percent. Landowners who used to grow black beans—the staple of the poor man's diet—for do-

---

[27] Schumacher, *Small is Beautiful,* from the Introduction.

[28] *Development and Environment* (The Hague: Mouton, 1972), pp. 6–7.

[29] Marcio Moreira Alves, "The Political Economy of the Brazilian Technocracy," *Berkeley Journal of Sociology* 19(1974–75):121, 118.

mestic consumption, now grow soya beans—a staple of the rich man's livestock—for export. The price of black beans has recently gone up 400 percent and potatoes 300 percent.

In an article brimming with enthusiasm over investment prospects in Brazil, *The Economist* is forced to comment that "as for public investment, the contrast between private affluence and public squalor in the industrial belt is unbelievable. The roads are full of flashy new cars, while most of the houses do not even have water supply or sewerage."[30] The article observes that "in Brazil's cities middle managers think nothing of pulling in $40,000 a year, and even secretaries in Rio de Janeiro can command up to $15,000 a year. But on the fringe of the cities, the poor live in shanty towns of incredible squalor and count themselves lucky if they earn $10 a week." In view of such extremes of wealth and poverty, *The Economist* flashes the insight that "it is an imbalance, which seems to be characteristic of other fast growing nations, like Japan."

In a country where one third of the population is outside the money market entirely, almost 30 percent being more or less marginal to the market, and overall 40 percent without minimum access to the possibilities offered by contemporary civilized life in Latin America,[31] 3 percent of the population holds 33 percent of the wealth and the poorest 40 percent holds only 9 percent of the wealth. Obeying the law of growth and inequality, the wealth gap has widened since 1960. In terms of income, the richest 5 percent receive 33 percent of the total and the top 20 percent receive 63 percent, contrasted to 3 percent of the income for the bottom 20 percent and 13 percent for the poorest 50 percent. Inequality in Latin America's growth paradise ranks with the most severe of the continent; but there is a bright side: "there are plenty of would-be Rockefellers on the make."[32]

The inverted relationship between growth and inequality in Brazil leads one to conclude with Marcio Alves that "even though the U.S. government presents Brazil as a symbol of triumph before the rest of the underdeveloped countries, a society in which the prosperity of a small minority is gained at the price of the growing misery of the ma-

---

[30] "The Next Japan Emerges From the Jungle," *The Economist*, December 15, 1973, pp. 90, 86.

[31] Cited in Andre Gunder Frank, *Lumpen-Bourgeoisie and Lumpen Development* (New York: Monthly Review Press, 1972), p. 117.

[32] "The Next Japan Emerges From the Jungle," p. 86.

jority does not offer a very seductive model for other Third World countries."[33] There is in Brazil a "harsh dichotomy between growth and well-being."

As with growth and equality in Brazil, so is the same pattern found in India and Pakistan. The material benefits of economic progress have not filtered down to the bottom half of the population, while the degree of inequality has widened since independence.[34] In India, growth since 1960 has been accompanied by increased polarization between the upper and lower thirds of the population.[35] Such polarization is one of the reasons why the Indian government has been spending one third of its budget on the military. Economic growth in the rural areas, where the bulk of the population lives, has meant an increase in the numbers of landless persons who, in turn, drift into the cities to swell the ranks of the unemployed.

What of the fabulous riches inundating the national treasuries of the oil-producing countries? Is there any reason to expect that the new windfall will result in real economic and social development? We should keep in mind that for decades the oil producers from Venezuela to Iran have had substantial flows of royalties into their treasuries with not the slightest indication of applying them toward self-sustaining, socially-productive economic growth. These royalties have been squandered on military supplies, luxury living for the few, real estate speculation, and invested in foreign banks. Will the enormity of the new revenues force redistributive, balanced socioeconomic development?

International oil economist Michael Tanzer doesn't think so: "The prospects for real economic development, in the sense of a rapidly rising standard of living for the great majority of people, are poor. Instead, what is likely to happen is that the increased oil revenues will lead to the handful of rich plus the state bureaucracy getting much richer, while the masses of poor will at best enjoy a marginal increase in living standard."[36] In addition to private and bureaucratic enrichment, Tanzer sees the money going for such things as a few major cap-

---

[33] Alves, "The Political Economy of the Brazilian Technocracy," p. 123.

[34] Angus Maddison, *Class Structure and Economic Growth* (London: George Allen & Unwin Ltd., 1971), p. 11.

[35] Cathleen Gough and Hari P. Sharma, eds., *Imperialism and Revolution in South Asia* (New York: Monthly Review Press, 1973), p. 6.

[36] Michael Tanzer, *The Energy Crisis: World Struggle For Power and Wealth* (New York: Monthly Review Press, 1974), p. 70.

ital-intensive projects in petrochemicals and steel which employ only a handful of people, for military equipment to fight internal threats and other rivals in the area, and for investment in other countries—mainly Europe and North America. A much smaller portion will go for welfare programs. Tanzer points out, by contrast, that the over 100 million Arabs of the oil-producing states could annually absorb billions of dollars worth of prefab houses and durables, capital equipment for broadly based industrialization, agricultural products, and personnel in technology and science. Even a sum as large as $25 billion for Saudi Arabia amounts to only $3,000 per person. If the Arab oil revenues were spread evenly over all Arab nations (the bulk of the revenue actually goes to states having only about 10 percent of the population), the average per capita GNP would amount to less than $800—hardly an embarrassment of riches.

If previous capitalist growth in Third World countries may be taken as a guide to what will happen in the oil-rich countries, including the previous growth patterns of these same countries, the distortion and imbalance in the latter is likely to exceed anything to have gone before it. In addition to the foreign financial adventures, Tanzer foresees a narrow kind of modernization taking place with "rapidly increasing wealth for the merchants and traders, real estate speculators, importers of luxury goods, wealthy landowners, and top bureaucrats and army officers." "Without a social revolution at home," writes Tanzer, "they can't use these funds productively for general social benefit."[37] The same applies to Venezuela, Indonesia, or any other major oil producer. Growing inequality symbolized by outlandish luxury spending in the midst of poverty will require increasing application of repression to hold together the old order. The stepped up activity of the secret police in Iran is indicative of this. The imperialist powers will sell ample arms and offer ample technical and ideological support ("retired" American military personnel are already training government forces in Iran and Saudi Arabia). Perhaps the old order can be held together long enough to suck out the last saleable barrel of oil; that will remove at least one cause for social revolution.

Another noteworthy case in the contentious relationship between growth and social development is that of Japan. Despite boasting the world's highest growth rate during the 1960s (11 percent), Japan's

---

[37] Ibid., pp. 71, 148. See also, Ray Vicker, "Easy Come, Easy Go," *The Wall Street Journal*, October 17, 1975, pp. 1, 21.

quality of development has given pause to many observers. One observer remarks that during the 1960s, environmental pollution and urban problems became severe, and creeping inflation set in.[38] At a time when corporations were making record profits (47 percent for the top 824) much of which was spent on purely speculative investments, the government made cutbacks in demand for housing, water supply, sewerage, public transportation, education, medicine, and welfare. On the other hand, government was investing 55 percent of its budget in industrial infrastructure such as roads, rail, factory sites, and industrial water supply. At the core of Japanese industry is heavy steel, chemical, and oil operations which, in Osaka, consume 50 to 60 percent of the energy and water supply but contribute only 22 percent of the economic value added.

Whereas Japanese agricultural self-sufficiency has dropped to only 40 percent, the urban population grew from 44 million to 75 million from 1950 to 1970. At the forefront of an American-style consumerist society is, of course, the automobile—of which there are 1,300 per hectare compared to a mere 120 in the United States. The picture of some of Tokyo's 22 million people cramming themselves into high-speed commuter trains is one not the result of enlightened foresight but rather of sheer survival requirements. If there were more space, there would perhaps be even more Toyotas and Datsuns idling in the Tokyo smog.

In view of the above developments, Ken'ichi Miyamoto writes, "Consequently, finding solutions to urban problems is becoming more and more difficult and it may be impossible to avoid catastrophe in Tokyo, Osaka, and other metropolises by the end of the present decade."[39]

Toward what ultimate point?

The most plausible answer to Mill's question "Toward what ultimate point is society tending?" is toward no point at all, at least not in any sense of a philosophy of history or ideology of progress. The only discernible trends are leading toward decay and destruction. The suicidal direction of present history reveals the very absence of any meaning or rationale to social evolution. The main tendencies within Western in-

---

[38] Ken'ichi Miyamoto, "Japanese Capitalism at a Turning Point," *Monthly Review* 26(December 1974):15.

[39] Ibid., p. 17.

dustrial society, and the entire world capitalist system, are essentially absurd. The system is literally senseless; it has no social vision, no cultural imagination, and no spiritual values. The prevailing society is numb to these larger human goals and ends. Its only real vision is that of more power, its only real imagery that of more goods, and its only real value that of more money. Ours is a history which looks only down, not paying any attention where it is headed. It is too busy accumulating power, goods, and money. Mill clearly realized this, and that is why he raised the question in the first place. It is a question which is intended to make people pause from their life routines and ask themselves what their activities mean, if indeed anything. Of what consequence is their action? Does it bind them into a socially secure, rewarding human group? Does it provide them with a feeling of purposive control over their lives? Does it encourage them to develop their individual talents and abilities in a satisfying manner? Does it harmonize them with their natural surroundings? Does it stir broad ranges of emotional and spiritual feeling?

The momentum of our society has not even allowed any sustained and serious discussion of these issues. The forward crush of growth has greatly diminished every other contender for societal attention. Growth is pressed upon us with the justification that it enhances social well-being, and the more growth the greater the extent of well-being. The tendency of society according to the prevailing wisdom then is toward greater and greater well-being. No future stopping point is designated, no attainable ideal is held out toward which we should direct our energies. We are led around in a vicious circle, supposedly an upward spiral vaguely leading to some yet unforeseen terminus which holds a short work week, plenty of material security, and a cornucopia of goods. What this is costing and shall cost us in terms of human community, cultural integration, and environmental viability cannot be considered. Nor is the desirability of pursuing such ends, at least as simple extensions of what we now know as work, security, and goods given over to debate. What the meaning and rewards of work might be for people, or how such work could relate to the rest of their lives, is not a legitimate topic either.

The upward spiral toward some technological utopia of material abundance is increasingly seen for what it really is: a futile and destructive descent into an unsustainable carnival of resource gluttony and ecological disruption which undermines all hope of creating a sense of human purpose and direction and of maintaining a durable society and environment. We are told salvation is to be found in an ever expanding output of goods and services and that growth means social progress. To ask about the nature and meaning of the goods and of the growth is to ask seemingly heretical questions.

If growth and social progress are not assumed to be opposite sides of the same coin, then it is only one step further to the notion that social progress has no direct relation to growth, at least after a certain point which may be long past. Growth beyond such a point, particularly artificially forced growth, may be seen to reverse previous progress, destroying the foundation upon which a socialist society and culture could be constructed. These are dangerous assumptions and thoughts, for once the link between growth and progress is broken, we are free to think of progress in wholly independent terms. Such an independent philosophy of life and history would in all likelihood lead to a complete reevaluation of growth and its place in human society. Further, it is also most likely (or should we say necessary) that an independent evaluation of growth would end in its dethronement, at least insofar as we have come to know it and lead to its redefinition to mean social, cultural, and spiritual expansion.

The severence of the idea of growth from that of progress and well-being is as heretical as it is necessary, for the ideological enthronement of growth is only a powerful gloss for an economic system which demands growth for its own survival. The challenges to human survival come originally and most forcefully from the economic system, and to respond effectively to these challenges—be they environmental, demographic, agricultural, technological, or psychological—requires, in turn, the challenging of that same economic system and its underlying growth drive. In these terms we are able to see why disuniting growth and well-being is a radical act. To challenge growth from any perspective, whether it be in terms of well-being or something else, is to challenge the pivot around which revolves social, cultural, and psychic relations. Thus, those who would challenge and redefine growth are acting as radically as those who directly pursue socialist political goals, inasmuch as the success of either requires thorough-going and far-reaching alterations in the organization of production and therefore in society and culture overall. By the same token a genuine socialism must itself ultimately view growth in sociocultural and individual terms.

The necessary linkage between capitalism and growth stands at the center of the foregoing line of thought. The centrality of this linkage, that is of growth to capitalism or vice versa, requires much clarification. There are a great many people who have never thought of placing growth and capitalism so closely together, or at least in such a vital and inseparable way. We have been taught that growth and well-being are partners, and that capitalism and well-being are partners as well; where instruction has been weak is on the subject of capitalism's dependency upon growth. This is artful and self-protective neglect, since to understand that capitalism requires growth may lead to the suspicion that neither has anything to do with well-being, but is merely in the unending service of the other. Indeed, it is precisely such a suspicion which is catching on, and it is precisely this movement which has brought out the growth advocates to further instruct us on the subject of growth and well-being. The emphasis now is on growth and well-being rather than capitalism and well-being, since the mounting gyrations of capitalism have already begun to undercut its claim as a partner to well-being.

Our next task, then, is to examine the linkage between growth and capitalism, and to see why capitalism as an economic system has such an insatiable appetite for growth.

3

The growth society

Hooked on growth

"Our system is hooked on growth per se," writes growth critic and economist Herman E. Daly, "and does *not* see growth as a temporary *means* of attaining some optimum level of stocks, but as an *end* in itself."[1] Being addicted to growth implies that its withdrawal would be painful, setting in motion a series of systemic reactions which would throw the entire society into a state of confusion and disarray. The longer the withdrawal of growth and the greater the reduction of the growth dosage, the more severe are the system's reactions. A fresh injection of growth stimulus turns the failing system around again and heads it healthily on its way upward. However, the new feeling of well-being is to a large extent illusory, since to sustain the euphoria requires ever larger growth doses. The increasing size of these doses soon overburdens the system, tightening up every possible loose end. The system cannot sustain any further growth dosages; in fact, it is already badly stretched out and overextended. It is time for a drying-out period, a withdrawal of growth inputs. The drying out will hurt everywhere, though some parts will suffer incomparably worse than others. But these are the less significant parts which must be sacrificed on behalf of the future; the important parts of the system weather the storm quite

---

[1] Herman E. Daly, ed., *Toward a Steady-State Economy* (San Francisco: W. H. Freeman and Company, 1973), p. 167.

well and courageously endure any hardships, knowing that the con-
tracting present is laying the grounds for an even greater expansion
than before. Thus, highs and lows are alternatingly manipulated toward
always better future highs.

The analogy of growth addiction, like most analogies, breaks down
at many points. The most fundamental difference between an addict
and an addicted economy is that the former *can* give up the drug following the drying-out period, whereas the latter cannot give up growth.
The addict can return to a stable and balanced life, provided there are
social conditions to encourage and allow it. The growth society cannot
enjoy stability and balance, for it is in as bad or worse shape at the end
of the drying-out period as it was during its illusory high. Without a
new growth dosage, the floundering growth society simply flounders
more and more, rising a little at the thought of receiving a new injection, but falling back down unless receiving a substantial dose. As the
health of the growth society continues to fail, the size of the dosage for
renewed viability must be correspondingly larger.

Our knowledge of the growth society's behavior comes from 150
years experience. We have seen it rise and fall over and over again. It
fell to an all time low in the 1930s, but heavy dosages of military spending for World War II put the growth society back on its feet (just as
spending for World War I had done previously).[2] It sometimes showed
signs of slipping again during the past three decades, only to be shored
up by more military spending, ten years of heavy warfare, a new wave
of automobilization,[3] and, increasingly, massive debt at all levels. Such
have been the main stimulants to continued growth and the avoidance
of systemic collapse.

The nature of the stimulants, however, are lethal in their own way,
and cannot be continuously applied without provoking a variety of
environmental, political, and economic repercussions which already
threaten collapse. Few stimulants are available to take up the mounting
threat of a heavy crash, for the stimulants acceptable to the society's
rulers have already been stretched to the breaking point. Even the traditional symptoms of highs and lows, of boom and recession are be-

---

[2] See Paul M. Sweezy and Harry Magdoff, "The Economic Crisis in Historical
Perspective," *Monthly Review* 26(March 1975):1–8.

[3] Automobilization includes not only the direct auto-related industries such as
steel, glass, fibers, electronics, and petroleum, but also the construction of highways and the entire suburban spawl made possible by the auto.

coming clouded and mixed. The growth system hardly knows whether it is going up or down anymore, as boom symptoms like inflation are associated with recession symptoms like unemployment. Advisors to the national economic health fear new injections for what these might do to worsen the destabilization caused by inflation, while they fear abstaining from new injections for what this might do to worsen the political threat caused by unemployment. Thus, a new term has appeared in our vocabulary: stagflation. Stagnation and inflation, the perennial threats to the growth society, have attacked the system simultaneously and with a new vengeance as they become immune to old remedies used too often and too much.

Why and how we grow

Why is it that capitalism must grow, or at least swing through cycles that recreate the conditions for growth? For centuries at a time other types of societies have persisted largely unchanged with regard to per capita wealth and level of technology. Then comes a system whose very essence is growth. Karl Marx constructed his entire economic and social theory around the logic of capitalist growth. He recognized the relentless drive toward accumulation and expansion within capitalism, and saw that this drive would wipe out virtually all remnants of the previous society and spread itself over the entire globe. Marx stressed that, whereas previous types of societies were not so much regulated by economic laws as by cultural value systems, capitalism obeyed economic laws of growth and development which were beyond the control of those subjected to them.

This inability to control and direct one's own social world, to be subject to the laws of economic growth, is the essence of what Marx meant by alienation. Under capitalism, producers are stripped of the ownership and control of their means of production; they are deprived of the decisions of when, what, how, and where to produce; the products of their labor are appropriated by another class; and they are unable to cooperatively organize the affairs of their workplaces and community. Nor are the capitalist owners, decision-makers, and appropriators free to act as they please. They, too, are bound to the laws of growth and development. If they fail to grow, they will be swallowed up by others who do grow, and their lives as capitalists will be ended.

Marx did not seek to end growth of this sort, at least not up to a point. Rather, growth eradicated backwardness of the old order and moved human productive capacities toward higher levels. The development of these productive capacities held the promise of liberation, of release from the realm of economic necessity. Alienation could be overcome as people stepped out from under the laws of growth and took charge of a powerful productive apparatus to make it work entirely for their own liberation. A socialist society is one freed from the dictates of growth and open to the possibilities of social, cultural, and personal development—that is, growth in the fullest sense.[4] The great problem of modern history is the transition from the growth society to the socialist society; it is the problem of socialist revolution.

Our concern here, however, is with the forces behind growth. Without entering into a discussion of what combination of factors initiated the growth society originally,[5] we may observe that the chief requirement for growth is profit. Profit represents net gain to the capitalist following his outlay for the factors of production, including machinery, raw materials, and labor. The fundamental source of profit lies in the fact that the cost of labor is less than the value which labor produces; labor is the "variable" aspect of production in that it produces more value than it costs to buy and replace it.

In this connection, Marx early emphasized that modern industrial labor is not to be conceived of in primarily individual terms, but rather in interdependent social terms (the "social individual"). The powerful productive machinery at the disposal of social labor is also capable of producing wealth far beyond the cost of the labor required to build it, although capitalists still must measure value in terms of labor time. If any other criteria were applied as a measure of value, say disposable or free time, it would negate the capitalist appropriation of surplus wealth, which is nothing other than surplus labor time beyond that required to support the worker. As we shall observe presently, a "no-growth" or noncapitalistic society would transform such surplus labor time (which capitalists must appropriate for growth) into disposable or free time available to all for the pursuit of self-development and social growth. Disposable time would become the measure of wealth, since during such

---

[4] See Karl Marx, *Grundrisse* (New York: Vintage Books, 1973), pp. 692–712.

[5] See Ernest Mandel, *Marxist Economic Theory*, vols. 1 and 2 (New York: Monthly Review Press, 1968).

time individuals could enlarge their own productive powers and understanding in arts and science, productive individuals (social individuals) being the real wealth of any society. Such a development would release an expansion of society's productive capacity far in excess of that forced by the laws of capitalist development.

Returning to the growth process, we see that the capitalist may deal in goods (industrial capitalists), services (service industry), or simply money (finance capitalist), as long as labor is hired in the process. Whatever the commodity might be, as long as profit arises out of the various exchanges, we have a capitalist relation and the basis for growth.

Profit cannot be consistently realized by one capitalist overcharging another or by overcharging other buyers. While this is frequently done and accounts for some part of individual firms' profits, the overall ability of the system as a whole to grow on such a basis is obviously impossible. This would merely involve shifting the same amount of wealth around in a circle of ever higher prices as each buyer passed on the excess charges to the next. Such a process may be going on by itself within a stagnating economy, thus producing inflation without growth; or it may be going on simultaneously with real growth, or conceivably, not at all.

Growth is harder to come by than swindling or tricks of bookkeeping, although swindlers and operators may grab a substantial share of real growth, particularly during an expansionary phase. Profit and growth come from the labor of human beings with the assistance of tools and machines. In advanced capitalism, machines assume an increasingly greater role in production vis-a-vis labor power until humans "only" design, help construct, assemble, maintain, and tend machines. The source of profit is not, however, changed. Without labor there can be no profit, no growth. To be sure, the individual worker produces mountains more of both products and profits with machines than without, and the more automated the machinery the higher is the worker's productivity. Such is precisely the basis for liberation from the laws of growth, since the labor time required to meet the material needs of a society steadily shrinks in relation to free time available to pursue social and self-development. However, the growth society must counteract the danger of free time being valued over more goods, for profit requires both labor and expanding consumption.

With profit the capitalist is able to invest in further production, or we should say he *must* invest in further production. If he did not, another capitalist somewhere else will invest, and by so doing raise the level of productivity of his workers and broaden his sales which, in turn, yields a greater volume of profit. The greater productivity and profit could then be turned against the backward capitalist either by driving him out of business with lower prices or buying him out. In developing capitalism, cutthroat competition leaves the weaker by the wayside and allows the stronger to grow ever larger.

Thus, competitive capitalism gives way to monopoly capitalism, a system whose sectors are dominated by a handful of industrial and financial giants. The transition to monopoly capitalism far from puts an end to competition or the growth drive. There are still a variety of threats to even the monopolist, not the least of these being foreign capitalists, small unbeaten domestic firms, and firms producing substitutable products.[6] Even monopolists in the same field, although largely in accord on regulating prices, battle each other for shares of the domestic market through expensive promotion and advertising. Abroad, the corporate monopolists scramble to expand in order to gain control over sources of raw materials and new markets. If they do not, other foreign firms will. Those giants who hesitate soon find themselves losing control over their supplies, markets, and worst of all, prices and profits. As Harry Magdoff observes, "The entire mechanism of a market economy . . . forces a restless drive of capital to expand."[7] It has been observed that the process of expansion becomes an ideological force.[8]

Within individual firms, growth is the chief means whereby opportunities arise for management personnel, the "technostructure," to use John Kenneth Galbraith's term. Growth of the firm or industry means more and better jobs for upwardly mobile executives and managers, higher salaries and bigger bonuses, larger expense accounts and retirement benefits, stock options, and more prestige and privilege. Take the bonus, which can amount to three times the six-figure salary a top company official draws; in 1973 69 top General Motors executives received compensation of $21 million, whereas in sagging 1974 they received $6.6 million, all in salaries. The chairman of the company, for example,

[6] Arthur MacEwan, "Capitalist Expansion, Ideology and Intervention," *Review of Radical Political Economics* 4(Winter 1972):36–58.

[7] Harry Magdoff, *The Age of Imperialism* (New York: Monthly Review Press, 1969), p. 24.

[8] MacEwan, "Capitalist Expansion, Ideology and Intervention," p. 38.

saw his $563,000 bonus of 1973 completely vanish in 1974, leaving him with only his $272,500 salary.

Thus, Galbraith can write that "the whole corpus of the technostructure is deeply committed to growth," and "its primary concern is with growth."[9] Galbraith points out that the technostructure seeks growth through the acquisition of other firms in order to increase size, financial reward, power, and prestige. There is also the need for growth if management is to receive a good rating and hold its position, if the firm is going to hold onto and recruit talent and find places for mobile persons, and is going to avoid being taken over by another firm.[10] A company must grow in order to expand its research and development program, to increase its advertising, to pay off interest and loans, and to maintain the confidence of banks and investors in general.

What drives the corporate elite, the corporation, and the corporate system may not be identical in all cases, but the forces are intertwined and mutually reinforcing. We are primarily concerned with the growth requirements of the system as such, since here are found the underpinnings of the growth society. It is the corporate system as such which must realize profit; top executives and individual firms can and often do fail.

The success of the growth society is by no means assured by the realization of profit, or by continued success over opponents. In order to realize each round of profits, the growth society must find a place to profitably invest its previous gains. As it turns out, the process of making profit, that is, of transforming labor into profit and appropriating it, is very easy compared to the process of finding places to reinvest that profit so as to again yield a satisfactory (maximum) return. This has always been, and more than ever continues to be, the great nemesis of the growth society. Marx early emphasized that the chief obstacle to the expansion of capital was capital itself, that is, the growth of capital makes each successive profitable reapplication of that capital more difficult. The larger and more mechanized the productive base the greater the volume of goods produced, the easier the markets saturated, the fewer the number of workers required and paid, and the lower the society's ability to buy. Stagnation threatens; inflation is stimulated by

---

[9] John Kenneth Galbraith, *Economics and the Public Purpose* (Boston: Houghton Mifflin Company, 1973), pp. 102–03.

[10] Neil W. Chamberlain, *The Limits of Corporate Responsibility* (New York: Basic Books, Inc., 1973), p. 6.

credit flows aimed at warding off depression. Under monopoly capitalism, prices are raised in an effort to compensate for slipping sales volume, a weapon which couldn't be applied under competitive conditions.

The entire growth sequence hinges on the ability of the economy to
absorb investment in the capital goods sector, the sector which produces
the productive machinery base itself. Growth requires that the investment be over and above that necessary for replacement of existing
stocks, that there be new net investment. During the building-up
process of an industrial society, the rate of growth is determined by the
amount of profit or gain which is plowed back into the expansion of the
capital goods sector. Building up the productive base of machines that
make machines and of machines that make consumer goods creates
employment and thus wage incomes which are, in turn, able to purchase the consumer goods.

Despite the fact that the whole production process is undertaken by
the capitalist for purposes of profit and not to meet social consumption
needs, it is also true that unless needs continue to exist and unless people have the money means to meet such needs, profit itself cannot possibly be realized. And if there is to be growth, which there must be if a
downward spiral of stagnation is to be avoided, not only must the customary needs continue to require regular replenishment and the money
means continue to be available, but new needs and additional money
means must also be created. More importantly, any new needs must be
amenable to profitable satisfaction; they cannot involve largely nonconsumptive activities, such as contemplative leisure, sociality and con-
versation, learning, local production of craft and food goods, art and
music.

During the initial building up of industrialization, a period which
can cover a relatively long time period or be greatly compacted depending upon the availability of the means and the proportion of new production which is plowed back into the base rather than consumed, the
obstacles to growth are comparatively small inasmuch as basic needs
are widespread, the demand for labor in heavy industry is great, and
there is sufficient money wages to buy what consumer goods are available. (Remember that the emphasis during build-up is on capital or
producer goods which consumers cannot buy.) In time, however, the
capital goods sector becomes large and powerful enough to make all
the machinery required to produce the consumer goods which people
need and want or have the money to buy. Firms which produce the

means of production are confined to replacement orders as consumer goods industries level off. Declining capital goods demand combined with on-going productivity gains reduce employment which, in turn, diminishes the amount of money available for consumer goods. A reduction in demand for consumer goods reverberates slack back to capital goods production and employment, and so the tendency toward stagnation and depression is reinforced.

To counter the tendency toward stagnation arising from the satisfaction of consumer needs, the growth interests employ heavy advertising campaigns, high pressure salesmanship, an unending stream of new products, built-in obsolescence, style obsolescence, and expansion into new markets. To counter the tendency toward stagnation arising from insufficient money among potential buyers, the growth system extends larger and larger amounts of credit resulting in rising mountains of debt for individuals, businesses, and government. The latter has become especially crucial in the battle against stagnation as a major buyer (especially of military equipment) and employer, and in the process has become the major debtor. In its battle against stagnation, the government fuels inflation. With varying degrees of success, the system plays out all possible acceptable alternatives to sustain or revive growth.

With every increase in size of the productive base the natural regenerative processes of the boom-bust cycle become more sluggish. By the 1930s these regenerative processes could not be activated even with unprecedented government intervention. Only World War II started the machinery rolling again. Since then every manner of government and corporate, economic, political and military activity at home and abroad has been required, including the exorbitant and disastrous Vietnam intervention. The result has been an economy, polity, environment, and society in such disarray as to threaten breakdown. The growth system is "up tight," thresholds of systemic tolerance are rapidly being approached, and another major drying-out spell could prove to be too traumatic for the system to survive. This danger is the reason why the onset of another major depression instills such morbid fear in the hearts of growth proponents.

Why must a society go about forcing such growth after the productive base has been sufficiently enlarged to meet normal needs? Why isn't it possible to simply shift additional profit or surplus wealth into individual and social growth, to eliminate public and private impoverishment, and to get about the business of creating a balanced world society and environment? In other words, why can't we utilize our productive resources to meet the needs of people instead of the needs of capital?

The answer to this question is so obvious it easily escapes us: to choose leisure over wage labor, to choose primarily nonconsumptive activities over primarily consumptive ones, and to emphasize human services over capital goods is to undermine the capitalist class whose very existence depends upon wage labor, consumption, and inequality. A shift to human development from capital development would involve nothing less than the end of the capitalist class. "It is tantamount," writes Robert Heilbroner, "to asking a dominant class to acquiesce in the elimination of the very activities that sustain it."[11]

Since the capitalist class and its representatives in the state hold power over the economy, it is perfectly understandable why a shift from economic to social growth cannot happen under capitalism. Social growth and capitalism are contradictory developments. This contradiction could be concealed as long as capital growth made indirect contributions to social growth; but once expanded to its mature form and plagued with increasingly intransigent stagnation, the completely self-serving function of capital and its owners becomes more and more evident. The contradiction between the needs of social development and those of capital growth openly collide.

The collision between the needs of balanced development and capital growth are manifest in widespread unemployment and enforced idleness, shoddy and harmful products, environmental degradation, resource waste, high rates of work-related injury and disease, urban blight, deteriorating medical services, juvenile delinquency, rising drug use, and deadening educational routines. The collision is also evident in housing shortages, high cost of basic necessities, expanding welfare roles, unmitigated racial conflict, the absence of efficient and inexpensive public transport; in short, the entire gamut of excesses and shortages which arise from the preoccupation of the growth system with profit as opposed to balanced social growth.

Why do we grow? Because we are cogs in an economic machinery which must grow in order to survive. We are forced to contend with all of the system's internal contradictions and needs as these are acted

---

[11] Robert L. Heilbroner, "Ecological Armageddon," in Warren A. Johnson and John Hardesty, eds., *Economic Growth vs The Environment* (Belmont, Cal.: Wadsworth Publishing Company, Inc., 1971), p. 44.

out in a series of accelerating crises which bring with them completely
unnecessary social decay and hardship. We are told to be thankful for
the circus of electric gadgets, throwaways, packaged foods, new chemicals, transistorized noise, plastic flowers, color television, film spectaculars, sports spectaculars, power mowers and power blowers, power
boats and power cars, trail bikes and snowmobiles, freeways and jets,
and interminable other socially, mentally, and ecologically erosive commodities. Any attempt to oppose the flow and expansion of "new and
better" things is denounced by growth enthusiasts as elitism, ridiculed
as faddism, and charged as un-American. If America represents nothing
more in the world than the epitome of the growth society, then indeed
it is un-American to channel wealth into social and self-development
and to conserve resources in an environmentally sound manner.

Just as planning for capital growth is done on a wide scale (believe
it or not), so must planning for social growth occur. However, whereas
planning for capital growth is done by the miniscule capitalist class,
planning for social growth by definition must involve everyone. Social
growth cannot be engineered from above. An important part of human
development is precisely the shedding of an alienated self, of stepping
out of dependency and powerlessness to play a role in shaping a new
society.

What are the chances of controlling and redirecting growth? Heilbroner, for one, is not hopeful: "The problem is that the challenge to
survival still lies sufficiently far in the future, and the inertial momentum of the present industrial order is still so great, that no substantial
voluntary diminution of growth, much less a planned reorganization
of society, is today even remotely imaginable."[12]

One may take issue with this assessment in several places. Firstly,
the challenge to survival is not far in the future; important aspects of
the challenge are already upon us and no one is sure just how much
time remains to avert various catastrophes. Secondly, the momentum
of the present order is not at all great; indeed, the state has had to enter into economic affairs in a massive way in an effort to keep up what
momentum is left. Deep recession and the threat of economic collapse
have become constant concerns. Thirdly, a voluntary diminution of
growth is a contradiction in terms; the capitalist class cannot cut off the

---

[12] Robert L. Heilbroner, *An Inquiry Into The Human Prospect* (New York:
W. W. Norton & Company, Inc., 1974), p. 133.

source of its own existence and reproduction. The growth system has no choice but to continue the pursuit of growth. Fourthly, given the above corrections, a planned reorganization of society is clearly imaginable. What is not conceivable is that the people will meekly follow the dictates of the growth system toward civilizational and ecological oblivion. Human beings have not yet been transformed into lemmings charging over a cliff into the sea. Something on this order is seemingly happening now, but there is reason to believe that an awakening, a coming to the social senses, is also taking place. Given a better understanding of why we grow and how the growth society works is a vital part of this awareness, of where we are and what we must do. Once we have come that far, there is again no reason to believe that the onetime subjects of growth cannot become its masters.

The stationary state

In the midst of the welter of growth proponents, spokesmen for a "stationary-state" economy have made an appearance. Thus, the concept of the stationary state has of late been the subject of some controversy. However, it is by no means a novel concept; economists had long ago given the stationary-state idea some thought. Classical economists such as Malthus and Ricardo, for example, feared that increasing scarcity of natural resources would render economic activity less productive and more costly, eventually resulting in the gradual diminution and cessation of investment and growth. Conversely, J. S. Mill much less feared the prospect of a stationary state than he welcomed it. Mill wrote, "It must always have been seen, more or less distinctly, by political economists, that the increase of wealth is not boundless; that at the end of what they term the progressive state lies the stationary state, that all progress in wealth is but a postponement of this, and that each step in advance is an approach to it."[13] In the following passage Mill elaborates his position:

> I cannot, therefore, regard the stationary state of capital and wealth with the unaffected aversion so generally manifested towards it by political economists of the old school. I am inclined to believe that it

---

[13] J. S. Mill, *Principles of Political Economy*, vol. 2 (New York: D. Appleton & Company, 1908), p. 334.

would be, on the whole, a very considerable improvement on our present condition. I confess I am not charmed with the ideal of life held out by those who think that the normal state of human beings is that of struggling to get on; that the trampling, crushing, elbowing, and treading on each other's heels, which form the existing type of social life, are the most desirable lot of human kind, or anything but the disagreeable symptoms of one of the phases of industrial progress.[14]

Mill's opposition to the growth society is founded upon a cultural argument against the moral and behavioral traits generated by "economic progress" as well as the recognition of the finite limits to growth. Thus, pressure toward a stationary-state society may come from the cultural and moral desirability of balance and from the physical and natural cost of growth. As to the most forceful of the two pressures, stationary-state advocate Daly argues that "although biophysical constraints on economic growth are the more easily recognizable, social and moral constraints are likely to be the more stringent. In other words, the economic steady state will be desirable socially long before physical limitations will make it a necessity."[15] The British historian Arnold Toynbee stresses that "more and more people are coming to realize that the growth of material wealth . . . cannot in truth be the 'wave of the future.' Nature is going to compel posterity to revert to a stable state on a material plane and to turn to the realm of the spirit for satisfying man's hunger for infinity."[16] Toynbee would, of course, hope that people turn to cultural and spiritual pursuits long before nature forces it— a point at which, we might add, it may well be too late to salvage anything but subcivilizational subsistence.

In economic terms, exactly what is a stationary, or steady, state? Daly defines the steady state as "an economy in which the total population and the total stock of physical wealth are maintained constant at some desired levels by a 'minimal' rate of maintenance throughput (i.e., by birth and death rates that are equal at the lowest feasible level, and by physical production and consumption rates that are equal at the lowest feasible level)."[17] From this definition we may proceed toward further elaboration of both the contents and the implications of the stationary state.

---

14 Ibid., p. 336.
15 Daly, ed., *Toward a Steady-State Economy*, p. 117.
16 Cited in Daly, ed., *Toward a Steady-State Economy*, p. 118.
17 Ibid., pp. 152–53.

Firstly, we may specify four major dimensions of the growth society which to various degrees must come under control in a stationary state: population, capital stocks, technology, and consumption. Within the growth society, all four of these dimensions have been increasing. Within a stationary state, all four must attain a stabilizing balance. One may easily see several possible combinations of growth, decline, and stability between the four dimensions. For example, a growing population with steady capital stocks and technology means lowered average consumption. Or a stationary population and capital stocks with improving technology could mean increased consumption; it could also mean steady consumption if the technological improvements just compensated for a declining stock of natural resources. While we could spell out other possible combinations and degrees of steadiness, let's stop with this latter combination of factors. Stationary population and capital stocks combined with improving technology to compensate for declining natural resources could preserve consumption levels. This would be, in fact, the most likely condition of an ongoing stationary state. Variations of the four dimensions over time there would naturally be, but the tendency would always be back toward an equilibrium.

Secondly, there is the question of what constitutes the optimal level of these dimensions. We shall subsequently deal at some length with population; suffice it to say here that most stationary-state advocates and anti-growth people regard the size of the world's population as already being beyond optimal from the standpoint of pressure upon resources and life quality. As to capital stocks, optimal size would hinge upon the cultural ideals and aspirations of those implicated. From a resources and environmental perspective, the optimal size of physical wealth would be the minimum required for a healthy and secure existence for all members of the society. From a social and cultural perspective the optimal size of physical wealth would be the minimum required for the pursuit of full individual and societal growth and development. The composition of the stocks would be quite drastically different from what we see before us today, a conservative one half of which is sheer waste required and produced by the growth system. Thus, given the same magnitude of today's capital stocks, a rationally ordered steady-state economy could accommodate a vast increase in the amount of wealth directed toward individual and societal growth, while at the same time greatly reducing the amount of wealth which is wasteful and destructive of resources and environment. That social growth may go on, in all likelihood accelerate, in a "no growth" society was early marked by Mill:

> It is scarcely necessary to remark that a stationary condition of capital and population implies no stationary state of human improvement. There would be as much scope as ever for all kinds of mental culture, and moral and social progress; as much room for improving the Art of Living, and much more likelihood of its being improved, when minds ceased to be engrossed by the art of getting on.[18]

Here Mill's ideas converge with those of Marx on disposable time and liberation.

As to technology, again we shall treat it separately and state here only that the stationary state by no means precludes technological advances. Rather, such improvements would be required to compensate for declining resource availability, to increase productivity when existing machinery is replaced so as to reduce the necessary size of stocks (particularly if there is any population growth), to reduce or eliminate undesirable labor, and to develop recycling and pollution control techniques. As in the case of the stocks themselves, the composition of technology would be altered significantly within a stationary state. Only a nongrowth, noncapitalist system can create the conditions required to develop a human-oriented technology both in its operation and application. To take just one example here, Daly points out that "taking the benefits of technological progress in the form of increased leisure is a reversal of the historical (capitalist) practice of taking the benefits mainly in the form of goods, and has extensive social implications."[19] To apply technology so as to increase leisure in the sense of positive free time requires overturning of the whole structure of wage labor, material goods incentive, economic inequality, and thus, the foundations of the capitalist class itself. The same logic holds true for a technology which places worker understanding and control above "efficiency" and environmental impact above profit.

Thirdly, the stationary state strives for stability not only in population, capital stocks, and technology, it also seeks to minimize throughput. The aims of the stationary state would fail if throughput were not minimized, even given constants in population, physical wealth, and

---

[18] Mill, *Principles of Political Economy*, vol. 2, pp. 339–40.

[19] Herman E. Daly, "Toward a Stationary-State Economy," in John Harte and Robert H. Socolow, eds., *Patient Earth* (New York: Holt, Rinehart and Winston, Inc., 1971), p. 238.

technology. For the aims of the stationary state are to conserve resources, minimize pollution, and free people to pursue primarily nonconsumptive sociocultural activities in their leisure time. The growth
society is the epitome of high throughput; its survival depends upon
high throughput and its goal is to maximize it. Otherwise, overproduction and stagnation will overcome us. Waste is a vital ingredient of economic growth. Throwaway and built-in obsolescence are essential to
"prosperity." One observer stresses that if sustained growth is dependent upon the proliferation of shoddy commodities, then a slowdown
and the production of goods that last would strike at the root of the
economic structure.[20] In his classic The Wastemakers, Vance Packard
took note that "the people of the United States are in a sense becoming
a nation on a tiger. They must learn to consume more and more or, they
are warned, their magnificent economic machine may turn and devour
them. They must be induced to step up their individual consumption
higher and higher, whether they have any pressing need for the goods
or not."[21] Mill's worst visions have come true.

The restriction of production to materially durable, socially necessary, and culturally supportive goods would immeasurably assist in
halting environmental deterioration and the achievement of ecological
balance. The value of permanence and quality for psychological and
emotional health should also not be underestimated, a fact almost forgotten in today's plastic world. The stationary state, observes Daly,
maximizes the time matter spends as wealth and minimizes the time it
spends as garbage.[22] How different this is from the mountains of garbage, much of it virtually indestructible, funneled through the growth
society and into watery and earthly graves (if it even gets that far).

Finally, the notion of the stationary state carries profound social and
political implications for the structure of class and power in the existing order. A stationary state would seriously undermine the position
of the capitalist class, for insofar as the stationary state remained capitalist, it would gradually (or suddenly) lose its ability to reproduce the
means of production and sustenance as the absence of profitable investment opportunities would reduce capitalist financial activity into
a downward spiral. In leading economist Kenneth Boulding's words,

[20] Harvey Salgo, "The Obsolescence of Growth: Capitalism and the Environmental Crisis," Review of Radical Political Economics 5(Fall 1973):28.
[21] Vance Packard, The Wastemakers (New York: Pocket Books, Inc., 1960), p. 6.
[22] Daly, ed., Toward a Steady-State Economy, p. 157.

"Thus, for a market society, there is a real danger that even the approach of a stationary state and the diminution of net investment could result in a very serious crisis of the kind which occurred in the United States between 1929 and 1932."[23] The ability of the capitalist class to preside over society would be in doubt and its own regenerative capacity would begin to erode. Capitalism would face extinction. Small wonder, then, that Heilbroner asserts "A 'stationary,' non-expanding capitalism has always been considered either as a prelude to its collapse or as a betrayal of its historic purpose."[24]

Yet this is not all which would be profound about the stationary state. The stationary state is by definition oriented toward social and cultural growth rather than capital growth. Certainly, *significant and substantial improvements in material condition and quality would become possible for the great majority of the population simply through elimination of waste and the transformation of investment and innovation.* How many sound but modest homes or apartments could be built for the cost of one skyscraper? How many rapid transit systems could be constructed for the cost of foreign military activity? To be sure, the stationary state would both give rise to and require material advance. Material advance would be required for the majority inasmuch as without overall growth there would have to be redistribution of wealth. There could be no more pacification through trickle down and promises of everybody "moving up." The stationary state would give rise to material advance insofar as there would be a release of free time for the pursuit of creative arts and science.

Without individual material gain coming primarily from wage labor, the entire system of individual materialist work incentives would crumble. Material gains would, as noted above, come through redistribution and social reinvestment. A stationary state would function largely upon social incentives and freely associated labor, since individuals could little or not at all increase their private consumption by additional wage labor. The creation of a stationary state in the first place would, unless imposed by force, assume the society is confident that redistribution and transformation of investment innovation would meet and improve material needs and that people are prepared to pursue social and cul-

[23] Kenneth E. Boulding, "The Shadow of the Stationary State," *Daedalus* 102 (Fall 1973):96.
[24] Heilbroner, *An Inquiry Into The Human Prospect*, p. 83.

tural goals over openly consumerist ones. The freely chosen stationary state would progressively move toward substantial material equality. How this could be accomplished without practicing full political democracy in the community and workers' control at the workplace is hard to conceive. In view of all this, it is not surprising that Daly should remark, "The economic and social implications of the stationary state are enormous and revolutionary."[25]

The critics of the stationary state fail to consider that the prevailing principles and values of capitalist society may be superceded in a stationary-state society. The critics go right on assuming that necessary wage labor, consumerist incentives, hierarchical control, and existing utilization of wealth continue as before. Given the continuation of capitalist values and requisites, Walter Heller is correct in saying that "short of a believable threat of human extinction, it is hard to imagine that the public would accept the tight controls, lowered material living standards, and large income transfers required to create and manage a stationary state."[26] However, since a freely chosen stationary state could not also be a capitalist one (some sort of stationary state-enforced capitalism is remotely conceivable), we may assume that the public *desires* tight controls on waste and speculative investment as well as the transformation of investment and the structure of inequality. Heller can also say that a no-growth society would continue to pollute in the same proportions as a growth society, but only so long as he also assumes an attempt is made to uphold capitalist relations in the no-growth society. One of the cardinal motivations to the creation of a stationary state is environmental, so why would those who chose it continue to pollute as before?

Criticisms and doubts surrounding the stationary state are many, but no one has said its development would be easy. All that has been said is that its development is necessary. One further criticism which deserves comment is Boulding's view that "the most fundamental and intractable problem of the stationary state is . . . that of dullness."[27] As an example, Boulding observes that once Beethoven has written the

---

[25] Daly, "Toward a Stationary-State Economy," p. 237.

[26] Walter W. Heller, "Coming to Terms with Growth and the Environment," in Sam H. Schurr, ed., *Energy, Economic Growth and the Environment* (Baltimore: Johns Hopkins University Press, 1972), p. 8.

[27] Boulding, "The Shadow of the Stationary State," p. 97.

Ninth Symphony, no one else can write it, implying that cultural creativity would soon come to an end in the stationary state. What Beethoven's musical genius had to do with the rate of net capital investment of the period is unclear. Perhaps Boulding disagrees with Mill's
contention that a stationary state would enhance the "Art of Living"
and Marx's theory that freedom from economic necessity liberates individual self-development. Perhaps he would disagree with the late Pitirim Sorokin's thesis of opposition between sensate (material growth)
and idealistic (cultural growth) periods of history.

This does not conclude our discussion of the stationary-state thesis.
We shall return again to it in our discussion of growth and socialism,
when we shall argue that *the stationary-state society is, in effect, a mature socialist society and, if it is to become a useful concept and effective practice, must be integrated into the general corpus of socialist
theory.*

Post-industrial and service society

Much has been said and written about "post-industrial" society with
the implication that traditional capitalism has ended and we have moved
on to another historical stage of development. What is meant by post-
industrial? What is its relationship to the growth society of capitalism?
How does it differ from a no-growth society or the stationary state?
Political scientist M. Donald Hancock defines the post-industrial society as "one which the primacy of capital accumulation and industrial
production yields to the potential primacy of redistribution—of wealth,
material goods, political influence, and social status."[28] If Hancock's
definition is to be accepted, then the post-industrial society would mark
the end of capitalism and the beginning of the stationary state. We have
seen what a diminution of capital growth means for capitalism, and we
have discussed the necessity of redistribution in the stationary state. If
the post-industrial society actually meant the beginning of the end for
capitalism and the onset of the stationary state, the concept of the post-
industrial society would arouse strong opposition from defenders of the
existing order instead of being promulgated by them. However, whereas

---

[28] M. Donald Hancock, *Sweden: The Politics of Postindustrial Change* (Hins-
dale, Ill.: The Dryden Press, 1973), p. 7.

"stationary state" sets off predictions of doom from the established strata, "post-industrial" rolls off their tongues like received truth.

It is not that Hancock's definition of post-industrial society is wrong. If that's what a post-industrial society is, so be it. The person most frequently associated with the term, Daniel Bell, would in all likelihood approve of it.[29] Bell's vision of a world dominated by scientists and technicians instead of industrial capitalists and financiers, by knowledge instead of wealth, by universities and government instead of business and corporations, by social welfare and community interest instead of profit and private interest, and by meritocracy instead of class conflict harmonizes with Hancock's definition. What is wrong in Hancock and Bell is that their post-industrial society concept has no reference point in the real world. The post-industrial society as they define and conceive it does not exist. What looks like a post-industrial society on the outside is not much more than a technological warfare state patched over troubled monopoly capitalism and a tacky welfare state patched over nasty unemployment, poverty, and racism. If we indeed were living in a post-industrial society, a systems analyst would dictate terms to the major stockholder, the faculty at the University of Delaware would be more powerful than that state's DuPonts, the State Department would overshadow the international oil corporations, Nelson Rockefeller would have derived his power from Henry Kissinger rather than vice versa, the poor would be getting richer and the rich poorer, investors would be watching university enrollments rather than the stock market. Need the fallacy of such a topsy-turvy world be further documented?[30]

An offshoot of the post-industrial society thesis is that of the service society.[31] The service society thesis focuses more upon the composition of the labor force and type of work being done than upon matters of power and wealth. Nevertheless, the two concepts contain very much the same content, that is, growth has shifted from industrial production to services, power has shifted from capitalists and corporations to

---

[29] Daniel Bell, *The Coming of Post-Industrial Society* (New York: Basic Books, Inc., 1973).

[30] For a further critique of Bell's work, see Richard Hill, "The Coming of Post-Industrial Society," *The Insurgent Sociologist* 4(Spring 1974):37–51; and Morris Janowitz, "Review Symposium: The Coming of Post-Industrial Society," *American Journal of Sociology* 80(July 1974).

[31] See, for example, Russell Lewis, *The New Service Society* (London: Longman, 1973).

civil servants and government, and privilege and status is being submerged in a homogeneous middle class. Again, appearances are taken at face value for reality. The service society is also considered by some to be the answer to the environmental obstacles to growth; they argue that capitalism can continue to grow if it emphasizes services, since services do not consume resources and pollute. The fallacy of this view shall be indicated presently.

The service society is, of course, set in contrast to the industrial society, therefore implying the service society is also post-industrial. Both concepts suggest that production and goods-related employment have been overshadowed by service employment. The implication is also present that such service employment is more characteristic, if not even more important, than industrially-related occupations. However, industrial employment, as found in the design, production, transport, and maintenance of industrial infrastructure, materials and goods, not only employs the majority of the labor force, but is so overridingly important to the existence of most other jobs that few of the latter are thinkable without the former. To be sure, *none* are thinkable without the industrial sector, for all real wealth arises from natural resources and human industry. What would support our top heavy government bureaucracies if not the taxes of workers and industries? What would the papers shuffled about in the Wall Street office buildings represent if not industrial and agricultural commodities and all that goes into their necessary support, production, and distribution? How long would government last in the event of a general strike by industrial and agricultural laborers; or armies, or beauty salons, or television studios, or insurance companies, or laundromats, or any of the so-called service sector operations? Service companies such as retirement homes or food catering run by capitalists may be profitable, but would soon fold up if abandoned by industry. Most services within the growth society are directly dependent on the continued operation of resource extraction, processing, manufacture, distribution, and maintenance. They are also dependent upon wages being paid to workers. The wealth of a society is ultimately derived from industrial production, and it is the surplus wealth which is not reinvested in industry, together with wages and taxes, which support the existence of the service sector. The greater the productivity of workers in the industrial sector, the greater will be the available surplus wealth over and above production required to reproduce these workers.

In order for capital to further grow, a portion of this surplus must be reinvested in production, be it production which involves goods for direct consumption (clothes, homes, appliances) or for the support of services (hospital supplies, schools, entertainment facilities). The production of "goods for services" may be as resource consumptive as goods for direct consumption. Specifically, the *kinds* of services which the growth society is willing and capable of delivering must be profitable, and most profitable services involve considerable industrial production and consumption. The kinds of services which rely largely upon the delivery of a person to person skill and involves relatively minor resource consumption tend either to be organized in a noncapitalist, petty exchange fee for service manner (for example, a barber) or is an entirely non-exchange or nonprofit activity paid for out of taxes or donations (for example, a social worker).

The delivery of "pure" or largely nonconsumptive services are only occasionally profitable and organized capitalistically. Thus, the growth of nonconsumptive services cannot be expected to be a way out for the growth society, depending as it does upon capital gains. One way or another, the growth of human services within a capitalist society depends upon the willingness of the capitalist class to turn over larger and larger portions of profits to public institutions and agencies organized to deliver these nonprofitable services. The mounting need for nonprofitable services has led to rising taxes on personal incomes, with corporations paying a declining share. Nevertheless, most public and private service institutions and agencies face debt and bankruptcy. The capitalist class cannot afford to hand over a larger proportion of surplus wealth to these service providers, since the growth system finds it increasingly difficult to satisfy its own expanding needs.

The only workable avenue of approach toward the growth of a genuine service society is the creation of a stationary state (more accurately, socialist) framework from which all wealth is controlled by the producers themselves and converted into equality, free time, and social growth. Otherwise only a pseudo-service society is possible, one in which workers pay high taxes and receive little in return and in which need is exploited for profit or neglected entirely if unprofitable. The pseudo-service society is also one in which the capitalist class and its allies consume a vastly disproportionate amount of surplus wealth and thus receive the full complement of services, whereas the vast majority of people involved in surplus production find that many urgently needed services are inordinately expensive or unattainable at all. It is also a society in which the few have the free time to pursue self-development, while the many spend their years in wage labor and "re-creating" themselves for yet more years of the same.

That is the nature of the growth society: a glut of services and free time for the minority, who have more purchasing power and leisure than they can justifiably use, and a dearth of services and undisturbed free time for the majority who are responsible for producing the surplus wealth and disposable time in the first place. The majority is supposed to be satisfied with a trickle-down of expensive second-rate services and escapist leisure, while making possible the immediate gratification of every interest and whim of the rich. To the rich, the service society means an elite school, private tutoring in the arts, a readily accessible physician, champagne flights to ski resorts and tropical islands, attentive politicians, and domestic servants; to the majority the service society means a high school diploma or a community college, "adult education," long waits in impersonal clinics, poor bus connections to polluted beaches, remote bureaucrats, and a fry cook. Such is the service society which the growth system can afford for its people.

If we, in fact, had a genuine service society, and a *social* growth society, college entrance scores would not be declining, the arts would not be deteriorating, medical delivery would not be worsening, public transport would not be gasping for survival, leisure time would not be consumed in all manner of escapism, there would not be small children home alone after school, old people would not rot to death in dingy flats, and voters would not have rejected politicians. The growth society literally does not have the time, space, or means for the delivery of services. It must concentrate relentlessly upon accumulation and high yield investment of surplus wealth. Today's service society is, in truth, a service society only to the privileged few. It remains a capitalist, industrial society for the many.

4

Anatomy of distortion

Threats to growth

Our task in this chapter will be to examine more closely why the growth system is faced with such severe internal problems. By internal we mean problems which concern the functioning of the economic system per se, such as debt, inflation, or unemployment, rather than the external impacts of growth as upon the environment, resources, and class conflicts. The internal difficulties of capitalism as a mode of production are really quite sufficient unto themselves to bring about the need for substantive change, not to mention the external impacts the growth system has upon the social and natural environment. The internal and external impacts are, however, closely related, since the internal economic problems bring various sorts of pressure to bear upon the social and natural environment. For example, pollution control may be regarded as too expensive given the available financing. Conversely, social and environmental pressures restrict the unlimited development of the growth economy. For example, the impoverished and dependent must be minimally sustained, or public water supplies must be protected against cheap but polluting waste disposal by cost-anxious industry (though such protection is rarely effectively achieved).

Whether the internal problems of the economic system are more threatening to the growth society's survival, or whether social and environmental pressures are greater, is a difficult question to answer. One can only safely go so far as to say that both internal and external pressures are increasing and are mutually reinforcing. However, in terms of immediate considerations, the internal economic threat is regarded by growth advocates, at least, to be the most serious and capable of producing the greatest disruption. Ecologists may disagree. Class aware sociologists may also disagree. Over the longer time span, it would seem that the external environmental and social threats may be decisive. The growth system may stagger through a number of further short-run economic crises, but the social and natural environment it leaves behind have limits of toleration. Class conflicts will intensify. Resources and environment will be extensively depleted and degraded. The harder the internal economic threat is to resolve, the more it will push against the limits of social and environmental toleration. The latter must always be sacrificed on behalf of the former.

A further question might be raised as to whether the social or natural environment poses the most severe threat to the continuation of growth. We would tend to agree with those who point to the greater immediacy of social pressures. Perhaps this is only because a sociologist better understands the social dangers than the ecological.

In any event, whether the constraints upon a continuation of existing growth patterns arise primarily from economic, social, or ecological sources is not the critical issue. All three work against growth, and they do so in an interrelated and mutually reinforcing manner. While it would seem that the immediacy of each follows in the order stated above, no one really knows what social or ecological surprises might usurp the economic pressures. Social classes treated most roughly by the growth system may quickly combine forces to put an end to it; or the ecosphere so roughly treated by the growth system may react with unexpected catastrophe.

An endowment of riches

In taking a close-up look at the economic system, the first question which might strike the interested observer is why we face such horrendous economic problems after a couple of centuries of economic progress in the West. Shouldn't we all be living on easy street, comfortable, satisfied, secure, and safe? To be sure, quite a large number of people are so living. But a much larger number find their situations less than acceptable and often deteriorating on all of these counts, and another much larger number have never known comfort, satisfaction, security, and safety.

Americans took over a continent so abundant in all aspects of natural wealth as to be almost unbelievable: vast accessible forests, great lakes and rivers, huge expanses of extremely fertile plains, a temperate climate with even rainfall, teeming fisheries, abundant wildlife, rich energy resources, and extensive mineral deposits. Not to be neglected is the fact that America has had no hostile border states to contend with after the English, Spanish, and French colonial threats were put to rout long before industrialization and economic growth really took hold (unlike, Russia which has had to face numerous land invasions and widespread disruption and destruction). On top of this, the country was to receive a constant stream of eager immigrants, top-heavy with young men and in later periods with skilled labor.

This sounds like a description of an automatic utopia, a Garden of Eden, where a population having 20 persons to the square mile could all live like kings. What happened? Why are we faced with city slums, rural poverty, high unemployment, enforced idleness, rampant inflation, housing shortages, water shortages, energy shortages, malnourished and hungry people, staggering public and private debt, and widespread needs for many basic goods and services? How could such a rich endowment end up witnessing such want, neglect, and shortages?

These facts should give us pause to think about the disparities between what is and what could be. Is what *is* inevitable, given the rich endowment, or have things been badly mismanaged? Certainly our troubles are *not* inevitable. Americans are capable of making more of their talents and resources than what we witness today. And although mismanagement is much in evidence, the heart of the problem is not so simply located in mismanagement.

The crux of the problem is to be found within the manner in which the economy works, or more properly, fails to work. Our economic machinery runs according to the laws of capitalist development. This development is now leading the system into deeper and deeper troubles, and thus the worse become our assortment of economic and social problems. It is not as if Americans, or any other people living in a growth society, deliberately set out to entangle themselves in a morass of self-defeating situations, or that even a few among us set out deliberately to confound things with their personal greed—although this *is* a partial truth. The truth is that we live in an economic system which grinds out its own logic, consigning (alienating) its participants within for better or worse. Surely there is a capitalist class which manipulates and exploits the system to its own best possible advantage; yet their *range* of action *as* capitalists is quite delimited by the system. Corporate elite, economists, and government officials can tamper as much as they like with the economic machinery, but the contradictions are too profound and numerous. Plugging a hole here (for example, government spending to counter recession) just creates enough pressure to spring another hole there (for example, inflation). A capitalist economy at the late stage is no longer amenable to successful repairs. Its machinery has outgrown human servicing in all but the tinkering sense. It displayed a harsh side in the 30s. Given all the years of expansion since 1940, the economic machinery is wound up exceedingly tight, and its would-be masters are awestruck at the thought of the force with which the taut machinery could spring. If the economy is not completely restyled to serve society rather than vice versa, the question is not if the mechanism will spring, but when. Present trends suggest that time is running out.

Economic fuel

The most fundamental thing to understand about our economy is that it is ultimately fueled entirely by profit. The emotion-charged defenses and attacks upon profit should not be allowed to conceal the completely necessary and logical position of profit within capitalism. Capitalism runs on profit; there can be no substitutes, no escapes. If profits shrink or disappear, so does the enterprise or society which has grounded its production system upon capitalism. Profits are crucial, so critical, that all must be sacrificed in their support. Nothing is too sacred or too important to be lost on behalf of profit. Profit is not a dirty word; it is simply the fulcrum of the entire society. No amount of verbal tricks should deter us from this fact, for if we are deceived here, there is no way we can comprehend all of the other things happening to the economy and to us.

What is profit? Without getting involved in any complex terminologies and categories, let us for simplicity's sake say that profit is the difference between what a capitalist lays out as direct costs of production for plant, materials, and labor and what is taken in as revenues from sales of the commodities produced. We understand that many claims will be made upon this profit, such as those by government in the form of taxes, banks in the form of interest, shareholders in the form of dividends, and top management in the form of bonuses. Salaries and expense accounts, like wages, even if they run into six-figures, are "costs" of production—which explains why companies which are going broke never have broke-looking managements. Precisely such claims on profits, themselves vital parts of the system, render profits all the more essential. If the government could not collect taxes out of profits and profit-stimulated wages, it would be all that less able to maintain a global military force to render profit-taking possible; if the banks could not collect interest owed them on loans out of profits, they would be faced with insolvency; if stockholders could not collect dividends out of profits, they would sell their holdings and collapse the stock market.

With so many big hands in the till, it might be surprising any profit is left over for reinvestment. (We might note that generous depletion allowances assist greatly in bolstering the real cash flows of business.) Actually, government, banks, and stockholders themselves turn around and reinvest much of their shares of the profits. And for the prudent and successful company, especially the monopolies, profits for investment are virtually counted before they are made. If profits are threatened, government can be persuaded to reduce corporate taxes (which it has from 23 percent of the total federal tax revenue in 1960 to 16 percent in 1974[1]), banks can be tapped for bigger loans (which has been done with increasing regularity), and shareholders' dividends can be limited for a while (the least attractive alternative inasmuch as the major shareholders are themselves big banks, holding companies, and ultimately multimillionaires). The dangers from these actions are becoming as menacing as insufficient profits. Reduced tax revenues for government means more inflation-fueling deficit spending, while more bank borrowing pushes up interest rates and then prices in order to pay off the higher interest obligations. Thus, a squeeze on profits jeopardizes the stability of the system in multiple ways.

---

[1] *The U.S. Fact Book* (New York: Grosset & Dunlap, for 1975), p. 221.

The trouble with success

At the same time a profit squeeze raises fears, there is the irony that big profits place the growth system in a bind as well. Big profits mean big investments and big investments require big markets in order to pay off. With each round of profit-taking and expansionary investment, the capacity for production becomes greater and greater. This happens even without increases in productivity per worker due to more advanced or automated machinery. If the replacement or expansion of plant and equipment involves technological advance, productivity becomes that much more powerful. With foreign producers, substitute products, and new upstarts in the field pressing ahead technologically for their own survival, the firm which fails to push up productivity and thus lower costs of production finds itself facing market and profit shrinkage as the more aggressive operators move in on the territory. Yet, with this all-around drive for greater productivity and profit, the market is confronted with the prospect and frequently the reality of glut. Exceptions to the productivity drive are cost-plus operations such as defense contractors and utilities who enjoy state-guaranteed profits, and hence pay big dividends, speculate in other fields, and invest little of their own money in research and development. For example, the huge utility Consolidated Edison increased dividend payments by 28 percent and interest payments by 45 percent from 1964 to 1969, but reduced plant investment by 10 percent at a time when power demands were increasing greatly.[2] The result has been both financial and delivery binds. Breakdowns of power delivery in the New York area pose obvious dangers to the social and physical continuity not only of this energy hungry metropolitan mass but to the far corners of the country with which it is vitally articulated.

The saturation of markets doesn't mean that individual and social needs have been saturated. All it means is that the commodities which are up for sale or would be produced for sale are not or would not be purchased. Why not? Reasons are diverse, and they vary depending upon the product and the potential purchaser. A major reason is insufficient purchasing power among the nonaffluent classes. Their purchasing power is insufficient for two closely related reasons. First, the wages paid them are substantially less than the exchange value of the com-

---

[2] James Ridgeway, The Last Play (New York: E. P. Dutton & Company, 1973).

modities they produce, so by definition producers can purchase only a portion of their product. What happens to the remainder? The remainder is, of course, profit and we have already seen what much of this goes for. In a sense, much of the difference (the profit) goes to support a "surplus class" and "surplus institutions" which exist either idly on profit or by actively manipulating profit and related monies.

Thus, one of the major functions of those who live off profit, whether it be government, finance, law, real estate, or insurance, is simply to help *consume* the difference between the costs and revenues of capital, that is, the surplus. If there is a class which produces more than it consumes, then there also must be a class which consumes more than it produces.[3] The most visible function of the surplus class and its institutions is to organize and manipulate the economy so as to preserve profit and surplus. It is something like a parasite which sees that its host is fed so that it can continue being a parasite.

A central tool in this organizing and manipulating activity is credit. Given the fact that the disposable income of the nonaffluent classes is insufficient to prevent glut or the threat of glut, one means of temporarily alleviating this gap is to lend them the money, essentially giving them an advance on wages to be paid back with interest. A whole string of "service" institutions is involved partially or entirely in solely money accounting exercises; these operations back up all the way from loan sharks to the Federal Reserve Bank and United States Treasury. The Treasury sells the Federal Reserve paper worth so much money, the Federal Reserve enters the amount in the Treasury's account, the latter spreads the new purchasing power unequally around, and much of it ends up in banks which are then able to extend many times again the amount in new loans.

The amount of public and private debt which has issued from vastly excessive credit (some credit is, of course, essential to the smooth operation of the economy, otherwise nothing new could be produced until everything already produced was sold) has in recent years become mountainous. The interest alone on the $486 billion federal debt in 1974 was $28 billion,[4] yet the federal government avoids raising taxes—indeed has continually cut them since the early 1960s—for fear of slicing

---

[3] See Martin Nicolaus, "Proletariat and Middle Class in Marx," *Studies on the Left* 7(January–February 1967):22–49.

[4] *The U.S. Fact Book*, pp. 221–22.

into precious profits. (State and local government has been unable to avoid raising the tax load to finance sharply rising costs.) Accordingly, commercial corporations have been borrowing so heavily in order to expand that their percentage of cash to liabilities had fallen from a secure 73 percent in 1946 to a shaky 19 percent by 1969.[5] Accordingly, commercial banks had jumped their lending from $198 billion in 1965 to $444 billion in 1973, leaving them with only about one dollar of available cash for ten dollars supposedly on deposit.[6] To add to this precarious situation, two thirds of the banks' loans are themselves accounted for by banks' own short-term borrowing. Consumer installment credit tripled from $8 billion to $21 billion from 1965 to 1973, and mortgage and remortgage debt went from $30 billion to $63 billion; the result has been that household debt has jumped from 65 percent of disposable income in 1955 to 93 percent in 1974. In brief, the limits to government, corporate, banking, and household debt are fast approaching. The economy is cannibalizing itself.

Paper money has been injected into the economy at a rate exceeding by several times the actual economic growth; indeed, the slower things get the more money is pumped in in hopes of averting a cataclysmic deflation. But the more excess paper fed into the economy the greater becomes the distortion between speculation and real economic production. If commercial credit was directed to people with real needs (a high marginal propensity to consume) and federal deficit spending was directed to the delivery of socially useful goods and services, the distortion would not be nearly so bad and would progressively eliminate itself as real demand converged with real production. As it is, we have credit being used extensively for speculative purposes to obtain quick profits such as in real estate and for war supplies, leaving in its wake mountains of bad debt which ultimately must come crashing down for lack of truly productive enterprise. Meanwhile, the real machinery of production, in particular that geared for providing necessities, stagnates and even withers.

The upshot of debt for speculative and military waste as opposed to useful production is why the nonaffluent classes have insufficient pur-

---

[5] Paul M. Sweezy and Harry Magdoff, *The Dynamics of U.S. Capitalism* (New York: Monthly Review Press, 1972), p. 186.

[6] Paul M. Sweezy and Harry Magdoff, "Keynesian Chickens Come Home to Roost," *Monthly Review* 25(April 1974); and "Banks—Skating on Thin Ice," *Monthly Review* 26(February 1975).

chasing power. The cure (credit) turns out to be another disease (inflation). As the glut of profitable-type commodities pushes the economy toward slump, the fast-burning fuel of economically baseless paper money, applied to avoid the slump, kindles the fires of inflation. Thus, the fourth quarter of 1974 recorded the second biggest drop on record (9.1 percent annual rate) of gross national product, while inflation rose to the highest recorded quarterly rate (13.7 percent annual rate). As Marxist economist Ernest Mandel puts it, "The dilemma confronting the state in an age of declining capitalism is *the choice between crisis and inflation*. The former cannot be avoided without intensifying the latter."[7]

We should note in this connection that inflation serves to redistribute income from nonaffluent classes and sectors to affluent classes and sectors. Price increases in an era of monopoly capitalism can move with much greater forcefulness and rapidity than can wage increases, especially the wages of the unorganized and the incomes of the retired, unemployed, and welfare recipients. Thus, these working and lower strata with the greatest needs and capacity to consume are the least able to influence what is produced, for their share of purchasing power continually shrinks.[8]

Exacerbating the matter of inadequate purchasing power is the deepening indebtedness of the nonaffluent classes, meaning that interest payments claim a rising portion of wages and income and renders their economic voice even weaker. At the corporate level, huge bank loans are made carrying equally huge interest payments; but the monopolies can much more easily raise prices to cover the interest demands upon profit than workers can raise wages to cover the resulting inflation and the interest demands on their incomes. The powerful, who have generated inflation to protect profits, are able to turn it into their own advantage. The powerless pit their paltry disposable incomes against one another to bid up prices on necessities such as food, clothing, and shelter costs. This so-called "demand-pull" inflation is not at all due to too

---

[7] Ernest Mandel, *Marxist Economic Theory* (New York: Monthly Review Press, 1968), p. 532.

[8] While manufacturing workers were increasing their productivity 139 percent from 1946 to 1969, their real take home pay rose by only 41 percent, indicating that their purchasing power as a percentage of the value produced diminished. Victor Perlo, *The Unstable Economy* (New York: International Publishers, 1973), p. 30.

many dollars chasing necessary goods shortages. It is the relatively meager purchasing power of the nonaffluent competing for essentials which the industrial system refuses to produce in sufficient quantity because of their low profitability. The poor pay more; the leftovers and seconds become relatively more expensive than the top of the line.

The reasons why the nonaffluent don't buy enough of the growth system's products differ markedly from why the affluent create inadequate demand to take up the slack between what is or could be produced and the society's capacity to purchase it. The problem with the affluent is not that they do not consume large quantities; it is that there is a human time and tolerance limit to what they are *able* to consume. Even though most women in the affluent classes are fulltime consumers, this is still not enough. Even though the affluent throw money away in a variety of excesses, this is still not enough. The affluent constitute the big and quick profit market, so that is the direction in which surplus capital is directed: to luxury goods, exclusive housing, expensive resorts, and tourist attractions; to high-rise office buildings, posh hotels and apartments, land deals, and shopping centers.

Since the affluent are affluent, the prices can be high, and we get a "cost-pull" inflation. If the pull was only on the affluent, no one would be too concerned. (The rich are not too worried about inflation, since it is their pocketbooks which are being inflated. Can one imagine a Rockefeller complaining about the price of a gallon of gas or a Hilton about the cost of a hotel room or a Borden about the price of milk or a Firestone about the cost of tires or a Johnson about the cost of a meal out or an Upjohn about the cost of drugs or a Mellon about the cost of a loan?) Cost-pull inflation is eventually inflation which hits everyone right down to the bottom: raised prices at the top bring raised prices next to the top which bring raised prices at the next rung, and so on down from a mansion to a one-bedroom flat. The bad trickles down just like the good.

So despite the frantic spending of the rich, their savings still pile up. They are unable to consume their own profits, up to an incredible all-time peak of $158 billion (at annual rates) in the third quarter of 1974, up from less than $40 billion in 1970. Some of this profit will shrink as inflation catches up with monopolies themselves when they replace their stocks. But very far from all of these windfall profits are "illusory." If the recent inflation-propelled profits were illusory, Chevrolet sales would not have been lagging badly, while Cadillac sales were enjoying new highs. The $15 a night small-town motel may have found business off, but not the $75 a night big-city hotel.

This is not to say that the capitalist class is uniformly happy about high rates of inflation; moderate inflation yes, runaway inflation no. Inflation has the capacity to destroy faith in long-term productive investment; to commit funds to production under today's prices may be financially disastrous by tomorrow, as costs of production continue to climb. (Venerable Rolls Royce went bankrupt by undertaking major production investments in jet engines.) The tendency is for investors to look for quick returns on speculative ventures, rather than go for long-term industrial capacity. This inflation and military parasitism upon the industrial base, especially that sector concerned with the production of necessities, further increases shortfalls and shortages in strategic consumer areas giving rise to still more inflation.

Government to the rescue

The government falls heir to the gathering financial and political storm, injecting stimulants here and withdrawing them elsewhere at an accelerating pace in an attempt to maintain a semblance of economic order. Government subsidizes failing giants, takes over those which are essential but unprofitable, but must avoid entering into production itself ("socialism"), even to supply urgently needed goods and services. Government must also avoid attempting any major redistribution of wealth from affluent to nonaffluent classes, since this would cut into the profits of the private sector; it might also reduce the "incentive" to work at any job among those enjoying the new security. Government must also limit spending in areas of social welfare, such as health care, housing, public transport, arts and culture, conservation, manpower retraining, and public assistance, which could indirectly redistribute and change well-being, security and work values. That such spending would increase health, morale, and skill, and thus in the long run, productivity, is of diminishing import to the get-rich-quick mentality prevalent today.

The major recipient of government financial inputs has been, of course, the military. Debt accumulation since 1940, which accounts for nearly all federal debt, has predominantly military origins. Military spending is ideally suited to the growth system since it pumps money into private production, redistributes income upward, and always finds an outlet, that is, there is never enough military power or sophisticated enough military hardware. Further, the military is, in effect, part of the industrial infrastructure of world capitalism; just as the machinery of production requires electrical power to keep running, so does the capitalist relations of production require military power to stay in control. The United States has assumed the immeasurably costly burden of policing the "free world." Aside from the devastating social impacts of militarization and war, the cost of world policeman has been inflation, decline of the dollar, and economic destabilization and distortion in general.

In dollar terms, military spending in 1974 may be added as follows: $80 billion for national defense, $28 billion for interest on the primarily militarily-incurred national debt, $13 billion for veterans' programs, $4 billion for "international affairs," and $3 billion for space, amounting to some 47 percent of the federal budget.[9] This sum of around $128 billion may be compared to such items as $108 million for low and moderate income housing, $400 million for rural housing and public facilities, $800 million for food for peace, $400 million for agricultural land and water resources, $800 million for school lunch, $400 million for prevention and control of health problems, $600 million for natural resources and environment, and $3 billion for manpower. Then there was the low-cost rat control program that was defeated. We need not go to military items to make these social items pale: $1.8 billion for investment tax credits, $5.6 billion for individual capital gains tax credit, $2.3 billion for corporate surtax exemption, $2.3 billion as partial farm subsidies, $2 billion for air transportation, $5.6 billion for highways, $2 billion for law enforcement, and $5.1 billion for interest and property tax deductions. How can liberal intellectuals call ours a service society with such a complete reversal of government spending goals?

Despite the military warp in federal spending, government economic activity involves some crucial welfare spending which provides both survival support for many dependent persons and direct stimulus to business involved in selling rudimentary necessities to the poor. If state and local welfare spending is added, the importance is magnified. Most so-called welfare programs such as social security, medicare, and unemployment compensation are paid for out of heavily regressive pay-

---

[9] *U.S. Fact Book*, pp. 222–25.

roll taxes; even education budgets, largely supported out of personal property taxes, are categorized as social welfare spending in an effort to create appearances of government humanitarianism.

The main point to remember is that without government spending (whether it accounts for more or less than one fourth of economic activity and employment is not critical), the growth system would collapse in an instant. On the other hand, government super-spending propels it toward financial insolvency and the economy toward hyper-inflation.[10] "The government can, and probably will," write Paul Sweezy and Harry Magdoff, "get deeper and deeper into the morass without ever finding a way out."[11] Given the magnitude of debt, the much larger urban concentration, and the vastly greater complexity of today's technological systems, the collapse of the 1930s would seem mild compared to that facing today's society. Unlike the 1930s, the impending shakedown has no new government card to play; it has already been played. The only alternative to unsustainable distortion is structural change of the economy and society, which must come sooner or later anyway. Must we have the modern counterparts of bread lines and WPA? The precursors are already upon us.

The manner in which the government finances its expenditures—taxes and borrowing—protects to the politically feasible maximum the interests of the affluent. The fact that major oil companies pay less than 2 percent taxation on an income of billions and some millionaires have been able to avoid paying anything may be taken as symbolic of tax inequity. Since 1960, corporations have accounted for a declining proportion of federal taxes, whereas the proportion of regressive social insurance deductions have doubled. On the other hand, the $28 billion in interest payments on the national debt amounts largely to a transfer of tax monies from the nonaffluent to affluent holders of government bonds and securities. As the debt has risen, so has the burden of taxation been shifted more and more to the wage and salary earners.

State uses of inflation

The manner in which the government spends its money, as well as the amount of deficit, does much to influence inflation. By pumping

---

[10] See James O'Connor, The Fiscal Crisis of the State (New York: St. Martin's Press, 1973).

[11] Sweezy and Magdoff, The Dynamics of U.S. Capitalism, p. 195.

money into military and affluent sectors of the economy instead of into areas of need, government worsens the imbalance between the insufficient purchasing power of the nonaffluent classes and the tendency of the industrial system to overproduce. Given the relatively paltry demand of the nonaffluent, the industrial system cuts back production for them, but raises prices to protect profits. This gives the appearance of inflation due to shortages, but the shortages themselves are artificially created and unnecessary. The surfeit of cash floating around the upper levels of the economy results in all manner of speculative ventures whose immediate success relies heavily upon further inflation.

As much as government claims it seeks to combat inflation, it only seeks to combat high rates of inflation which threaten to destroy confidence in the growth system. The most vocal government opposition to inflation occurs not when the actual act of inflation is performed, that is, when corporations raise prices, or when the conditions for such increases are established, that is, when the government itself injects more paper money into the economy than it collects in taxes. This is an intentional tactic which serves to transfer wealth to the big corporations which can instantly garner the state's deficit spending with monopoly pricing. Inflation becomes government's number one enemy when the nation's workers want pay increases to avoid backsliding. And backsliding they have been; even the better off earners, those with 1973 incomes of around $16,000, saw their purchasing power dwindle by nearly 20 percent compared to 1970 incomes.[12]

Not only do the top layers of the growth system make off with the lion's share of the new money, inflation considerably eases the government's own existence. With the use of inflation the state is able to do things which would be impossible if it had to do them with taxation, like deficit spending for unpopular military adventures. If Americans had known in 1965 how much Vietnam was going to pick their pockets through inflation in the 1970s, majority opposition would have been much quicker in coming (not that majority opposition, when it finally did come, ended the war). The Gulf of Tonkin resolution was a blank check issued by Congress to President Johnson to start running the printing presses without regard to taxation or real economic production. The result has been economic disaster from which world capitalism may never fully recover. Viewed in this manner, inflation is an unlegislated, hidden military tax on the working class.

---

[12] *U.S. News and World Report*, October 14, 1974, p. 45.

As profits and then wages go up with inflation, taxation itself yields higher revenues without raising tax rates. Government also benefits from inflation by paying back its debts with shrunken dollars. From the combined effect of debasing the currency with "funny money," collecting inflated taxes, and saving in diluted interest payments on debt, the government realized, according to the conservative University of Chicago economist Milton Friedman's calculations, $25 billion in 1973 alone.[13] Yet, with the state's gigantic tasks of keeping the economic mechanisms going, combined with the restrictions placed upon it to raise funds through higher real taxation on big business and the wealthy, it must to an increasing extent rely upon inflation to help finance operations. The state could hardly raise any more taxes from the working class without setting off a tax revolt, whereas the affluent classes *are* the government and can hardly be expected to raise taxes on themselves.

It is unfortunate that the excess monies of the affluent, who stimulate speculation and more inflation, could not be transferred to the non-affluent, who stimulate productive capital investment and thus lower inflation. But if this were the economic objective of government, it would subsidize the working class rather than the capitalist class to begin with. This would, of course, be labeled as "socialism," which is in our system reserved mainly for the capitalist class. (Government spending, however, should not under any circumstances be equated with socialism, a system in which the producers and consumers of wealth are largely one and the same people.)

In the field of foreign affairs, government utilizes inflation by paying its military bills around the world with debased currency, while American corporations make investments and buy up foreign firms with the same paper.[14] Such accounting tricks eventually backfired as mountains of increasingly unwanted dollars accumulated in foreign banks, devalued the dollar against stronger currencies, and made imports from these countries more expensive. More expensive imports are taken as a cue to raise domestic prices, giving inflation still another stimulus. The exporting of debased dollars is the exporting of inflation, since much of this money finds its way into the other country's money supply and

---

[13] *Fortune*, July 1974.

[14] See Ronald Segal, *The Decline and Fall of the American Dollar* (New York: Bantam Books, 1974).

thus dilutes it as well. Owing to excessive paper dollar distribution abroad, serious American balance of payments deficits soon had to be attacked by exporting agricultural products at bargain prices—creating price-raising shortages on the domestic market. Increasing U.S. dependence on oil imports assures the need for maximum agricultural exports to pay for them, meaning no downward pressures on food prices from agricultural surpluses.

Capitalism is an interrelated world system, and destabilization in its major representative is bound to ramify throughout the entire system. Governments of most smaller states, the major oil producers excepted, find themselves increasingly impotent to channel economic events in their own countries. Only economies operating largely outside the market mechanism may proceed as before.

Distortion through concentration

The cycles of prosperity and decline have continued with considerable regularity for well over a century, but with planned intervention of government the ups and down have assumed a somewhat different nature. The postwar recessions have been less deep and of shorter duration than had previously been the case. The normal cleaning out of bad debt and surplus production has been avoided or minimized by the willingness of government to continue to extend itself on behalf of prosperity. However, the same laws of capitalism are at work underneath the floor of government protectionism. When the day of reckoning comes again, its severity will be all the worse owing to the artificial bandages government has been administering in ever greater quantities. America has been living far beyond its means for some time now, but especially since the escalation of the Vietnam war. The economic debts began to be collected by the early 70s. Environmental debts have also accumulated to precarious sums; days of reckoning which shall balance the environmental books cannot be too far off either.

Another of the main reasons why the normal cycles of the growth system have been unable to work themselves through is the rise of monopoly power in many sectors of the economy. With the market glutted at the end of a boom period and recessionary forces coming into play, the traditional processes of deflation and price declines no longer serve their regenerative purposes. Instead of prices coming down in order to clear out glutted markets, monopolies restrict production and raise prices in order to compensate for sales declines. In concentration-dominated industries, prices rose 27 percent (manufacturing wages only 10 percent) during a period of economic turndown from September 1973 to September 1974, whereas among competitive industries the increase was less than 5 percent.[15] As the president of a Canadian steel company points out, "Monopoly means no choice for the consumer, price is whatever may be demanded and supply depends on whether the consumer can meet the price." Hence, the unorthdox phenomenon of deep recession, high unemployment, and record high price inflation—a juxtaposition of events which would be unthinkable prior to the rise of monopoly capitalism.

In industry after industry, three or four firms almost completely dominate their respective markets. For example, one to four giants account for 90 to 100 percent of sales in aluminum, autos, synthetic fibers, flat glass, electric bulbs, copper, telephone equipment, cereal foods, and electrical tubing.[16] Scarcely more than 100 firms account for over one half of industrial assets in the United States, a country which alone has one half of the world's 50 largest industrial companies.[17] Add the next largest 100 and account for two thirds of assets. Add another 100 and account for approximately three fourths of industrial assets. Galbraith refers to these monopolies as the planning system and the some 12 million smaller firms as the market system. The market system can be competitive only within definite limits, since it relies heavily upon the planning system to supply goods and technology and must pay their price. The market system can afford to be competitive only in bankruptcy and closing-out sales.

The domination of the economy by a limited number of firms has of late been accentuated by conglomerate mergers which go beyond the ordinary limits of expansion within a given industry and branch out in all varieties of ventures. With the concentration ratios already scraping the ceiling in most sectors, the conglomerate merger now predominates. Some of the new giants are nothing but a melange of diverse companies; for example, over four fifths of Gulf & Western's total assets are

---

15 Robert Lekachman, "The House is Burning: Notes on a Three-Alarm Economy," *The Nation*, April 5, 1975, p. 398.

16 John M. Blair, *Economic Concentration* (New York: Harcourt Brace Jovanovich, Inc., 1972), p. 331; Alan Wolfe, *The Seamy Side of Democracy* (New York: David McKay Company, Inc., 1973).

17 John Kenneth Galbraith, *Economics and the Public Purpose* (Boston: Houghton Mifflin Company, 1973), p. 43; *Fortune*, August 1974, p. 185.

acquired, three fourths of Ling-Temco-Vought, three fifths of ITT, and so on.[18] In this carnival atmosphere, speculation prevails over production, inflation over price stability.

The world of high finance is equally centralized; for example, a bare 100 commercial bank trust departments hold 85 percent of approximately $400 billion worth of trust assets, of which one third comes from employee pension funds.[19] A mere ten New York banks hold sway over $114 billion trust dollars; one company, J. P. Morgan, disposes of $23.5 billion surplus investment dollars. And to think that Thomas Jefferson had the audacity to oppose the creation of the First Bank of the United States on the grounds that it might become a monopoly![20] The growth system is unstoppable, until it meets its own internal contradictions and limitations.

The power of monopolization over prices is not confined to industry. As Robert Lekachman points out, "It is not an exaggeration to assert that wherever an observer's eye falls, it registers a situation of market control or actual dominance by a small number of individuals, corporations, health insurers, trade unions, business associations, or professional societies."[21] Lower prices through competition face the hopeless task of fighting their way through organized interests, credential barriers, tariffs and quotas, subsidies, regulations, unions, and monopolies. In every case the tactic is the restriction of supply, the artificial preservation of scarcity, and the prevention of deflation and lower prices. Considering the bloated financial structure, the increases in productivity, and the pressing needs of so many people and things, we may expect mounting opposition to the monopolization of society by vested interests. America was created and developed by immigrants who sought to escape the hegemonic restrictions of rigid organizations; but they have recreated for themselves another set of monopolies, guilds, and castes which destroy the free movement and play of human possibilities. This is not to say that the Jeffersonian ideal of independent farmers and tradesmen is possible or desirable to recapture today. The dismantling of concentrated power, however awesome a task, *is* attainable; it is essential if the challenges to survival are to be met.

---

[18] Blair, *Economic Concentration*, pp. 285–88.

[19] "Trust Busting?" *Forbes*, July 1, 1974, pp. 54–62.

[20] See Louis M. Hacker, *The Course of American Growth and Development* (New York: John Wiley & Sons, Inc., 1970), for a discussion of early American opposition to corporatism.

[21] Robert Lekachman, *Inflation: The Permanent Problems of Boom and Bust* (New York: Random House, Inc., 1973), p. 48.

5

Technology and growth

The nature of technology

Before examining the relationship between technology and growth, a definitional word regarding technology is in order. John Kenneth Galbraith defines technology as "the development and application of scientific or systematic knowledge to practical tasks."[1] This is an acceptable definition as long as we take the time to spell out its implications more fully. We may regard technology most simply as "know-how" and, of course, the material means to carry it out; one tends to imply the other. The existence of know-how and means implies that at some prior point in time a need was felt which demanded satisfaction. In the process of struggle to meet the need, both know-how and means are gradually developed and systemized as they are applied to the problem of need satisfaction.

Knowledge of how to solve practical tasks must be accompanied not only by material means but also by successful technique or skill processes. The technology of house building may be fully understood by someone with the equipment to accomplish the task, but the knowledge and means can be effectively combined only by successful technique. The presence of automatic machinery does not eliminate the need

---

[1] John Kenneth Galbraith, *Economics and the Public Purpose* (Boston: Houghton Mifflin Company, 1973), 38–39.

for technique, but rather shifts it to the design, construction, monitoring, and maintenance of technology.

In brief, know-how implies both knowledge of task solution and technical application, which also implies the existence of means. It is readily conceivable how the means essential to a given technology become exhausted or unavailable, thus forcing the development of a new technology. Indeed, one of the chief concerns of survival involves the conservation of exhaustible material means, whether they take the form of raw materials or finished products. The technology of modern agriculture, for example, relies heavily upon petroleum to operate its machinery and for fertilizer. Yet, this precious substance is wasted on the most ludicrous and destructive activities which the growth system recognizes as necessary for its survival. Replete with contradictions, the growth system's uncontrollable appetite for resources lays the groundwork for its own destruction. Permanent survival requires rational use of resources appropriate to existing technology, *and* the development of *new* technology which minimizes the consumption of nonrenewable resources.

The growth system would soon starve to death on this technological recipe. It must combat the very emergence of ideas which promote the development of "radical" technology, of conservative and human-oriented know-how. We shall presently discuss how large-scale and inefficient technology serves the needs of the growth system in an even more important way than maximizing consumption, that is, in preserving the class power of the owners of technology over those who actually apply it.

A further point of definitional clarification concerns the fact that know-how and technique may be applied to social organization and to solving social tasks as well as to material ends. In advanced technological production, a related form of social organization has been advanced which itself operates something akin to a machine and embodies administrative know-how and technique. Such a social machine may operate either as an adjunct to industrial production (a corporation) or as an independent entity (government). The concept of *bureaucracy* comes to mind when discussing social machinery, and in our own society the two are usually interchangeable (see Chapter 6 for further discussion of bureaucracy). However, social machinery need not necessarily be organized bureaucratically. Democratic know-how and technique may also give direction to the accomplishment of material and social tasks. Yet, the growth system thrives on the bureaucratic form and has consciously cultivated bureaucracy as a means of directing and controlling the elements of growth. Bureaucracy is by definition a hierarchical system of unequal power and privilege, and so is the growth society. Bureaucratic techniques, while used in several precapitalist societies and therefore clearly amenable to other societal types, are ideally suited for use in the growth society and have become virtually synonymous with its industrial organization and government. The social machinery of bureaucracy has been taken over by the state-planned economies of the Soviet type as well.

This should not be interpreted to mean that hierarchic rigidity of a bureaucratic kind is an inevitable and necessary means of social organization; it is, however, necessary for modern growth systems, private or state-planned, which require and necessitate hierarchic control and social inequality. Radical democracy, that is, decision-making which goes right down to the individuals and groups involved in social and material production, is the social technology of a liberated and practicing socialist society. Democratic know-how and technique is also the only kind of social technology compatible with a workable stationary-state society, for no bureaucracy could effectively dictate the kinds of decisions required for the redistribution of wealth and the transformation of investment into social growth. Such fundamental changes would have to be carried out with the full participation and approval of virtually everyone involved. The growth society, on the other hand, requires just the opposite: the acquiescence of the many to the decisions of the few. Granted, democratic know-how places more responsibility and demands upon people; but to develop as individuals, people must cultivate the arts of independence and self-control and stop wasting away as cogs and wards of industrial and administrative bureaucracies.

A final point of clarification in the definition of technology concerns that of science. Prior to the early stages of industrialization, science and technology had a relatively tenuous connection. Science occupied an elevated position over and above the dirty work of production, of technology. Science had customarily been practiced as an art rather than as an effort on behalf of material production. The scientific understanding of technology and the application of science to technological problems provided an enormous impetus to industrialization and the rapid increase in the productivity of labor. Thus, while technology has always incorporated systematized knowledge, its fulltime use of science is a relatively recent historical development.

Today, technology and science are closely linked. One usually thinks of science as "research" and technology as "development" in the impressive "R & D" department. The bulk of research, however, is not pure but rather directly oriented to the solving of preconceived practical tasks which typically have military or profit ends in mind. The need is for the full-scale application of science to the solution of environmental, agricultural, industrial, demographic, medical, and urgent social tasks. We need a science for society, a *social* science, which aids in the development of human-oriented technology, a technology which conserves resources, brightens the physical landscape, and brings people into innovative relationships with the means of social and material production. Such a science and technology would permit survival; more than that, it would establish the conditions for the full development of personality and the integration of person with person and person with the life-support system. It would overcome the false dichotomy which the growth system imposes between work and leisure and between mental and material production.

From our discussion of technology thus far we may begin to see that it is not something with an independent life and development of its own. The development of technology is shaped by the mode of production within which it finds itself. That is, the kind of technology which has been and shall be developed by the growth system is very different from the kind of technology which would prevail within a socialist society. Above all the growth system requires a technology which reduces human beings to the needs of profit, expansion, and control. This means that the technology of growth as found in capitalism puts productivity above mental health and physical safety, extension of power above the consolidation of cooperation and equality, and fragmented submissiveness above individual responsibility and participation. All of this is put upon us as if technology had a life of its own and demanded that we place ourselves at its service.

This is not the way it is, for technology is at the service of the growth, putting us in the service of both. Under the kind of society required for survival and social growth, technology is at the service of pressing social and environmental needs, taking on a radically new image and position within society. Technology appropriate to a viable mode of production would be geared to smaller-scale, comprehensible, and energy-rational kinds of units. It must be a technology which, as widely as possible, meets routine needs through collective rather than personal means, and places human and environmental costs above monetary costs in its application.

The social shape given to technology does not mean that technology is a totally malleable aspect of human life. Obviously, technology and particularly its scientific component have a significant universal aspect to it. Electrical technology must adhere to the same principles under either capitalism or socialism, the growth society or the stationary-state society. But the application of this technology may involve the proliferation of transistor radios and fifty-story elevators or language learning aids and tube wells for agriculture; it may supply the current for 100 households, each equipped with a half dozen major appliances or the current to meet the same needs at a single neighborhood center. Certainly a socially-oriented technology would make extensive use of today's technological storeroom; but it would transform current usages and develop entirely new directions in the future.

Given these qualifications, we may agree with Murray Bookchin's assertion that "modern technology has now reached so advanced a level of development that it permits humanity to reconstruct urban life along lines that could foster a balanced, well-rounded, and harmonious community of interests among people and between humanity and nature."[2] Bookchin refers to the existence of an ecocommunity rather than a city, which suggests that the kinds of technological changes required to achieve the reconstruction he envisages is so profound as to suggest a redefinition of traditional social concepts and categories. There is no doubt, however, that the continuation of the current exponential growth of technology under the existing mode of production would *also* necessitate new concepts and categories of thought. The choice between an ecocommunity and a technocracy is not simply a matter of preference; it is a matter of survival.

Technology, population, and well-being

A cardinal assumption of the growth society is that the advance of technology is always accompanied by an improvement in the life of

[2] Murray Bookchin, *The Limits of the City* (New York: Harper & Row, Publishers, 1974), p. 138.

the people affected. Increasingly, economic growth is dependent upon technological growth, and we have previously observed the firm conviction on the part of growth proponents that economic growth produces well-being. We shall return to the ties between economy and technology in the next section. It will only be noted in this connection that economic growth is driven by technological change in two ways: first, technological advance raises productivity and profit volume, provided wages can be held in relative check and the increased production can be sold; second, technology is instrumental in the development of new products and the creation of new needs which are of critical importance to the perpetuation of growth and the avoidance of stagnation and decline. If technology was unable to devise novel appearances and commodities and cultivate new needs, the growth system would soon grind to a halt as existing investment and capacity absorbed existing demand.

However, if all of the technological change we witness in exponentially increasing amounts is to our advantage, why would anyone want to call a halt to it and jeopardize the growth system? J. S. Mill, who as we have already learned is not exactly the life of the party, was long ago a doubter:

> Hitherto it is questionable if all the mechanical inventions yet made have lightened the day's toil of any human being. They have enabled a greater population to live the same life of drudgery and imprisonment, and an increased number of manufacturers and others to make fortunes.[3]

This is another way of asking whether all of the growth we have witnessed over the past, say, 30 years, has palpably improved the lot of the average person, the answer to which is in all likelihood, no. Indeed, what has been suggested thus far is that such superfluous growth poses a threat to survival, hardly a development which would be called progress. An argument could be made that recent developments in technology permit a larger number of people to live not at the same level of living as before, but at a lower level.

Demographer Kingsly Davis argues in a similar vein that, instead of using technology to support a limited number of people in a rational sense,

---

[3] J. S. Mill, *Principles of Political Economy*, vol. 2 (New York: D. Appleton & Company, 1908), p. 340.

the human species is now in the preposterous situation of using an extremely advanced technology to maintain nearly four billion people at a low average level of living while stripping the world of its resources, contaminating its water, soil, and air, and driving most other species into extinction, parasitism, or domestication.[4]

Kenneth Boulding has phrased the argument as the "utterly dismal theorem": any improvement in technological productivity, if not accompanied by population limitation, will eventually allow only for a greater number of people to live at the same or lower level as before.[5] Donella Meadows sees humanity as reaching a given consumption and size limit, only to have technology raise the limit and the population expand once again up to the new limit—a cycle which is continuously repeated.[6] Why not be content with existing limits? Why pursue the chimera of a better life through growth? As has previously been stressed, the answers to these questions are not something individuals per se decide upon. Our society as such is a growth society; it cannot even go so far as to ask such questions. It *must* raise the limits of growth out of self-preservation.

As if to further complicate our search for a workable and satisfying social order, it has been observed that the technology which has allowed greater numbers of people to live on earth also precludes the possibility of returning to a previous way of life.[7] The pressures against the existing limits of life-support would not allow a retreat to earlier modes of living without sharp reductions of numbers and amounts of resources consumed. Certain prognosticators foresee precisely such reductions impending. While the amounts of resources consumed will certainly have to be reduced in the developed societies, an increase is required for the underdeveloped countries. However, there is no reason why the latter must be chained to the utterly dismal theorum which says that increases in productivity are accompanied by larger numbers of people living in the same misery as before. Population can be controlled, and our argument is that it is precisely such increases in productivity which,

---

[4] Kingsly Davis, "Zero Population Growth: The Goal and the Means," *Daedalus* 102(Fall 1973):26.

[5] Kenneth E. Boulding, "The Shadow of the Stationary State," *Daedalus* 102 (Fall 1973):92.

[6] Donella H. Meadows et al., *The Limits to Growth* (New York: Universe Books, 1972).

[7] Arnold Toynbee, *Surviving the Future* (London: Oxford University Press, 1971), pp. 32–33.

within a rationally ordered society, increase well-being and bring about a reduction in population growth. Given such a society, technological advance can remove all limits to *social* growth, a growth which in itself counteracts the need for economic growth. And a society whose priorities are social growth will come to the realization of the need for a stable or even declining population.

The idea of new population filling up the margin of living created by technological innovation may be turned around and argued that expanding population forces advances in technology, that "necessity is the mother of invention." Applying this theme to the history of agriculture, Danish scholar Ester Boserup contends that "the growth of population is a major determinant of technological change in agriculture."[8] She argues that agricultural revolutions follow rapid population increases. Others would prefer to interpret the historic relationship between agricultural technology and population the other way around: agricultural revolutions pave the way for rapid population increases.[9]

Both approaches may retain validity, depending upon the frame of reference. Boserup's view of population forcing technological change in agriculture has applicability to situations where available land has been used up, leaving no alternative but to devise and utilize new, more productive methods of land usage. This situation has existed in densely populated regions in the past and over much of Asia and Europe today. The opposite view of technological advance in agriculture opening up room for more people has been the more general condition in historical and global perspective. No mode of agricultural production has ever realized its global population maximum before another more productive mode was established. For example, before food gathering had exhausted its population carrying capacity, primitive cultivation appeared; and before it had existed long enough to people the earth at its maximum capacity, more advanced forms of cultivation appeared. With each technological advance in productivity, the earth's population limits were stretched further. This is the reason why it is impossible to state how many people can survive on the earth; new technologies force upward revisions of the number.

---

[8] Ester Boserup, *The Conditions of Agricultural Growth* (London: George Allen & Unwin Ltd., 1965), p. 56.

[9] Harrison Brown and Edward Hutchings, Jr., eds., *Are Our Descendants Doomed? Technological Change and Population Growth* (New York: The Viking Press, 1972), pp. 4–8.

The validity of both themes may be accepted insofar as population pressures within a given community or society stimulate agricultural innovation, innovations which not only permit an expansion of population within the inventing community but elsewhere in the world where the innovation is applicable and borrowed. Nevertheless, productivity-raising innovations may occur in communities which don't require more productivity, at least for normal human requirements and leave a margin for population growth. In the past, such innovations may have arisen more or less fortuitously within the footsteps of an innovation which logically preceded it.

But the main tendency today, at least in the growth system, is "invention is the mother of necessity"; technological change pushes purposively ahead and leaves a host of new needs in its wake. Instead of the crash programs of agricultural change which are so urgently required by the exploding populations of the underdeveloped world, we get crash programs of superficial need creation among the world's affluent. The "advance" of technology allows them to fill an ever larger margin of excess consumption of agricultural products, industrial goods, and services. In the case of the affluent, technology has far outdistanced population needs, but it presses forward for economic reasons. In the case of the poor, technology lags far behind population needs whether they be agricultural, industrial, or services. The rich are drawn forward by innovation into a glut of consumption; the poor push against their technological limits in an effort to survive. A major breakthrough in agricultural productivity, without major change in social organization, would in all likelihood result in the confirmation of the utterly dismal theorem—more people living at the same low level as before.[10] However, major breakthroughs in Third World agricultural productivity today are in the first place dependent upon the transformation of the social order.

In short, well-being is dependent upon the development of technology, but it must be a socially-oriented and environmentally rational kind of technology. The development of technology simply for growth's

---

[10] Taking the position that, under existing social circumstances, marked increases in Indian agricultural productivity would add 200 million instead of an expected 150 million in ten years, Georg Borgstrom supports the second thesis. Georg Borgstrom, *Focal Points: A Global Food Strategy* (New York: Macmillan Publishing Company, Inc., 1973), p. 199.

sake is increasingly detrimental to well-being and if pursued much further may well prove lethal.

Technology and economy

Just as science was previously considered as independent from technology, so was technology regarded as a development external to the economy. The importance of technology to the economy was, of course, understood; the production and distribution of goods and services requires technology. Yet prior to World War II technological change was viewed as following its own independent course and impinging upon the economy from without.[11] The idea that economic interests could consciously and effectively manipulate technological development and bring it directly under their own control is of comparatively recent origin. The enormous impact of technology upon economic productivity and growth had long been obvious, but the idea of "domesticating" technological innovation rather than absorbing it from the outside has only recently been institutionalized.

The previously external position of technology is indicated by the long interval between the discovery and industrial application of early inventions. For example, 112 years elapsed between the invention of photography and its commercial use, 65 years for the electric motor, 56 years for the telephone, 35 years for the radio, 33 years for the vacuum tube, and recently, only 3 years for the transistor.[12] Today the growth system has literally hired science and technology for its own ends, channeling invention out of its traditional independent course and running it through the purposive institutions of industry and government—industry with profit in mind and government with military power. Thus, as Nathan Rosenberg declares, "Whereas technological change was once regarded as an exogenous phenomenon moving along without any direct influence by economic forces, it is now coming to be regarded as something which can be *entirely* explained by economic forces."[13]

---

[11] Nathan Rosenberg, "Science, Invention, and Economic Growth," *The Economic Journal* 84(March, 1974):90–108.

[12] John McHale, *World Facts and Trends* (New York: The Macmillan Company, 1972), p. 2.

[13] Rosenberg, "Science, Technology, and Economic Growth," p. 91.

The most systematic statement of the dependency of technology upon economic needs is that made by Jacob Schmookler.[14] Schmookler emphasizes the economic demand side of the technology-economy relationship, viewing technology as being largely a passive supplier of inventions. Technology is seen as a reservoir of know-how large and versatile enough to accommodate a variety of disparate economic demands, either directly or through applied research. Yet, it is evident that human needs and economic demands cannot always be met upon command. Demands for medical cures, for example, may exist for centuries without being met. The demand for practically usable solar energy must also await further scientific and technological development. Science and technology cannot make leaps, but must build up from foundations.

Nevertheless, given the size of today's scientific and technological foundations, a great deal of innovation hinges upon what is emphasized, invested in, and worked upon. This is precisely the reason why technology has today become subordinated to economy; there would be no reason to have hired technology in the first place if it could not do for you what you wanted it to do. Previously, when the smaller base of knowledge and know-how existed, the economy waited patiently for things to turn up that looked promising. Today little patience is required; we didn't have to wait long to get to the moon. New chemicals, synthetics, and power equipment are upon us almost everyday.

But while space technology and chemistry can deliver fantastic results in a short time, we wait and wait for pollution-free transportation and quality housing for the nonaffluent classes. It's obvious that getting to the moon is an incomparably more advanced technological task than getting around a city conveniently and enjoyably; yet moon flights are already old hat, while travel in central cities has virtually slowed to a speed of horse and buggy days.

Science and technology have been bought by the highest and most powerful bidders, and they serve their masters well. The rest of us endure the consequences. If you would prefer clean lakes and rivers over the C5A transport, too bad. If you would prefer quiet, clean, safe electrical-powered transportation over foul, noisy, gas-guzzling autos, too bad. If you prefer clothes made of renewable resources like cotton or

---

[14] Jacob Schmookler, *Invention and Economic Growth* (Cambridge: Harvard University Press, 1966).

wool rather than from petroleum-based synthetics, too bad. If you would prefer that the inner cities be rebuilt with attractive housing and recreational facilities rather than having the business district piling up ugly skyscrapers, too bad. Profit and power come first in the growth society; other things can wait for their technological needs to be met.

The critical point to be made is that with today's existing and potential technology two very different kinds of societies could be built. These two societies, let's call them the growth society as we know it now and the stationary-state society as it could be, could be almost totally different in their uses and development of technology. The same invention might occupy a completely different place and be applied in a completely different manner. Technological change could take two entirely different lines of development. Technology can either contribute to centralization or decentralization of people and power; it can promote inequality or equality; it can make life miserable or enjoyable; it can impose walls of indifference between people or bring them into mutually cooperative endeavors. Advanced technology is capable of promoting these opposing ends in the extreme, unlike its relatively impotent forerunners. Before technology can be put into the service of humanity, it has to be taken out of the service of the growth system. Thus, the technological revolution awaits social reconstruction.

Putting technological development into the context of the overall industrialization process, we may observe that innovation is directed toward and taken up first by the agricultural sector. The resulting food surpluses release large segments of the rural population for urban employment, and the demand for goods shifts toward basic industrial products.[15] Once these needs have been met, the technological effort shifts toward the creation of new products and "services" and the concomitant development of new needs. Now, instead of traditional needs calling forth technological assistance, technology is used to call forth new and artificial needs.

A stationary-state society, or a socialist one, does not have to use its surplus in such a manner; rather than call forth new consumption needs, the socialist society is able to meet the historic desires of people for freedom to pursue sociality, skills, learning, and the arts. Instead of distorting technology for growth purposes, technology is advanced to

---

[15] Robert L. Heilbroner, "Work and Technological Priorities: A Historical Perspective," in Fred Best, ed., *The Future of Work* (Englewood Cliffs, N.J.: Prentice-Hall, Inc., 1973), pp. 50–57.

relieve drudgery, improve health and security, restore and preserve the environment, and assist in individual self-development. The limits to the growth of such useful socially-oriented technology are mainly those of the human vision.

Technological giganticism

Among the most actively promoted myths of the growth society is that modern technology requires bigness. If the sacred cow of technology requires that organizations be big, who could possibly challenge the necessity of large-scale operations? Actually, very few single organizational units are notoriously large; General Motors is massive, but its individual plants, scattered as they are around the world, are not inordinately oversized. If bigness were required by technological efficiency, then General Motors would manufacture all of its cars in one place.[16] Technologically, nothing is lost by dispersal of production, while efficiency is in all likelihood increased. As a president of General Motors has said, "With fewer people we find that management can do a better job of organizing facilities and personnel. This results in lower manufacturing costs and better production control."[17]

Nor have large organizations been noteworthy for technological inventiveness itself. John Blair finds that "the contribution of large corporations to technical progress has fallen far short of what would have been expected in view of their resources, their facilities, and their shares of the market."[18] More often than not it is the smaller firms which run innovative risks and then if they are successful, the invention or the entire firm is purchased by the giant. The giants literally have too much invested in old technology to render it prematurely obsolete by new and expensive replacements.

Giganticism within the growth system can be explained in only small part by the requirements of technology and efficiency, both of which typically suffer from bigness. The real source of giganticism is to be

---

[16] Robert Lekachman, *Inflation: The Permanent Problems of Boom and Bust* (New York: Random House, Inc., 1973), p. 64.

[17] John M. Blair, *Economic Concentration* (New York: Harcourt Brace Jovanovich, Inc., 1972), p. 383.

[18] Ibid., p. 228.

found in the requirements of profit and power, that is, in socioeconomic relationships rather than in technology. Bigger investments yield both higher rates and larger volumes of profits; economies of scale are good for growth. With bigness comes power over suppliers, prices, markets, competitors, employees, communities, and governments. When it comes to such things, nothing is too big. No organization is ever able to say that it exercises enough control over its social, political, and economic environment. The bigger the better in the growth system, if not for the public, certainly for the profits and power of the organization. As discussed previously, concentration of power over production is a process built into the logic of the growth system.

Economic organizations are not the only manifestations of giganticism in the growth society. As the archetypical organization, the corporate model has been emulated by other power and prestige hungry social institutions, public and private. Giganticism overflows into every dimension of modern society: farms, dams, cities, buildings, towers, autos, freeways, airplanes, airports, tankers, bridges, tunnels, shopping centers, stadiums, and atomic bombs. The Guinness Book of World Records must be revised every day as old records are smashed. Technology has given us all of this and much more. The question is, how long can record-breaking technological giganticism persist before the monster turns and consumes itself? Breaking a record is one thing; returning day after day to uphold what has been achieved is another. Gigantic achievements may give way to gigantic failures. Further, with all of these giant organizations and technological wonders all around us, what sort of guarantee have we against their dynamically and synergistically interacting with one another to produce a sequence of gigantic disasters?

Technology need not be huge to be impressive. Technological giganticism, in either its organizational or material forms, seems increasingly idiotic and suicidal. But then, this *is* the growth system. Survival requires technological simplicity and directness. It is this simplicity and directness which is impressive, because to achieve this is much more difficult than to add another layer of programmed routines onto a sprawling organizational or mechanical network. Small-scale technology permits the individual to take an active part in innovation and production. Today's trends, in both mechanical and social construction, relegate the individual to a passive observer or automaton.

Training for growth

As technology becomes integrated into the process of economic growth, the production of scientists, engineers, and technicians must be routinized so as to assure a steady flow of trained personnel into the research, development, and application of technology. Education in the growth society performs a number of important functions. Thus it was following World War II that higher education entered into a period of sustained growth which still continues, albeit at a slower rate. Prior to this time, higher education like technology had not generally been considered as a direct tool of growth to be consciously applied to capital accumulation by economic rulers. Education was, in fact, much further removed from economic consideration than technology. Higher education served mainly as credentials for social status and privilege.

The institutionalization of technological development thus required a revamping of educational goals, for it was to be within the educational context that the training for large-scale technological employment was to take place. From 1940 to 1974 college enrollments jumped from under two to over eight million. That a sizeable proportion of this increase was due to increasing affluence and the capacity of the economic surplus to support larger numbers of students is not in doubt; the whole structure of higher education may be viewed at least in part as performing surplus consumption, or as a hedge against unemployment and stagnation. The more immediate role of education, however, is to prepare a labor force capable of greater economic productivity which, in turn, increases surplus wealth and the capacity for further educational support. Education is, in effect, an investment of social surplus into longer-range growth potential.

As long as educational investments seem to be paying off in growth dividends, support remains enthusiastic. However, should there be indications that the labor force is receiving too much education over and above that required to develop and operate growth-oriented technology, support is bound to dwindle. The general inability of society to profitably absorb the new technologically-produced surplus wealth, that is the tendency toward stagnation, will also undermine educational investment: if the existing technology and economic plant overproduces, why use more of precious profits to raise productivity continually higher unless forced into it by unscrupulous competitors? The tendency toward stagnation and consequent government spending to stem the tendency cuts into available funds for education. College and university budgets may be frozen or even cut back, while increases fail to compensate for inflation. The above trends have all been very much in evidence since 1970, frequently painfully so, as the lavish support for training in the 1960s left growing numbers of graduates facing gloomy job prospects in the 1970s.

In order to reduce the amount of overeducation for job requirements and prune down educational costs without igniting a revolt among the millions of young people anticipating college educations, there has been a massive shift of enrollments to two-year community or junior colleges. By the fall of 1974 over one half of all college freshmen were enrolled in community colleges and the number is expected to reach 70 percent by 1980.[19] Not only is the cost of educating a community college student significantly less than that for a four-year institution and especially a university, but only about one third of community college students transfer to a four-year institution.

An essential cost-reducing aspect of the shift to community colleges is the minimization of "academic" course work and the concentration upon strictly vocational training.[20] This vocationalization of education is not limited to two-year colleges, but is being promoted in other colleges and universities as well. After all, the growth system only wants technically competent manpower, not a corps of free-thinking liberal arts graduates. Given mainly technical training, the products should know their place in the system and not harbor any unrealistic aspirations about pursuing a challenging and rewarding career infused with autonomy and opportunity. Everyone can't be on top and most of the work to be done is highly routine; general scientific and social knowledge can only serve to instill unrealistic mobility aspirations and may lead to widespread rebellions against the priorities of the growth system. The classic American dream of education as a ladder for social mobility must be preserved in the defense of social stability and the status quo, yet to actually maintain such a ladder is itself potentially disrupting.

When higher education was almost the sole prerogative of the upper social strata and considered as polish for preordained privilege, the sys-

---

[19] Fred Pincus, "Tracking in Community Colleges," *Insurgent Sociologist* 4 (Spring 1974):17–35.

[20] See Michael W. Miles, "Student Alienation in the U.S. Higher Education Industry," *Politics and Society* 4(3, 1974):311–41.

tem of class inequality was only reinforced. However, with large numbers of people eyeing advanced degrees, the whole educational prop for class certification is challenged. The promotion of the community college counteracts this challenge by telling its students their subordinate place, while still seemingly living up to the equality of opportunity the system promises to its members. However, as Harvard researcher Jerome Karabel is quick to point out, "Without the benefit of a sociologist telling them, junior college students sense that the manual, technical, and semi-professional jobs of the new working class mark a denial of opportunity for genuine upward mobility."[21] (The "new working class" refers to the technically-trained, usually college-educated, segment of employees, as opposed to the traditional factory worker and manual laborer.) In a sense, we may speak of educational inflation in connection with the community college; those participating are only apparently moving up the social scale, when in actuality no real changes are taking place in their overall social positions.[22] Thus, the second function of education becomes readily apparent (the first being the production of necessary skills): the reproduction of class inequality upon which the growth society ultimately rests.[23]

With the extra trimmings of education removed, the necessary scientific and technological work can be concentrated in a few universities and research centers. This pattern fits nicely into the growth society's penchant for centralization and giganticism. It also fits nicely into the preservation of social inequality; thus, the relationship between class background and type of college attended is positive and strong. The strategy is to return higher education to its previous untroublesome, subservient status, and help avoid a social revolution in the process. The financial squeeze and tracking tactics may heighten caution and conservatism among many faculty members, but such tactics are unlikely to cool off the aspirations of the majority of students in the community and state colleges.

Among the most urgently needed changes within higher education is the infusion of large numbers of adults who have been in the labor force for a period of time or housewives. The prime responsibility of

---

21 Jerome Karabel, "Protecting the Portals: Class and the Community College," *Social Policy*, May–June 1974, p. 18.

22 Ellen Kay Trimberger, "Open Admissions: A New Form of Tracking?" *Insurgent Sociologist* 4(Fall 1973):29–43.

23 Samuel Bowles, "The Integration of Higher Education Into The Wage Labor System," *Review of Radical Political Economics* 6(Spring 1974):100–33.

America's colleges and universities should become education of adults
—on either a part-time or full-time basis.[24] This means regular curriculum participation, not "continuing education." Higher education greatly
needs the injection of broader ranges of social and occupational experience into the classroom, whereas older people need context for intelli-
gent dialogue and the enlargement of intellectual skills.

The difficulty with this proposal from the growth system's standpoint is that it would be a waste to invest money on people already
placed in the organization of production. Adults are too crucial to the
maintenance and operation of the growth system, whether executives,
laborers, or housewives, to be allowed to return to college or the university. The objective of higher education today is primarily to train
youth for entrance into the labor force, not to expand the minds of
employees and housewives. Only a no-growth society could afford the
time and money to provide the support for widespread adult education,
that is, for social growth. Yet, even within the growth system, it is
questionable how much would be lost if, say, one half of today's students could be placed in the labor force and their place taken by employees and housewives. In all likelihood, both the labor force and the
university would receive equal amounts of talent and the changeover
would offer a fresh impetus to both. Later on these displaced students
could bring their outside experiences back to the classroom and the
older students could revitalize their workplaces and communities. But
it is the latter possibility which is considered as a threat to those who
administer the growth system.

The grand design for the university in an era of technologically-
induced growth is that of the growth system itself: a machine, a factory, a knowledge factory.[25] Like other organizations in the growth
society, the university has a concrete task to perform, in its case the
reproduction of the labor force and the class structure. In fulfilling these
functions, the university is encouraged to follow the lead of the corporation and strive for efficiency through maximum use of technology,
the consumption of which itself assists profit and growth.[26] After the

---

[24] Stephen Gravbard, "Thoughts on Higher Educational Purposes and Goals:
A Memorandum," Daedalus 103(Fall 1974):7.

[25] See Irving Louis Horowitz and William H. Friedland, The Knowledge Factory (Chicago: Aldine Publishing Company, 1970).

[26] Sidney M. Willhelm, "The Political Economy of Professional Sociology," Insurgent Sociologist 4(Fall 1973):15–28.

102   *The sociology of survival: Social problems of growth*

campus uprisings of the 60s, the power structure of American society concluded there was too much education and too little training going on. The productivity of higher education, the Carnegie Commission on Higher Education concluded in 1972, must be raised: expand the community college system, develop the tracking system, utilize more technology in teaching, reduce academic and increase vocational departments, downgrade the instructional staff, increase the size of classes and schools, and streamline and industrialize higher education.[27]

Such a design for higher education seems to lack the necessary ingredients for success. The campus uprisings of the 60s were in some part motivated by this very sort of industrialization and proletarianization of education. To programmatically reinforce these trends could hardly be judged sagacious. But what other course is there to follow within the limitations of the growth system? It would seem equally risky strategy to strengthen and broaden the liberal arts curriculum, a move which might also raise the level of critical thinking.

From any point of view, the integration of higher education into the growth system is bound to encounter a host of difficulties in the immediate future. The narrow training requirements of the growth system and the broad educational requirements of viable democracy are still on a collision course.

As important as the integration of education to the growth system is, the central area of concern over technological impact must necessarily be the labor force itself. It is with the labor force proper where the links between technology and growth are the most crucial and decisive. To an examination of these links we next turn.

---

[27] See Miles, "Student Alienation in the U.S. Higher Education Industry."

6

Technology and work

Specialization and hierarchy

Among the most important issues in the debate over growth is that concerning the role of technology in creating a highly specialized and hierarchical society. Since the origins of the growth society, there has been a continuous and marked development of occupational specialization and hierarchy throughout all sections of the labor force. We know that general occupational differentiation and inequality emerged with surplus agricultural production, so that artisans and craftsmen developed their specialities and skills on a fulltime basis. However, craft specialization and hierarchy, say as found in the guild system which preceded the capitalist order, involved the workman in the creation of the complete product and a possible line of advance from apprentice to master craftsman. The craft specialist decided upon all aspects of production and distribution. The ideals were quality production and economic stability. Critics of the guild system correctly observe the frequency of rigid local monopolies and lack of technological innovation, though there was certainly no absence of much creative workmanship.

The specialization and hierarchy which developed within the capitalist mode of production were of an entirely different nature. Here the workman specialized not in the creation of the entire product, but only in the performance of a fragmented task within the overall production process. Craftsman becomes semi- or unskilled laborer. The line of advance from apprentice to master is destroyed and replaced by a mass of more or less undifferentiated workers. Instead of a hierarchy of skill mastery we have a hierarchy of power including capitalists, managers, supervisors, and workers. Instead of an integrated division of labor where producers decide and regulate their own production, we get an alienated mass of powerless wage laborers who are unable to organize and control the production process. Whereas the craftsman could decide what to produce and how to construct the product, as well as how much to work and not work, the laborer has no choice in these matters. The laborer has only one choice: whether to work or starve. All the other important decisions have been stripped from the producing class.

The historical and socioeconomic processes which gave rise to capitalism are beyond the scope of the present study. Our concern is with the reasons why specialization and hierarchy were key aspects of early capitalism and have proceeded to such extreme lengths. The reason most commonly given for specialization is its superior efficiency, that is, when an individual performs a single task rather than a larger complex one, more output is achieved for the same amount of input. Thus, so the argument goes, the early capitalist recognized the efficiency advantages of breaking down the production process into pieces and assigning workers to the respective components. By so doing he raised the level of his profits. It is further asserted that technology required workers to specialize in order to operate it. The complexity of technology is considered not only as a cause of specialization but also as the reason for hierarchy: technology purportedly creates a great variety of skill levels which give rise to hierarchical organizations of production. In brief, efficiency and complexity force an extreme division of labor.

From the perspective of radical criticism, this account of the development of specialization and hierarchy is wholly unacceptable. Neither efficiency, in the sense of getting more output for the same amount of input, nor complexity required the development of specialization and hierarchy. Later on, as the entire organization of production and the development of technology became planned around and wedded to specialization and hierarchy, it was inevitable and automatic that efficiency and complexity demanded specialization and hierarchy. But this is self-fulfilling prophecy. Had the entire organization of production and the development of technology been geared toward groups of integrated and equal producers, there is no question that we would have before us today a radically different situation with respect to specialization and hierarchy.

That greater technical efficiency is unable to explain the rise of specialization in the division of labor is evident from the fact that prior to capitalism the craftsmen did break down the production process into specialized tasks or steps and worked for a given period of time in finishing a large number of items to a certain point before returning to the first item and proceeding to complete the rest of the items to the next stage, and so forth. A potter would prepare his clay one day, throw the next day, bisque-fire on the next, glaze them, and on another day fire them. The technical efficiency of pottery-making under the guild system was the same as if a capitalist hired five different people to do five different tasks *all* of the time. Nor can technological complexity account for either specialization or hierarchy, since the same technology was applied in the early capitalist period as was used immediately prior to it. Capitalism as a mode of production was well established prior to the introduction of industrial machinery, so the latter could not possibly be the reason for the emergence of specialization and hierarchy.

If technical efficiency and technological complexity cannot account for the rise of specialization and hierarchy, what *are* the sources? The central source or reason for both specialization and hierarchy was originally, and continues to be, the need of capitalists to control the growth process. Specialization and hierarchy were means through which capitalists consolidated their power over workers. As long as the producers were able to master the technology of production themselves, the status and power of the capitalist remained in jeopardy. The capitalist might put up the money to carry out production, but beyond that he occupied an essentially superfluous position; actually, the workers themselves could pool their financial resources, borrow money, or take over from the capitalist. What's worse, given mastery of the production process and thus control over it, workers might decide against further accumulation (growth) and in favor of free time. This course of action would, of course, be disastrous to the capitalist, whose existence depends upon accumulation.

By bringing workers together into a factory situation and breaking down the production process into minute and isolated fragments, capitalists were able to destroy the workers' knowledge and generalized skills of production. This rendered workers powerless and dependent upon capitalists for organizing and directing the production process; capitalists had guaranteed their own necessity by expropriating from the workers, not only the means, but also the knowledge of production. With labor placed in a dependent condition, capital gained complete control over the accumulation process; free time over more work was no longer an option to producers, an option which producers traditionally have taken.[1] Now growth could be unreservedly pursued.

Gathering workers within the factory, as opposed to independent craft or cottage production, allowed the capitalist to apply rigid supervision and discipline over the work process. Herein, as Stephen Marglin points out in his seminal study of the factory system, lies the explanation for the greater "efficiency" and competitive success of the factory system over independent producers: "The key to the success of the factory, as well as its inspiration, was the substitution of capitalists' for workers' control of the production process; discipline and supervision could and did reduce costs without being technologically superior."[2] The handloom was taken out of the cottage and put into the factory long before the appearance of the power loom. That the early alienation of labor was resisted by workers finds expression in an 1838 quotation: "They have driven us away from our houses and gardens to work as prisoners in their factories and seminaries of vice."[3] Later on, given the specialization of the factory system, industrial technology took shape around these demands and greatly accentuated the fragmentation and dependency of labor.

The power of capital, then, adhered to the principle of divide and conquer. However, the increasing fragmentation of tasks led to greater homogeneity among workers; skill differentials were reduced as the great majority of workers were leveled to semi- or unskilled repetitive tasks. While narrow specialization robbed the workers of an understanding of production, the accompanying leveling threatened to pro-

---

[1] See Stephen A. Marglin, "What Bosses Do? The Origins and Functions of Hierarchy in Capitalist Production," *Review of Radical Political Economics* 6(Summer 1974). Marglin points out that "a backward bending labor-supply curve is a most natural phenomenon as long as the individual worker controls the supply of labor" (p. 92). (The backward bending labor-supply curve refers to the tendency of workers to take larger amounts of free time once their wages have passed a given level of sufficiency.)

[2] Ibid., p. 84.

[3] Ibid., p. 89.

duce a bond of collectivism among them. To counteract this threat, capital further pursued the strategy of divide and conquer, this time in the form of a false hierarchy. A management over labor hierarchy had already been created by the specialization which took control and knowledge of production from the workers and placed it into the hands of capital. Taylorism, named for the individual who devoted his life to the breakdown and analysis of each motion in a production process, developed the expropriation of knowledge from workers to management into a science.[4] Then, to counteract collectivism, hierarchy was introduced among the factory workers themselves. As Katherine Stone skillfully demonstrates in her historical analysis of the steel industry, hierarchy among workers was not a response to complexity of jobs, but rather a device to counter the increased simplicity and homogeneity of jobs.[5] The process continues today, particularly in the area of job titles so that the illusion of upward mobility can be invoked by a simple upgrading of a name—the secretary becomes the administrative assistant.

Thus, the entire job hierarchy from unskilled labor through management was artificially created to protect the power and position of capital. Workers' skills had been lost to specialization, their knowledge of production had been lost to management, and their control over their lives had been lost to capital. Wherever remnants of workers' control stood in the way of capitalists' control, these remnants were smashed. Stone documents how the steel industry very early smashed its remnants of workers' control, an amount of control which would, in fact, seem unthinkable today.

In a subsequent section, we shall see how hierarchy has itself become a focus of discontent and rebellion: the very hierarchical supervision and discipline which enabled capitalists to wring every ounce of value out of labor has today become a major obstacle to productivity. What began as a relatively simple hierarchy has ballooned into huge, top-heavy bureaucracy. This contemporary bureaucracy is a specific product of capitalist organization of work and reflects not primar-

---

[4] See Harry Braverman's detailed and informative review of the development of Taylorism in "Labor and Monopoly Capital," *Monthly Review* 26(July–August 1974):12–47.

[5] Katherine Stone, "The Origins of Job Structures in the Steel Industry," *Review of Radical Political Economics* 6(Summer 1974):114, 134.

ily the needs of large-scale production but the social antagonism between capital and labor.[6]

What the above discussion adds up to with regard to technology is that the growth system has developed a technological base which is largely unique to the system's own needs and has created an organization of work and division of labor which is accordingly unique.[7] The emancipation of labor and its integration into a social whole requires extensive changes in technological organization and development, not to mention the prerequisite of workers' control of the means of production. A *technology* of liberation is as important to disalienation and survival as is a *politics* of liberation. Both are required to put an end to the power of capital over the life of society, and to alter course from the entrapment of destructive economic growth to the freedom of sustainable social growth.

Bureaucracy

Our concern with bureaucracy here will only be to specify its relationship to growth and technology. As alluded to in the previous chapter, bureaucracy as a form of social organization is characterized chiefly by a formalized hierarchy of superordinate and subordinate positions which carry specific rights and duties and which follow a line of advance from lower to higher status. The lower the position the greater the duties in proportion to rights, while the higher the position the greater the rights in proportion to duties. Bureaucracy is purportedly the most efficient way to apply human resources to the solution of social tasks. Bureaucracy is a social machine, a mechanism of social technology.

While bureaucracy is a highly formalized kind of social machinery, its efficiency lies primarily in the way in which it centralizes and enhances power rather than in getting things done smoothly and effectively. In this it is another way of looking at the effects of the division of labor as applied in the factory. Bureaucracy is thus a component of the division of labor, and is normally thought of as the white-collar

---

[6] Braverman, "Labor and Monopoly Capital," p. 45.

[7] See Andre Gorz, *Socialism and Revolution* (Garden City, N.Y.: Anchor Books, 1973), pp. 25–27.

side of industry or government. Prior to the development of bureaucracy in industry, which was extensively elaborated only in the 20th century, bureaucracy and government (the state) were virtually synonymous terms. The first bureaucracies were, in fact, state administrations which grew up upon and administered the surpluses produced by early agricultural civilizations. Contemporary bureaucracies, whether they be public or private, also exist upon surplus wealth and function mainly in the administration of the surplus. Thus, bureaucracy is self-justifying; it comes into being by appropriating surplus wealth and then justifies its existence as the administrator of such wealth.

The contemporary relationship between bureaucracy and growth is fairly evident. The larger the surplus wealth the greater is the base for the elaboration of bureaucracy. Growth permits the expansion of bureaucratic positions and enlarges the scope of power for those whose positions are elevated up the bureaucratic pyramid. "Career opportunities" mean that one's organization promises to grow. If the organization did not grow, opportunities for upward advance would wither as higher positions became clogged up with those who arrived earlier. Bureaucratic organization itself thus provides a strong impetus to the growth society. Bureaucracy feeds on growth; growth nourishes bureaucracy. The surplus wealth generated by industry requires the expansion of private and public bureaucracy to both consume and administer the surplus wealth. The growth society inevitably gives rise to larger and larger bureaucratic organizations devoted to managing and manipulating the mountains of distributional, financial, legal, and paper problems generated by growth and efforts to promote growth and to deal with the consequences of growth.

Once the bureaucratic social machinery has been erected and set in motion, it appears to be completely natural and the only possible way to organize social life. Ostensibly democratic institutions are themselves bureaucratized and lose most of their participatory aspects. Large-scale organizations are created, and then their very existence is used to demonstrate the impossibility of workable democracy. Bureaucracies are not only self-justifying and destructive to democracy, but are self-perpetuating. In the growth society, even the most ardent opponents of big government end up presiding over even bigger governments. In the growth society, even the most individualistic entrepreneur ends up being absorbed by a corporate bureaucracy. His success guarantees it. In the mature growth society, the size and weight of bureaucracy almost overshadows the means of material production upon which it rests. The modern skyscrapers towering over antiquated factories symbolize the illusory ascendancy of paper over production. The price for this illusion must eventually be paid in full, even though we pay in part with inflation every day.

Bureaucracy is not always and necessarily compatible with growth. In precapitalist eras, for example, state bureaucracy was the chief obstacle to the accumulation of wealth by private groups, insofar as the bureaucracy parasitically absorbed and wastefully expended the surplus wealth, frequently crushing those classes which opposed state hegemony. Or, at a time when early English capitalism was flourishing quite independently, French society was burdened with a sprawling civil bureaucracy. However, as capitalism matures, the state enters not as a burden upon limited private wealth but as a necessary consumer of private wealth which would not otherwise have been produced.

As far as the conception of bureaucracy as being efficient is concerned, its capacity to exercise power cannot be questioned, but its capacity to get the most out of available social and economic resources has achieved a veritably humorous reputation. The gross inefficiency, waste, and bungling of today's bureaucratic behemoths is notorious. The most impressive aspect about contemporary bureaucracy is that it functions at all, inefficiency aside.

The contemporary link between bureaucracy and technology, as between bureaucracy and growth, tends to be direct and positive. However, in precapitalist society, bureaucratic development often proceeded to great lengths without any marked corresponding technological advance. Precapitalist bureaucratization, as noted above, is associated with the state, and with two state-related institutions, the church and military; the role of technology in these cases is relatively minor. We may note, however, that the governmental bureaucracies of the early agricultural civilizations grew up around advances in agricultural technology and played prominent roles in the administration of the far-flung irrigation systems.

In capitalist bureaucratization, technology comes to play a prominent role both in producing surplus wealth for the support of bureaucracy and in providing means for consolidating the operative power of bureaucracy. Consider the importance of advanced communications systems for the development of national and global bureaucracies. The organization and development of science and technology is itself incorporated into the bureaucratic framework. Bureaucracy is, in effect, a kingdom of information, and increasingly of computer technology specifically designed for the classification, storage, retrieval, and application of information. In this fashion, bureaucratic power is able to extend the effective scope of its tentacles even into a person's most private sphere of thought and action (note the recent revelations regarding the CIA, FBI, and IRS). Just as capitalist economic organization shapes the development of industrial technology, so does bureaucratic social organization draw in its train the technology of social control.

The trend of bureaucratic growth is unmistakable. Even in the bastion of Western social democracy, Scandinavia, bureaucratic centralization moves inexorably forward. In close observer Lars-Erik Karlsson's words, "In spite of some noteworthy experiments with school and university democracy and intense discussion of municipal and industrial democracy, the signs in fact point to Sweden progressing more and more toward management by elite, centralization, and bureaucracy. In spite of the 'democratic breakthrough,' most of the society's institutions still retain their basically authoritarian character."[8]

The only structural force working against bureaucratic expansion is the general tendency of the growth system toward stagnation. The threat to profit and surplus wealth in general restricts the ability of the state to expand and forces private corporations to rationalize (reduce) white-collar and management jobs. We may expect to see much more of the unemployed clerk, salesman, manager and even executive. Yet, to carry bureaucratic rationalization too far is to alienate people who have been among the strongest supporters of the growth system, another of the many insoluble contradictions of capitalist society.

Alienation

The growth society breeds alienation in many ways. Alienation may be defined as the separation of producers from their means of production and from what they produce. By separation from the means of production is meant that workers do not own what they work with, are not able to control the production process, and perform fragmented

---

[8] Lars-Erik Karlsson, "Industrial Democracy in Sweden," in Gerry Hunnius, G. David Garson, and John Case, eds., *Workers' Control* (New York: Random House, Inc., 1973), p. 177.

tasks which renders production as a whole incomprehensible. By separation from what they produce is meant that workers do not decide what is to be produced, how much is to be produced, and how the product is to be distributed. Alienation is powerlessness; it heightens the capitalists' power over labor as the latter is increasingly removed from a position of objective evaluation and potential criticism of the system. Alienation further includes the structural cleavages which arise between people, and the rift between people and their natural environment. Capitalist society views both people and nature as objects of exploitation to be used in whatever manner promotes accumulation of wealth. A main theme of this study, however, is that the growth society is rapidly approaching the limits of human and environmental exploitation, and that the negative returns far surpass the positive. Rather than making the required alterations, however, capitalism pushes all the harder in the same direction in repeated attempts to make exploitation pay off. The result is still a larger harvest of alienation.

That alienation exists under capitalism is true by definition. We might ask, however, the extent to which the objective condition of alienation is experienced subjectively. The widespread feeling of powerlessness among people, and especially workers, suggests that alienation is a commonplace experience. Among factory workers and manual laborers indicators of alienation run significantly higher than among white-collar employees, although alienated responses are increasingly present among the latter as well, especially among *lower* white-collar workers.[9] (In the ensuing discussions, "worker" and "working class" refer in most instances to white-collar as well as blue-collar people.)

Adam Smith had early spelled out the fate of the industrial worker: "The man whose life is spent in performing a few simple operations has no occasion to exert his understanding. He generally becomes as stupid and ignorant as it is possible for a human creature to become."[10] The following are auto workers' descriptions of their jobs:

> Factory work is so monotonous. You are always being told where to go and what to do. It slows them up; they can't think for themselves;

[9] Among recent studies, see Dorothy Wedderburn and Rosemary Crompton, *Workers' Attitudes and Technology* (Cambridge: Cambridge University Press, 1972); Michael Young and Peter Willmott, *The Symmetrical Family* (London: Routledge and Kegan Paul Ltd., 1973); and Geoffrey K. Ingham, *Size of Industrial Organization and Worker Behavior* (Cambridge: Cambridge University Press, 1970).

[10] Cited in Daniel Bell, *Work and Its Discontents* (Boston: Beacon Press, 1956), p. 7.

they are like machines or robots. A man does the same thing over and over again so many times he just doesn't care any more. It seems I just don't care anymore; I am there and that's all. It weakens their mind. Many men when they first come here were sharp and alert; after a few years they are not the same; their mind is dull. It sure has weakened me; it has taken the life out of me. Some days I feel I'm 70 years old.

It's dirty work and monotonous. Everyone is your boss. The work doesn't require any thinking. You more or less lose your individuality; you're just part of a machine. It burns you out. When I was on production it made me too tired to enjoy anything; I couldn't even enjoy reading the newspaper.[11]

English food production workers respond as follows:

You're just doing the same thing every day. It would be different if you were making something. It's just the same old thing. There's no chance to get on, either. It's just the same old thing, all around you, stretching out for ever. That's what get's me most I think—that it will go on for ever.

This job just doesn't seem important to me at all. There doesn't seem to be any achievement. I don't want a fantastic career but I'd like to see something done. I feel like I'm dying here; smothering or something.[12]

In response to the question "Are there features of the job that give a sense of achievement?" most of the food production workers said no. A nationwide sample of American workers were asked "How often do you feel you leave work with a good feeling that you have done something particularly well?" Less than one fourth of those under 30 years old said very often and two fifths of those between 30 and 64.[13] The large majority of blue-collar workers would not choose the same job again if they had the choice. While many studies show that a sizeable number of workers are "satisfied" with their job, being satisfied is hardly an indication of commitment and integration. After all, what other choice is there? Workers had better be satisfied with their jobs, since the alternative is ruination. Income and material benefits are also the aspects of work which growth advocates continually promote. An alternative may be to change jobs, and a large proportion wish to and do change; but they tend to realize that another job would be just the

[11] Arthur Kornhauser, Mental Health of the Industrial Worker (New York: John Wiley & Sons, Inc., 1965), p. 80.

[12] H. Beynon and R. M. Blackburn, Perceptions of Work: Variations Within a Factory (Cambridge: Cambridge University Press, 1972), pp. 76, 53, 73.

[13] Work in America (Cambridge, Mass.: M.I.T. Press, 1973), p. 45.

other side of the same coin. There is some evidence, however, that workers in smaller firms find overall occupational rewards higher than those in large plants.[14] There are also indications that workers in automated plants are more integrated to their jobs than those working as operatives.[15] Professional and managerial personnel also report relatively higher positive work orientation.[16]

A major study of American workers concludes that "What workers want most . . . is to become masters of their immediate environments and to feel that their work and they themselves are important—the twin ingredients of self-esteem."[17] That which is disliked most is constant supervision and coercion, lack of variety, monotonous and meaningless tasks, and isolation. Workers desire greater autonomy in tasks, greater opportunity for increasing skills, and greater participation in the design of work and the formulation of tasks. The message is that workers want more control, more power. Actually, the results of studies of worker alienation indicate that worker demands are relatively modest; most could be largely met within the framework of capitalism. Yet, there is little to suggest that capitalists are willing to make anything but the most token kind of concessions. By failing to liberalize the work setting, capitalists may be laying the foundation for more total kinds of alterations within the organization of production, that is, for workers' control.

In evaluating research on worker alienation, we should always be cognizant of the fact that answers to questions on work take the existing economic framework as a benchmark. It is therefore not surprising that things such as pay, job security, and material comforts are placed at the top of the list of priorities. As people dependent upon wages and benefits for survival, these kinds of things must come first. To even think about autonomy, control, self-development, social relevance, and other considerations which lie completely outside the logic of the growth society, with the force of all of its ideologies and cultural manipulation, requires a leap of consciousness.

That workers should find more meaning in their home and family life than on the job is to be expected; the system strongly encourages

---

[14] Ingham, *Size of Industrial Organization and Worker Behavior.*
[15] Wedderburn and Crompton, *Workers' Attitudes and Technology.*
[16] Young and Willmott, *The Symmetrical Family.*
[17] *Work In America*, p. 13.

it, for it diverts attention away from issues critical to capital which deals with wealth and power. But try as one might, it is impossible to sever one's work from one's life. Work is too encompassing and too central to be compartmentalized. Work claims the best hours of the day and the best years of life. It overflows into every other aspect of personality, family, and social relationships. Work must be disalienated and workers liberated before the whole person can develop. As it stands today, there exists all too much of the opposite: self-destructive behavior as illustrated by excessive drinking, drug use, and even murder. The dehumanizing nature of the workplace may often be held to account.

Since automated work settings reportedly produce lesser feelings of alienation, could we expect technological change to take care of the problem of alienation by itself? In the first place, advanced technology maintains all of the objective conditions of alienation as the most primitive factory. Secondly, the evidence is not entirely uniform that automation reduces feelings of alienation; automated work has its own kind of problems.[18] Thirdly, the growth society does not consciously pursue automation as an end in itself; as long as labor power is cheaper than automation, automation will not spread much. Indeed, the past 20 years has not seen much of a decline in the percentage of manual or blue-collar workers. As the authors of the government contracted study *Work in America* put it, "The automation revolution that was to increase the demand for skilled workers (while decreasing the need for humans to do the worst jobs of society) has not occurred." The study points out that "it is illusory to believe that technology is opening new high-level jobs that are replacing low-level jobs. Most new jobs offer little in the way of 'career' mobility—lab technicians do not advance along a path to become doctors."[19] Like the early phases of capitalist transformation which reduced skill differentials among workers, the stage of advanced technology also has the effect of flattening out job hierarchies. Certainly automation has much to do with unemployment, and this is just the point: automation doesn't create nearly as many jobs, high-skilled or otherwise, as it eliminates. In brief, advanced technology as it has developed in the growth society may ease the physical burden of work for some, but for these and the majority of others, it only means a different kind of alienating work.

---

[18] See J. K. Chadwick-Jones, *Automation and Behaviour* (London: Wiley-Interscience, 1969).

[19] *Work In America*, p. 20.

Outside the logic of the growth society, automation could be pursued strictly as a means of eliminated drudgery and dangerous and undesirable labor. Automation could play a major role in enlarging the amount of free time available for the pursuit of social and self-development. Advanced technology in all of its forms could be harnessed for the goals of liberation. Then work could begin to take on voluntary and creative aspects, and become integrated with the rest of the human personality and community. In order to move toward the goals of enlightened automation and the social use of technology, a transformation of power must take place and the logic of the growth society must be reconstructed. Control of wealth and technological resources must be transferred from owners to workers. Only then can the goals of economic growth be replaced by those of social growth.

Workers' control

"The working class in this the richest country in the world," write Paul Sweezy and Harry Magdoff, "is quite literally facing a struggle for survival."[20] In view of the criticalness of workers' situation, it may seem inappropriate to be discussing such things as workers' control. Yet it is precisely the absence of workers' control, their powerlessness which has rendered their situation critical. As the growth society confronts deepening stagnation, profits are protected by the reduction of social spending, inflation, lay-offs, and relative wage decline, all of which erode working-class security. As long as there is a facsimile of prosperity, the working class is not squeezed unduly hard. But when economic conditions deteriorate, workers are among the first to feel the pinch. Until the working class, defined as all those who depend upon jobs to meet their daily needs, takes charge of production and distribution and places human need above growth, we may expect its own survival crisis to deepen.

Workers' control should not be confused with job enrichment, that is, programs to humanize the structure of the work setting through job rotation, work teams, job enlargement, reduction of supervision, re-

---

[20] Paul M. Sweezy and Harry Magdoff, "The Economic Crisis in Historical Perspective—Part II," *Monthly Review* 26(April 1975):12.

moval of time clocks, and so forth.[21] Swedish motor firms Volvo and
Saab have taken the lead in job enrichment innovations, and the results
for worker morale and productivity have been favorable. It is, of
course, productivity which lies behind management's desire to raise
morale, and enlightened management will extend job enrichment as far
as possible without endangering its own decision-making powers.

Herein lies the difference between workers' control and job enrichment: workers' control begins when workers begin to assume power
over the utilization of capital and surplus wealth produced therefrom.
And this does not mean that a few workers sit in on management ses-
sions or board meetings playing the growth game according to the rules
of private ownership.[22] It means that workers (in cooperation with the
larger community) own and run the entire operation from beginning
to end according to their own needs and the needs of the larger society.
It means that fundamental changes take place in the manner in which
decisions are reached and plans are implemented. In time it means an
end to specialization, hierarchy, and wage labor itself. The development of workers' control will require time because the crippling effects
of minute division of labor cannot be overcome in a day. The acquisition of confidence and knowledge to replace alienation and fragmentation requires a transitional period. However, the cases of China and
Cuba both suggest that seemingly unprepared laborers can quickly
learn the various skills of economic and technological administration
once the responsibility is thrust upon them.

Although some job enrichment programs may produce positive results, others may not. The lack of success should not be interpreted as
a blow against workers' control. As long as worker innovations and
productivity increases largely accrue financially to the owners of capital, there is slight reason to expect workers to be enthusiastic about
job enrichment. Indeed, workers tend to view job enrichment programs
with considerable skepticism.[23] By and large, the relatively few job enrichment experiments which have been tried involve what could only

---

[21] For a summary of recent job enrichment programs, see *Work In America*, pp.
188–201.

[22] See Andre Gorz, "Workers' Control is More Than Just That," in Hunnius
et al., *Workers' Control*, as well as his discussions of workers' control in *Socialism and Revolution*.

[23] See Howard M. Wachtel, "Class Consciousness and Stratification in the Labor Process," *Review of Radical Political Economics* 6(Spring 1974):1–31.

be viewed as tangential aspects of production. To proceed into major areas of economic organization and production is too risky for management, insofar as success with a major innovation of worker participation in decision-making would in all likelihood lead to demands for further inroads on the power of capital over production. The process could culminate in a challenge to the entire principle of private ownership.

Thus, capital faces still another contradiction: if workers are held in subjugation beneath the levels of their capacities, morale and productivity will suffer; if workers are given responsibilities up to their potential, confidence and knowledge will grow to dangerous proportions. This power struggle is more explosive than the struggle with economic contradictions, even though the latter dominates the headlines. As long as the working class is acquiescent in the midst of economic turmoil, the capitalist class will always manage to "suffer" through the squeeze. A permanent 20 percent of real unemployment and consequent annual declines in purchasing power is still economically feasible, indeed has already been an established fact, as long as it continues to be politically feasible. However, the struggle for survival which the working class now faces makes the long-run political feasibility of the growth society seem highly improbable.

7

Growth meets the environment

The exploit of nature

Just where the ethos of "man over nature" originated is unclear. Some would locate it in Western religious history beginning with the Book of Genesis, which states that God created man to "have dominion over the fish of the sea and over the birds of the air and over every living thing that moves upon the earth." If this were the original battle inscription, it has taken almost two millennia for it to bring about an environmental crisis. Moreover, the early Jews lived no more rapaciously off the land than did their Mediterranean neighbors, certainly less so than the Romans. It is also asserted that Christianity destroyed animism, the view that every aspect of nature has its own guardian spirit which must be placated prior to using or consuming it.[1] While Christianity may have destroyed animism, and even this may be questioned in view of a strong tradition within Christianity of spiritual concern with nature,[2] animism or any other complex of religio-spiritual ideas per se was no guarantee against environmental degradation. The deforestation and soil erosion which fatally crippled ancient agricultural civilizations attests to this.

---

[1] Robert T. Roelofs, Joseph N. Crowley, and Donald L. Hardesty, eds., *Environment and Society* (Englewood Cliffs, N.J.: Prentice-Hall, Inc., 1974), pp. 11–13.

[2] The Holy Ghost side of the Trinity is not unimaginably far removed from animistic notions of spiritual inhabitance of the earth.

Certainly it must be granted that Christianity was very easily put into the service of environmental exploitation; given its anthropocentric emphasis, the path could be made clear and safe for the human assault against nature. But as a moving force in itself, neither Christianity nor any other religion can be held to account for the natural degradation we witness today. Natural pacifism may just as well be the logical extension of Christianity as environmental aggression. With a wholly different religious history, Japan pursues a course against nature which is more suicidal than anything found in Europe.

Another much more direct source of the man over nature ethos may be found in the secular philosophers of the 16th and 17th centuries such as Bacon, Descartes, and Leibnitz. Here we have an activist secular reversal to centuries of religious passivity. Bacon's *New Atlantis* may be considered as Western society's manifesto of human determinism, while Descartes exhorted men to make themselves "lords and masters of nature."[3] These thinkers sought to utilize science as a means of submitting nature to the practical needs of society. Yet, even these early proponents of progress espoused views which are quite incompatible with the environmental aggression of the growth society. The secular philosophers sought only to liberate humanity from the dead hand of religious fatalism, not to convert people into environmental terrorists. No, the ruthlessness of the growth society toward nature cannot be laid at the feet of philosophy, although the concept of nature serving man through science was given systematic articulation for the first time.

Secular philosophy sought to rationalize society's relationship to the external world and to relieve humanity from natural capriciousness and uncertainty. The answer to the way in which Western society runs roughshod over the earth must be found in an ethos of irrationality and of exploitation. This ethos is the ethos of the growth society itself, the one Max Weber referred to as the spirit of capitalism. The spirit of capitalism is a spirit of accumulation as an end in itself without regard to the consequences of the accumulative activity. There is not so much a directive to conquer nature as to conquer the economic competition and to survive the other requirements of the capitalist structure as previously discussed.

The mandate to accumulate capital has created the assumption that natural phenomena are there for the taking on something of a first

---

[3] Roelofs et al., *Environment and Society*, pp. 19–20.

come first serve basis. If he were to survive, the capitalist had to move forcefully against nature in order to exploit as rapidly and cheaply as possible its "free" supply of raw materials before someone else did. Any environmental destruction which might follow the exploitation of nature could not be of much concern, since protective or reconstitutive measures would only add to costs and reduce profits. Capitalism never was developed as a means for anything other than accumulation of financial and industrial wealth; in the process, nature ended up as an innocent victim, much as did the masses of peasants and villagers who were swept into the grinding factories.

But like the workers themselves, nature has turned out to be much less than a completely passive aspect of the accumulation process. Frederick Engels was much more cautious regarding the alleged victory of man over nature: "Let us not, however, be very hopeful about our human conquest over nature. For each such victory, nature manages to take her revenge."[4] Engels observed past results of human economic activity upon the earth, and correctly concluded that survival required a calculated respect for natural processes. Departing from the prevailing "rip-off" approach to nature, Marx and Engels held natural phenomena to be capital, and they reasoned that environmental and biological costs must be reckoned concurrently along with all others. A rational accumulation process would thus place the long-range value of nature's capital ahead of the short-term economic gain. However, the growth society can tolerate no such distant and unprofitable calculations; if nature fights back, the growth society raises the ante further.

We have already alluded to the fact that the exploit of nature was not originated by the growth society. People have always left their mark upon the environment, most commonly in the form of deforestation and soil erosion. Deforestation throughout the ancient world heightened flooding and soil erosion. Overcultivating and overgrazing the land also contributed to the loss of precious top soils. Vast irrigation networks resulted in salinization of the soil and extensive silting. From Mayan civilization to the Mediterranean, India, and China, man left denuded hillsides and infertile fields in his wake.[5] Much of the ancient world's grainery is today's wasteland. The extent to which population

---

[4] Frederick Engels, *Dialectics of Nature* (New York: International Publishers, 1940), pp. 291–92.

[5] John A. Loraine, *The Death of Tomorrow* (Philadelphia: J. B. Lippincott Company, 1972), p. 186.

pressures strain man's relationship to the environment will be examined momentarily; we have previously suggested in our discussion of
technology that in more densely settled agricultural societies, population growth forces more intensive land use, encroachment on forests
and marginal land, and other changes which threaten environmental
viability. Many ancient civilizations crumbled owing to excessive burdens placed upon the land which supported them.

Environmental problems in the form of sewage disposal have been
perennial, and the filth of many medieval cities made epidemics a constant threat. However, the viability of the earth's water resources was
never in question. And while air pollution made an initial appearance
in 13th century London with the burning of soft coal, it wasn't until
the industrial period that this form of environmental erosion began
taking shape.[6] Industrialization as pursued in the growth society, and
especially given today's technological developments, represents an environmental onslaught which, if continued, will end the earth's human
inhabitability. Obviously, nothing of this sort could be said of earlier
societies, although the earth's bountifulness had indeed been variously
tarnished. Thus, it is absurd to attempt to slough off today's destruction by suggesting that man "has always been polluting." We are today
witnessing an assault on nature of a different degree and, most significantly, of a different kind. The kinds of technological changes made
since the 1940's challenges the environment in ways much more severe
than even those in the preceding industrial period. We shall take specific note of the more recent technological challenges to the environment presently.

Growth through waste

A built-in essential of the growth society is waste. As the polar opposite to the stationary-state society, the growth society maximizes
throughput of materials. Throughput means consumption, and consumption is necessary to growth. The maximization of throughput gives
rise to tremendous volumes of waste. As the threat of stagnation

---

[6] In 1273 Edward I enacted a law designed to prevent the use of soft coal for
domestic heating. The seriousness with which air pollution was taken at this early
time is suggested by the execution of a London citizen in 1306 for domestic coal
burning (Loraine, *The Death of Tomorrow*, p. 1).

mounts, so does the need for throughput increase in order to maintain tolerable growth rates. Thus, the volume of waste produced each year by the average American household doubled between 1920 and 1970, and it was expected to increase by one half again between 1970 and 1980.[7] Each American produces on the average one ton of waste per year and at a given time accounts for 11 tons of steel in personal possessions, most of which are designed to become junk as soon as possible. Some 48 billion metal cans and 26 billion bottles are discarded annually. Hundreds of pounds of paper and hundreds more in plastics and other materials are used up per person just for wrapping and packaging purposes. Paper wastes from commercial sources which used to be recycled for income are now dumped. The returnable bottle and recyclable paper became too costly for the growth society to bother with, and such conservation practices retarded consumption and growth. Throwaway means profit. There is even profit to be had in cleaning up after the throwaway society, as billions of dollars are spent on solid waste disposal.

A major waste factor of the growth society is animal manure, of which one billion tons a year are produced in the United States alone, the equivalent waste product of *two billion* human beings.[8] Slaughterhouse refuse adds another one billion tons of waste. Rather than greatly extending the nation's sewage run-off which it now does, animal manure could all be used for fertilizer or fuel. Manure, and wood and paper (cellulose) waste as well, has substantial energy value.[9] Like other throwaway products, collecting manure (even though 80 percent of it is concentrated in feedlots) is considered to be uneconomical; furthermore, it would interfere with the profits of the chemical fertilizer business. Animal manure is a superior fertilizer not only in terms of crop productivity, but more importantly, it helps restore the natural regenerative processes of the soil rather than damage them as does chemical fertilizer. What is rational environmentally is frequently irrational from the standpoint of short-term financial gain. In the long-term, however, the wasteful short-cut strategy will prove to be far more costly.

---

[7] Barbara Ward and René Dubois, *Only One Earth* (London: Andre Deutsch Limited, 1972), p. 129.

[8] Sterling Brubaker, *To Live on Earth* (Baltimore: Johns Hopkins Press, 1972), p. 28.

[9] Cathy Kaufman, "Cellulose to Glucose: Food and Fuel From Trash," *The Nation*, July 20, 1974, pp. 50–52.

The problem of animal waste and pollution, of course, stems in large part from the gross inefficiency of heavy meat diets. When one considers that the bulk of American farmland is used to raise corn, oats, alfalfa, soybeans, and other high protein crops to feed animals, and that only 10 percent of the protein in these crops reaches humans through meat consumption, we may see how inefficient our agricultural operations and eating habits indeed are. Few people are conscious of the environmental and soil problems their voracious meat-eating creates. Our soil is being depleted ten times faster for a pound of animal protein than for a pound of grain or bean protein. We may be eating "high off the hog" now, but the real price per pound is far higher than that listed on the package. Agriculture, like urban industry, aims not at meeting needs in an environmentally sound manner, but in the most profitable manner possible. Even at that, agriculture has for the most part been a failure, owing to its ability to overproduce and its competitive market structure. Both of these aspects, however, have been changing rapidly, as world grain markets tighten up and large-scale agribusiness moves into food production. Rural America hasn't really seen anything yet in terms of what technology has in store for it and its environment.

Recycling of all sorts, not just that involving organic wastes, is an essential part of any environmentally balanced society. Recycling is an area where technology is lagging badly, and quite expectedly for the growth society, for to recycle or reuse anything is to diminish through-put and consumption. If the determination were present, there is very little which society needs and consumes which cannot be salvaged and reused in one form or another. When profit dominates decisions, however, much of what is reusable figures out to be "too costly." But what is too costly for capitalism is not necessarily too costly for a need-oriented social order. What does "too costly" mean? Basically, it means that the investment in recycling technology and labor is not as profitable as in new production. But in a society geared to meet human and environmental needs, profit is not the arbiter of resource and labor utilization; rather, what should be done can be done. Actually, what should be done will be the cheapest route to follow in the long run anyway.

Still, recycling can only play a minor role in creating an environmentally balanced society. Conservation in the broadest sense is the key to successful environmental adaptation: this means that we should consume only what is necessary for a stable and secure material life, and do everything possible to restore the environmental damage which has already been wreaked by an irresponsible, growth-mad society. Ecological viability depends upon the restructuring of bourgeois life styles and priorities and calls for a revolution in technology and consumption. Such a revolution by no means implies a return to primitive living, something which awaits the growth society itself once it overburdens the ecosphere. Rather, such a revolution would greatly enrich life's meaning and satisfaction, as people began to feel themselves a part of an historic rebuilding process and cease to feel themselves part of a debasing cycle of alienating work and wasteful consumption. The members of a viable society must be able to define for themselves, in their own groups, what a high standard of living consists of rather than sit passively while the latest images of the good life are purveyed in gloss and color.

Air, water, and growth

The impact of growth upon the environment is highlighted in air and water quality decline, although these only head a longer list. The decline of these most fundamental elements also stems from the necessity of waste in the growth society. For example, the gases and particulate matter which constitute air pollution contain minerals which if recovered constitute solid wastes of substantial value. The 125 million tons of fly ash which spews from North American incinerators each year contain 9 million tons of recoverable metal worth more per ton than many working mines produce. Yet, as with other wastes, the recovery of mineral wealth from industrial combustion processes is "uneconomical."

Instead, the environment and public pick up the costs in the form of depletion and pollution. The 140 million annual tons of pollutants in the United States are spread around at an estimated cost of between $15 billion and $30 billion a year in the form of vegetational, property, and health damages.[10] We need not go into the sordid list of toxic chemicals which make up the blanket of pollution;[11] suffice it to say

---

[10] Paul R. Ehrlich, Anne H. Ehrlich, and John P. Holdren, *Human Ecology* (San Francisco: W. H. Freeman and Company, 1973), p. 115.

[11] Paul R. Ehrlich and Anne Ehrlich, *Population Resources Environment* (San Francisco: W. H. Freeman and Company, 1972), pp. 147–52.

that many greatly exceed federal safety standards in the large cities and respiratory, heart, and tumor problems show correlation with density of pollutants. The source of air pollution varies from place to place, but the automobile and industry variously share top honors. In areas subject to frequent temperature inversions, relatively small amounts of daily pollution can build up to sun-occluding thickness. During these periods, people with chronic health problems suffer excessively, while normally healthy persons find themselves combating a variety of discomforts and mental and physical slowdowns. What air pollutions cost the economy in terms of lost work time, mistakes, and lowered productivity is inestimable.

Beyond the earthly damages of air pollution, the amount of carbon dioxide and particulate matter being emitted into the atmosphere by an energy hungry society has raised questions among scientists regarding the possibility of climatic changes due to changes in the heating and cooling qualities of the atmosphere. Carbon dioxide, the atmospheric level of which has increased by 15 percent in this century, produces a "greenhouse effect" by holding heat in and thus raising the earth's temperature; clouds and particulate matter also reradiate heat back to earth and help maintain a warmer temperature. Too much reradiation, however, could raise the earth's temperature and substantially alter the agricultural situation; or a mere two degrees centigrade increase could destabilize or melt the polar ice caps, raising the oceans 50 meters and flooding coastal populations and agricultural areas. There is already evidence, perhaps unrelated to the greenhouse effect from pollution, that the Antarctic icecap has a slushy bottom and may eventually slide into the sea. Conversely, carbon dioxide and atmospheric particles and clouds have an albedo, or a reflectivity effect, which works in the opposite direction of the greenhouse effect by preventing the sun's energy waves from reaching the earth and thus cools the atmosphere. Two degrees centigrade drop would also greatly alter agricultural conditions on the earth and initiate a new ice age. (Massive polar ice afloat in the oceans could also significantly lower the earth's temperature by reflectivity.) Which direction the vast amounts of atmospheric pollution increasingly veiling the planet will take us is uncertain. Each thesis has its proponents. (Incidentally, jet contrails add 10 to 15 percent to cirrus cloud cover which, of course, contributes to either the albedo or the greenhouse effect.)

As with other forms of environmental degradation, the full effects of air pollution are not yet known. It would be much too hasty to conclude from this that nothing inimical to life will result from atmospheric changes, or that nature will balance things out for us. With the world's population moving toward six billion in another generation, any heating or cooling changes in the earth's climate, man-made or otherwise, are bound to exacerbate an already critical food situation.

As dangerous as the problem of air pollution is today, it is still overshadowed in importance by water pollution. To date, the amount of pollutants put into the air has not overwhelmed the atmosphere's self-cleansing capacities, despite striking declines in air quality over sustained periods of time and extensive geographic regions. With water, however, the amount of pollutants has in lake after lake, river after river, and bay after bay overwhelmed nature's self-cleansing capacities and turned the water into stagnant death. With 97 percent of the earth's water in the salty seas, and three fourths of the remainder locked up in glacial ice, the less than 1 percent of available fresh water appears as a mighty small resource to serve the world's growing industrial and agricultural needs. Thus, it is not surprising that three fourths of the world's population is without even an adequate or safe water supply.[12]

The world's fresh water takes a heavy load of pollution, since it is the lakes and rivers which are the drainage systems into which industry, agriculture, and municipalities dump their wastes. Bays, estuaries, and coastal waters also receive heavy inputs directly and from the rivers; even though this is not yet a problem with human water consumption uses, coastal water pollution has greatly reduced marine life and fisheries, while ruining recreational pleasures in many key urban areas.

Fresh water supply has assumed critical proportions throughout America, as per capita usage has more than tripled since 1900, while pollution has changed such water resources as the Hudson River from a producer of salmon, sea sturgeon, and 20 million annual pounds of oysters to an open sewer.[13] Water tables in some urban areas are down by hundreds of feet and still lowering. Almost the entire West faces critical water shortages in the near future. Rural areas, especially the corn belt and California's agricultural valleys, confront serious water quality problems as a result of nitrate runoff from the soil in heavily

---

[12] John McHale, *The Ecological Context* (George Braziller: New York, 1970), p. 13.

[13] Gus Hall, *Ecology: Can We Survive Under Capitalism?* (New York: International Publishers, 1972), p. 12.

fertilized agricultural areas. The nitrogen content of the Midwest's water drainage system is equal to the sewage of 20 million people, or twice that of the Lake Erie basin population.[14] Because nitrate in drinking water can be converted to highly toxic nitrites by intestinal bacteria, the tenfold increase in nitrogen fertilizer predicted from 1970 to 2000 will increasingly present health problems of major proportions. Already physicians in some areas recommend bottled water for infants. Yet, nitrogen hungry corn plants are fed on chemical fertilizer (the Midwest's soils have already lost one half of their original nitrogen content), and cattle and hogs are fattened up rapidly on corn so stockmen and meat packers can make money and a meat hungry populace can fill up on beef and pork.

If the artificial fertilizer runoff from the fields were the only source of animal-related water pollution, the problem would be bad enough; but there is also the water contamination from the runoff of excreta from commercial feedlots, a pollution equivalent of 800 million people.[15] Packed like sardines in a sea of manure and urea, feedlot cattle attract disease agents and parasites which require increased pesticide use and require a variety of drugs and antibiotics which in all likelihood affect meat quality and safety. However, with per capita meat consumption up by three fourths since 1950, and with the traditional pasture grazing too slow a weight-gaining process for profit-minded producers, the feedlot has become the central focus of the American cattle industry. In single massive feedlots, the annual grain crop from many large farms are consumed in a matter of hours. The entire process of one pound of meat production requires 2,500 to 6,000 gallons of water compared to only 60 gallons for one pound of wheat. It is evident that the feeding process of both livestock and humans will have to change if the water pollution and supply problem is going to be met.

In addition to a host of chemicals and mineral poisons such as mercury, lead, DDT, and cyanides flushed into waterways, organic wastes in sewage from industry, agriculture, and municipalities place heavy oxygen demands upon the waters into which they run. The oxygen in the rivers and lakes is used up in decomposing these organic wastes into inorganic substances, phosphates and nitrates in particular but other nutrients as well, which in turn act as fertilizer for aquatic plant

---

[14] Ehrlich et al., *Human Ecology,* p. 185.
[15] Ward and Dubois, *Only One Earth,* pp. 116–17.

growth and give rise to algae blooms. These blooms themselves use up oxygen in their decomposition process, as bacteria go to work on the dead plant life. When sewage treatment is used to supply the bacteria and oxygen prior to the emitting of effluents, unless the inorganic phosphates and nitrates are removed afterwards (tertiary treatment), the water fertilization effect still takes place and the oxygen levels are ultimately reduced nevertheless. Industrial wastes account for three times the oxygen demand rate upon American waters as do municipal effluents—40 percent of which itself comes from industry. Industry also accounts for most of the heated water or thermal pollution which raises water temperatures and destroys fish life. If effluents from feedlots are added, Barbara Ward and René Dubois point out that "industry emerges as the main source of water-borne effluents, with municipalities supplying most of the rest."[16] Substantial amounts of organic sewage could be readily recycled as fertilizer to surrounding farmland or processed for feed and fuel value, rather than overburdening rivers and lakes.

As oxygen levels decline and vanish, so does the ability of water to purify itself. Bodies of water which are normally viable for millions of years may undergo eutrophication in a few decades or even years time. Lake Erie and the Baltic Sea are prime examples, but the number of unheralded smaller instances abound. Numerous are the previously viable lakes, ponds, and rivers where all that now lives are the anaerobic bacteria giving off their stinking gases as they finish off what is left of the decomposition work to be done. No more fishing, boating, or swimming in these places now given over to algae, muck, and the lowest forms of aquatic life. To render water potable from most lakes and rivers today requires extensive purification measures, and even then the water may not meet federal safety standards. In certain waterfront and river locations, Cleveland for example, the water is so polluted as to have caught fire or posed a fire hazard.

The oceans themselves are threatened by pollution. In addition to the sewage, garbage dumping, and river pollution deposited in the sea, the major pollutant is oil, of which up to ten million tons are washed in annually. The chief source of oil pollution is tankers which flush out their tanks at sea to avoid port laws prohibiting it. By the end of the century, it is estimated that annual oil pollution could reach anywhere

---

[16] Ibid.

from 24 to 80 million tons.[17] Oil in the oceans retards the development of phytoplankton, the basis of the marine food chain and the source of most of the world's oxygen. On top of the millions of tons of oil, garbage, lead, phosphates, nitrates, iron, mercury, acids, insecticides, and DDT running into the seas, Americans have dumped hundreds of large containers of nerve gas into the Atlantic, and Europeans have dumped thousands of tons of radioactive waste into the same sink.

In a hungry world, and one that is bound to grow a lot hungrier in the years to come, water pollution has made major reductions in the ability of the seas to produce food. Oxygen supplies have been cut beneath survival level, water temperatures have risen above spawning toleration, and estuary food chains have been modified. Like air pollution, water pollution follows in large measure from the dictates of the growth society; waste is a way of life, as is the minimization of short-term costs.

Nuclear power is often held out as a solution to the growth society's energy hunger. However, nuclear fission poses environmental dangers which exceed any of those discussed previously. Thermal pollution from atomic power plants could attain disastrous proportions, while the disposal of radioactive wastes raises seemingly insoluble problems. The failure of an energy program which has already invested billions of dollars and years of research time strongly hints at the unfeasibility of nuclear fission as a means of satisfying the growth society's energy appetite. As to fusion, which many also hold out as the ultimate answer to the energy and pollution problem, there is little evidence so far that anyone is interested or convinced enough in its development potential to promise delivery within an accountable time period.

No one who makes a serious appraisal of the environmental crisis can avoid the conclusion that errant technological development on behalf of maximum economic growth underlies ecological deterioration. A solution will certainly require the utilization of technology, but a technology which has environmental needs and ends in mind rather than capital accumulation. A solution will require the development of restorative technology plus an entirely new technology of production which gradually diminishes the need for restorative environmental measures. A new, environmentally integrated technology assumes the prior

---

[17] Tiny Bennett and Wade Rowland, The Pollution Guide (Toronto: Clarke, Irwin & Company Limited, 1972), p. 54.

emergence of an equally new set of social and cultural values governing production, consumption, and the use of time. In other words, the growth society itself can never come up with technological solutions to the overall environmental crisis. For the crisis is comprehensive, and its solution demands changes on an equally comprehensive scale. There simply isn't sufficient time or margin to permit today's way of life to halfheartedly stumble through a series of conservation measures, environmental penalties and laws, and environmental technology for profit. An all-out campaign against ecological suicide is necessary, and this will require a society which places environmental balance above financial gain. Such a priority runs against the grain of the growth society.

Growth and environmental decline

In searching for the contributive causes of the ecology crisis, both Barry Commoner and Paul Erhlich see total environmental impact or damage amounting to the product of population $\times$ per capita wealth $\times$ technological damage per unit of wealth.[18] It is stressed that the relationship between population, affluence, and technology is multiplicative rather than additive, thus raising the impact of each factor. Erhlich and associates calculate that since 1945 the relative environmental impact of population growth, economic growth (rising affluence), and technological change have been more or less equal, though rising affluence is given the highest impact rating.[19] Erhlich stresses economic growth and population growth as *causally* more dominant than technological change, viewing the latter as being responsive to demands made upon it by the former.

Economic growth has increased the development and utilization of more damaging technologies, as when highly energy-consumptive and nondegradable synthetics are substituted for natural products. Thus, per capita consumption and pollution have been growing at a rate considerably faster than population since 1940. Population growth raises the demand on natural resources and overall environmental pressures. Population growth also raises environmental impact by way of the law

---

[18] Barry Commoner, *The Closing Circle* (New York: Alfred A. Knopf, 1971), pp. 175–76.

[19] Ehrlich et al., *Human Ecology,* pp. 213–15.

of diminishing returns: increasing population requires more and more input to achieve less and less output. For example, if more and more people are to be fed from a given land area, more and more fertilizer must be applied to the soil, yet the increase in crop yields diminish in relation to the increase in the amount of fertilizer used. A case in point is Illinois between 1962 and 1968 when the nitrogen fertilizer level doubled but the corn crop yield rose only 10 to 15 percent.[20] Each additional gain in plant growth can be achieved only by progressively increasing the amount of fertilizer. Although crop increases steadily diminish, negative soil modification and water pollution increase.

Erhlich also draws our attention to the fact that each additional unit of population does not simply require a single additional unit of a resource or service for that unit to be integrated into the community; additional population units each further *compounds* the costs of a resource or service, as every growing city has found out. For example, to integrate a new telephone receiver into a network of ten involves not just one additional line but 11. Further, population growth raises the possibility of the threshold effect; the wastes of 500 people may not overload a lake, whereas that of 550 may exceed the lake self-purification capacity.

Of the three environmental impact factors, Commoner places overwhelming importance on technological change—the increasing output of pollution and environmental damage per economic good produced. Compared to the roughly 50 percent gain in population and per capita GNP in the period from 1946–66, per capita pollution increased sevenfold.[21] "Thus, the chief reason," argues Commoner, "for the sharp increase in environmental stress in the United States is the sweeping transformation in production technology in the postwar period. Productive activities with intense environmental impacts have displaced activities with less serious environmental impacts; the growth pattern has been counter-ecological."[22] Commoner contends that basic needs are being met at about the same level today as they were in 1946, but that the technology used to meet these needs has changed drastically. For example, rail transport has been replaced by truck (trucks require

---

[20] "The Environment Cost of Economic Growth," in Sam H. Schurr, ed., *Energy, Economic Growth, and the Environment* (Baltimore: Johns Hopkins University Press, 1972), p. 44.

[21] Commoner, *The Closing Circle*, p. 136.

[22] Schurr, ed., "The Environment Cost of Economic Growth," p. 63.

six times the energy to move one ton of freight one mile), natural fibers by synthetic ones, steel and lumber by aluminum (15 times more energy-consumptive than steel) and plastics, low power by high power cars, soap by detergents, and organic by chemical fertilizer. In all cases, resource and energy consumption is vastly increased, while the pollutants produced are greatly expanded or, what is worse, environmentally unassimilable. The result is the overburdening of self-regulating environmental processes or the disruption of these cycles by unassimilable pollutants. Since 1945 the increases in environmentally destructive technologies and products range anywhere from 200 to 6,000 percent. Commoner concludes that "this pattern of economic growth is the major reason for the environmental crisis."[23]

In saying this, Commoner does not seem to locate the roots of the crisis within technology per se, but rather within the particular technological manifestations of economic growth. His previous observation regarding the continuity of the standard of living in the postwar period as opposed to the drastic changes in the technology designed to achieve this standard would seem to contradict the above quote on economic growth as cause. However, economic and technological growth are actually two sides of the same coin. Whereas pollution and environmental degradation have proceeded far more rapidly than simple economic growth statistics would suggest, the achieved rate of economic growth in the postwar period *has been made possible only through the drastic technological changes* pinpointed by Commoner. New technologies and products have been absolutely essential to the prevention of economic stagnation and the maintenance of a modest growth rate. Old technologies and products soon saturate the profit market, and the perennial menace of the growth society, overproduction and stagnation, sets in. Growthmen must put their scientists and technologists to work to discover "new and better" commodities to market, commodities whose production increases the producer's control over supply costs and profits, as in the case of synthetics.

While the new technologies and products increase control and lower production costs, they tend to be far more energy-consumptive and wasteful than their predecessors. However, up until most recently, energy has been cheap and abundant; petroleum products, both as raw material for chemicals and synthetics and as energy for industry and

---

[23] Commoner, *The Closing Circle*, p. 143.

transport, have formed the backbone of the new technology. And the profligate usage of petroleum has been essential to the economic "prosperity" of the postwar period. A temporary oil shortage and sharp increase in oil prices sent the growth society into a state of near panic, and its utter dependence on oil became acutely painful. It remains in doubt whether the world capitalist economy can make the necessary adjustments to the finances and limitations of the new energy situation.

The fact that per capita affluence or economic growth has increased far less than the large increases in the environmentally hostile technologies during the postwar period should not becloud the equally important fact that economic growth in this period began upon a very sizeable base figure, whereas the huge percentage increases in dangerous technologies arose from a base of little or nothing. In assessing environmental impact, then, a doubling of constant dollar GNP in the postwar period may mean environmental degradation worse than tenfold increases in a new technology or even a tenfold increase in all new technologies combined. The point to be made again, however, is that this doubling of capital stocks could not have been possible without the tenfold increase in new technologies which, in turn, laid the foundation for economic growth on top of an already mature capitalist society—an impressive but environmentally costly feat.

What of Erhlich's emphasis upon population? Is this, then, misplaced? We shall examine the link between population and economic growth in Chapter 9. Here we shall only take time to record our agreement with Erhlich's population concerns. It is only common sense to accept the fact that more people pose greater environmental problems, not only in areas burdened with new technologies, but also in agrarian regions where population increases place destructive pressures upon land use. When one considers also that the agrarian societies are pursuing industrialization, every low polluting villager of today is a potential high polluting urbanite of tomorrow. Population growth thus means that future living standards can never be as high as they might have been without such growth. Every addition to the world's population means a further division of the earth's resources and further pressures upon the environment, particularly if the long term aims of world industrialization are in view.

This should not be interpreted to mean that Asia is a greater threat to the environment than North America or Europe. Quite to the contrary, while the underdeveloped countries have serious environmental problems and prospects,[24] they nowhere nearly approach the environmental exhaustion and destruction perpetrated in the industrialized world. It is also in this industrialized world where additional population has the greatest environmental impact. How many newborn Asians it would take to match the lifetime environmental impact of one newborn American is uncertain, but the number would surely be large, if indeed it could be matched at all. Millions of American Indians came and went from North America and left only a trace, but one person's decisions and actions from today's society is capable of leaving behind a trail of waste and destruction which transforms the earth. The next 30 million Americans augur greater ill to the environment than the next 300 million Asians.

Not surprisingly, much of the environmental damage which has taken place in the underdeveloped world has been the work of foreign growth supervisors and their local converts. Wherever Western industrial investment has taken place, particularly in major Latin American and Asian cities, environmental problems have developed with alarming alacrity. Foreign investors have inadequate concern for the environment of their own countries let alone those of other countries. When the health and sanitation problems arising from chaotic urbanization are included in the environmental picture, the environmental problems of many cities are extreme.

Also in the underdeveloped world, there is the silting and pollution of rivers from acid runoffs from mining operations, plus the scars from indiscriminate exploration and mining. Second to nothing as an environmental problem in the underdeveloped world has been the construction of huge dams and massive irrigation projects. The classic case is that of the Soviet engineered Aswan Dam on the Nile in Egypt, though the Middle East has had previous experience on a smaller scale. The monster dams have created a host of serious environmental side effects, including the spawning of waterborne diseases in the slow-moving irrigation channels, the spreading of salinization and water-logging in the irrigation projects, the sedimentation of the reservoirs, the displacement of population, the inundation of upstream agricultural land, the drying up of downstream fisheries with the suspension of nutrient flow, and an ending to the spring flood silt deposits on delta farm land with the resulting need for artificial fertilizer and erosion of delta farm land

---

[24] See *Development and Environment* (The Hague: Mouton, 1972).

by the sea.[25] All in all, the food, economic, and environmental losses from nature-altering dams will in all likelihood exceed any short-term gains. Certain rivers may lend themselves to dams and their hydro-electric, reservoir, irrigation and flood control purposes; but dam construction in the underdeveloped world has been marked by inadequate impact evaluation and nearsightedness.

The environment as an issue

The magnitude of the environmental challenge has begun to make inroads into the public mind. The growing awareness of environmental deterioration is only in small part due to the dissemination of scientific knowledge about the problem; such awareness has been stimulated much more by direct experience of large numbers of people, particularly those living in urban areas. Urban dwellers have seen their environment fundamentally transformed in recent decades. Urban society has attempted to virtually eliminate the natural environment, a trend which is having disastrous consequences for that environment and for the people compelled to deal with the effects.

The decline in the quality of life discussed earlier is closely associated with the growing awareness of environmental degradation. Technological and economic expansion have placed unprecedented demands and stresses upon the environment, and the environment has responded with diminished capacity to support the quality of life which previous generations took almost for granted. This is not to say that technological and economic growth have had uniformly regressive effects upon the environment; in some instances the effects have been manifestly positive. The balance sheet for the past quarter century, however, has without question shown a sizeable environmental loss at the hands of growth, and a corresponding decline in the livability of human surroundings.

The environment, or ecosphere, consists of the system of earth's living things and their thin global habitat of air, water, and soil. The environmental system is composed of numerous subsystems which are each in themselves in delicate balance and in complex articulation with other subsystems. These are functional systems in the sense that they

---

[25] Bennett and Rowland, *Pollution Guide*, p. 25.

have the capacity to maintain an equilibrium or stable state in response to internal and external changes affecting them. Although a delicate balance, the ecosphere demonstrates an impressive degree of resilience; it can return itself to a viable or steady state despite relatively serious changes or interferences with its normal self-regulating processes. Both water and air, for example, display powerful self-cleansing capacities, but the self-regulating processes of either can be overwhelmed by inordinate amounts of human waste products—by pollution. The environment is rapidly losing its regenerative powers as new overpowering inputs weigh down upon it. Many argue that a point of no return could be relatively close at hand.

Out of environmental decline has arisen an ever broadening concern with ecology; the concern with ecology and environment has even been awarded the status of a movement. World conferences on environment are held and international agencies established. Locally active conservation groups proliferate. Laurence Rockefeller views the environmental movement as a force of great vigor and excitement.[26] Dow Chemical Company co-sponsors a university symposium on "Environmental Quality and Social Responsibility." Opinion polls disclose a profound shift in public attitudes accepting the seriousness of pollution and in the willingness to take the necessary restitutive measures.[27] Environmental bills of rights have been ratified in Massachusetts and Washington, while New York and Florida have passed major environmental bond issues. One writer observes that "it is significant that, at this critical juncture in human affairs, man now turns to 'ecology' as a guide toward rethinking his overall relationship to his environment—rather than to the more traditional political and economic viewpoints which have guided and measured his large-scale actions before."[28]

If ecology can replace political economy as a guide to social action, it is easily understandable why Rockefeller or Dow Chemical could be enthusiastic about an environmental movement. However, as this book argues throughout, the political economy of the growth society is inherently anti-ecological and for Rockefeller or Dow Chemical to be *serious* environmentalists is as contradictory as an anti-growth capital-

---

[26] William K. Reilly, *The Use of Land: A Citizen's Policy Guide to Urban Growth* (New York: Thomas Y. Crowell Company, 1973), p. 1.

[27] Louis Harris, *The Anguish of Change* (New York: W. W. Norton & Company, Inc., 1973), pp. 112–15.

[28] McHale, *Ecological Context*, p. 1.

ist. (Capitalists may and presumably do want *control* over environmental use and abuse, but never an end to the growth of consumerism.) If ecology can get people's minds off qualitative social changes, so much the better. The pitfall of pushing eoclogy, however, is that if environmentalism is taken seriously and pursued to its logical conclusion, one ends up with a radical political critique of the growth society after all. Environmentalism and capitalist growth turn out to be incompatible, a point in social understanding which has not yet been reached along a broad front. When this point is reached, we may expect Rockefeller's and Dow Chemical's support for the environmental movement to expire. So long as environmentalism remains at the strictly conservation level of action, little more can be expected from it than isolated attacks on isolated problems—hardly a means of achieving an end to the extensive processes of ecological breakdown. In order to be effective, the environmental movement must become a part of a broadly based political movement oriented toward fundamental economic reconstruction. Only then can the assault upon the environment be reversed.

Despite the reverberations made by environmentalists, there is reason to doubt the real strength and support of the movement. It may well be true that "the great mass of the world's producers and consumers continue their habitual behaviors devoid of any ecological ethic or awareness."[29] People may approve of cleaning up the environment in the abstract sense of reducing pollution, but few have thought out the full implications of reversing ecological demise. Cleaning up the environment in the sense of reestablishing a permanently viable relationship between society and nature requires an almost complete transformation of bourgeois culture, the entire way of life of the growth society. How many people are environmentalists in this necessary sense? Even with the slightest financial pressures, not to mention a threat to a long accepted life style, would-be environmentalists fall by the wayside in droves.

Thus, Rutgers sociologist Irving Louis Horowitz may well be right in asserting that "there are few people who would give up a single jetport and fewer people still who would give up their family automobile for the sake of cleaning the atmosphere."[30] Horowitz continues, "It is

---

[29] Lynton Caldwell, "The Coming Polity of Spaceship Earth," in Roelofs et al., *Environment and Society*, p. 259.

[30] Irving Louis Horowitz, "The Environmental Cleavage: Social Ecology versus Political Economy," *Social Theory and Practice* 2(Spring 1972):125–234.

well known that no people will endure for long lower standards of income or return to more primitive economic forms, in exchange for either clean atmosphere or clean water." What Horowitz does not mention is that if we continue to degrade the environment at the present rate, we will have no choice but to endure lower living standards and to return to more primitive economic forms. But Horowitz is evidently not the man to inform us on this matter, since he is of the opinion that "if in fact the levels of pollution in the United States are much higher, so too are the comforts and the life style superior to anything known in the past." Anyone who sees a positive relationship between pollution and life quality, even if only indirectly, is not likely to sympathize with an ecology movement. Thus, Horowitz views the ecology movement as a product of "rural ideals and troglodyte values."

Horowitz, of course, is not against ecology or a sound environment; he only opposes giving them priority over such things as the elimination of poverty and other social inequities. There is good reason to fear that, given the growth society's need for social inequality, it might attempt to divert attention toward isolated environmental clean-up programs. This has already been suggested by the favorable disposition of Rockefeller and Dow Chemical to solving environmental problems. The fact is that environmental degradation and social inequality are interrelated in numerous ways and neither can be reversed without fundamentally altering the course of the other. Environmental deterioration will continue as long as there is a class system, since the profits of environmental neglect accrue primarily to one class whereas the costs are borne primarily by another.

Thus, to attend to the problems of social inequality is also to attend to the problem of environmental degradation. The working class and poor are degraded in the growth society right along with the environment; to strengthen the position of either is to strengthen the position of the other. It is not a matter of priorities; even if class inequality and environment could be dealt with separately, it would still be impossible to establish the priority of one over the other. Both must be attacked simultaneously. Think, for example, what workers' control (an issue of social inequality) would mean for decisions regarding the safety of the work setting (an issue of environment).

A powerful environmental movement can materialize only within the broader scope of a powerful political movement, for the roots of the environmental crisis lie within the political economy of the growth society. Such a political movement has not yet been forthcoming. In the meantime, the culture of capitalism continues on its path of environmental destruction and ecological suicide.

Environmental debts

The growth society operates as if it had tunnel vision and nearsightedness; the accumulation of capital is pursued without regard for side effects or for long-range consequences, leaving to nature and the larger community these uncalculated costs. A quarter century ago, K. William Kapp phrased the point succinctly: "Capitalism must be regarded as an economy of unpaid costs, 'unpaid' in so far as a substantial portion of the actual costs of production remain unaccounted for in entrepreneurial outlays; instead they are shifted to, and ultimately borne by, third persons or by the community as a whole."[31] Kapp points to costs in the form of waste and duplicity, environmental exploitation, resource depletion, unemployment, health and injury problems, and retardation of constructive science and technology. Our concern in this chapter is primarily with environmental costs; these costs have been the most dear and the most dangerous.

Marx originally dealt with the problem of "externalities," the imposition of unpaid costs upon nature or the larger community by the capitalist class.[32] Marx wrote that "labour is not the source of all wealth. Nature is just as much the source of use values (and it is surely of such that material wealth consists!) as labour, which itself is only the manifestation of a force of nature, human labour power." Natural resources are a stock of capital which may be augmented or depleted much as any other capital formation. Modern agriculture, charged Marx, is as guilty of soil exploitation as it is of labor exploitation; the capitalist extracts a fictitious surplus from the soil by taking more wealth out than he restores. Thus, just as workers produce more value than they are paid in return, and thus perform unpaid labor, so has nature been forced to yield up its capital stock at a rate far in excess of actual or

---

[31] K. William Kapp, *The Social Costs of Private Enterprise* (Cambridge, Mass.: Harvard University Press, 1950), p. 231.

[32] See Michael Perelman, "An Application of Marxian Theory to Environmental Economics," *Review of Radical Political Economics* 6(Fall 1974):75–77.

restorative costs. The unpaid costs to the environment underlie the ecological challenge to survival.

In truth, however, these environmental costs are already being borne by the earth and its entire population, especially that part and those people laboring under the logic of the growth society. Soil depletion costs us in the form of lost nutrients and lowered production; deforestation costs us in the form of soil erosion, decline in rainfall and water supply, and loss of beauty and recreational enjoyment; depletion of fish and wildlife costs us in terms of food, ecological balance, and biological richness; pollution costs us in terms of health, recreation, and productivity. Aside from the day to day economic, social, and physical costs borne by the natural and human victims of growth for quick gain, an unpaid debt is being recorded with the environment which will soon come due. The magnitude of this debt is unknown, although we know it is already of extensive proportions.

Commoner sees the next quarter century as a final grace period before nature collects its unpaid costs in the form of ecological disaster. During this period, the United States, for example, would have to make *all* new investments under ecological rather than economic imperatives and spend at least $40 billion a year on environmental reconstruction if the country is to avoid disaster. Already five years have passed since he wrote these recommendations, while the survival requirements have been all but ignored. A growth society can never base investments upon ecological imperatives rather than economic, since it is the laws of capital accumulation which it must obey. And given the already huge financial debts of government, from where shall come $40 billion a year for environmental clean-up?

"Wealth has been gained," writes Commoner, "by rapid short-term exploitation of the environmental system, but it has blindly accumulated a debt to nature—a debt so large and so pervasive that in the next generation it may, if unpaid, wipe out most of the wealth it has gained us. In effect, the account books of modern society are drastically out of balance, so that, largely unconsciously, a huge fraud has been perpetrated on the people of the world."[33] The idea is that we have been living on borrowed natural capital for some time now, and the borrowing has been especially heavy since the 1940s. The surplus wealth

---

[33] Commoner, *The Closing Circle*, p. 295.

which has been extracted from labor and nature has permitted an unprecedented amount of so-called luxury living.

Labor has not yet made any serious demands about collecting the debt owed it; by and large, the working class continues to be confused over its role in capitalist society. How much more squeezing the working class will take in the support of the growth system is uncertain. Nature, on the other hand, *must* collect soon, for it is a self-regulating system which has definite limits of toleration to exploitation and abuse. The injustice of this debt is that payment will not be made by the generations which piled up the environmental IOUs, but by their offspring.

While the environmental crisis stems first and foremost from the nature of the economic system under which we are compelled to live, science and technology have raised the environmental crisis to lethal proportions. But it is not science and technology per se which are responsible for the survival challenge. Science and technology are not in themselves anti-ecological, although many primitivists would vent their rage against science and technology as the chief villains. Science and technology have, of course, been in existence long prior to the survival crisis and will continue to develop if the crisis is surmounted. It is not science and technology in the general sense which have heightened the survival crisis, but the particular kind of science and technology which develops within the growth society. The economic laws of capitalism have pushed forward the development of an openly exploitative and destructive science and technology geared toward the maximization of surplus wealth and the minimization of immediate financial cost.

Modern science, and technology in particular, have been almost synonymous with military power, itself a means towards the accumulation of global economic profit. The nonmilitary technology has been dominated by the search for and development of higher profit chemical and synthetic products to replace lower profit natural products. Aluminum and plastics are more profitable than steel and wood, synthetic fibers more so than wool and cotton, and detergents more so than soap.[34] As a result of the new marketing and profit structures, such renewable and biodegradable wood, wool, and soap products are in diminishing supply and expensive, whereas nonrenewable and nondegradable plastics, synthetics, and detergents are driving their predecessors from the market.

---

[34] Ibid., p. 259.

A rationally ordered economic system could put science and technology to use in an environmentally constructive manner and reduce the ecological debt while simultaneously raising life quality. The environmental impact of technology hinges upon the nature of the technology in use, and the nature of technology in use hinges upon the requirements and priorities of the economic system. If an economic system is made to be the servant of society and its natural environment, rather than the other way around, then an ecologically sensitive technology can indeed be developed.

Economics of neutrality

Bourgeois economics tends to wash its hands of the environmental crisis. As Walter Heller writes of the conclusions reached by economists Nordhaus and Tobin, "With respect to global ecological collapse, they appropriately conclude that 'there is probably very little that economists can say.' "[35] Economists steadfastly maintain their "neutrality" as the economy they purport to understand systematically destroys the earth. The furthest our economic sages venture is to engage in "cost-benefit analysis." Heller defines the economist's position on growth and the environment as follows: "As he (the economist) sees it, the right solution in striking a balance between nature and man, between environment and growth, and between technology and ecology, would be the one that pushes depollution to, but not beyond, the point where the costs—the foregone satisfactions of a greater supply of additional goods and services—just equal the benefits—the gained satisfactions of clear air, water, landscape, and sound waves."[36]

Cost-benefit analysis assumes diverse forms, and may be viewed in terms of an "optimal level" at which further expansion increases costs more than benefits, or in terms of an "efficiency criterion" whereby a point is reached where it is not possible to rearrange things so as to benefit one person without harming others.[37] The trouble with cost-

---

[35] Walter W. Heller, "Coming to Terms with Growth and the Environment," in Schurr, Energy, Economic Growth, and the Environment, p. 9.

[36] Ibid., p. 4.

[37] Larry E. Ruff, "The Economic Common Sense of Pollution," in Robert Dorfman and Nancy S. Dorfman, eds., Economics of the Environment (New York: W. W. Norton & Company, Inc., 1972), pp. 3–20.

benefit analysis is that there are no objective criteria with which to measure costs and benefits. As Kapp points out, "The final determination of the magnitude of specific social costs [or benefits] for purposes of practical policy remains a matter of collective evaluation and social value."[38] However, the idea that social values decide the course of economic development is as alien to economists as it is impossible within the logic of capitalism.

Since the logic of capitalism has only one criterion of success, growth, Robert and Nancy Dorfman thus conclude that optimal level or efficiency is best gauged by the degree to which an economy is producing as much of every good and service as is technically possible: "The GNP-maximization criterion . . . is the only one that is much used or of practical importance."[39] This is at least an honest evaluation of how the system actually works. Economists who develop elaborate cost-benefit schemes are largely engaging in academic exercises, since the growth system only calculates costs and benefits from its own needs and perspectives and ignores the needs and perspectives of the environment and the larger community. The powerful grab the benefits and impose the costs on environment and society. There is no social Solomon to stand in judgement over the neutrality stance posed by cost-benefit analysis. The environment always loses.

The economist's neutrality on the cost-benefit scheme is carried to ends which clearly expose its bias for growth and against the environment. The Dorfmans argue, for example, that "the question of whose right shall prevail—Able's [right to meditation] or Baker's [right to play stereo at resounding volume], birdwatchers' or snowmobilers' . . . is a question of equity. Any production measure will constrict or revoke some people's long-standing right to use the environment as they see fit—and thus reduce their welfare for the benefit of other people."[40] Is it any accident that bourgeois economists fail to see that meditation and birdwatching do not contribute to the maximization of GNP, whereas overpowered electronics and snowmobiles do? And how can their neutrality guise be maintained in the face of such obviously diverse environmental impacts as birdwatching and snowmobiling? If economists cannot outrightly decide cost-benefit correctness in such

---

38 Kapp, *The Social Costs of Private Enterprise*, p. 232.
39 Dorfman, *Economics of the Environment*, pp. xxvii, xxxi.
40 Ibid., p. xxxii.

cases, we may count ourselves fortunate that they have little to say about global ecological collapse. The environment's death warrant is signed by the Dorfmans when they assert that "the proper use of environmental resources is more a matter of economics than of morals."[41]

The propriety of economics as arbiter of resource use has already left a record so dismal that it should take little persuasion to jettison this approach. It is axiomatic that any resource use or investment which does not contribute to economic growth cannot successfully compete with growth-producing utilization. Nonmonetary benefits have no way of entering the calculus of capitalism; indeed, all nonmonetary benefits must be considered as costs to capital. To set aside natural resources and economic investment for purely social, aesthetic, or spiritual use is to subtract from capital growth. Irreplaceable craftsmanship completed decades or even centuries ago may be destroyed in the name of economic progress; culture is a cost, growth is benefit. When social values gain ascendancy over the laws of capital accumulation, only then will environmental and cultural survival have a chance. Until then the Dorfmans must count dollars and cents, telling us how well off we are by the magnitude of the total.

Those whose faith in the growth society remains unshaken usually set forth some variation of a "pollution tax" as a means of avoiding ecological disaster. The idea here is to use the market mechanism to redistribute social costs and reduce environmental abuse, that is, make the exploiters and polluters pay for their unpaid costs. One such argument for example, runs that environmental balance must be "reached by methods which harness the strong human motivations—the greed, avarice, and self-interest of individuals within the ranks of business and government. . . . The business system, private property, and the profit motive" must be strengthened.[42] This approach may also suggest that *all* resources should be privitized so that responsibility can be pinned down.[43] But would anyone really expect from this that privitization of the Great Lakes would reverse their death processes, or that privitization of the national parks would preserve the resources and beauty contained therein? Why should we think that pollution taxes

---

[41] Ibid., p. xl.

[42] Edwin Dolan, *TANSTAAFL* (New York: Holt, Rinehart & Winston, Inc., 1971), p. 13.

[43] See, for example, J. H. Dales, *Pollution, Property, and Prices* (Toronto: University of Toronto Press, 1968).

would do anything more than raise consumer prices, just as other taxes levied on business tend to do? Certainly it is plausible that particular cases of pollution might be overcome through financial pressure, but it is inconceivable that the ecological crisis, rooted as it is in an entire mode of production and consumption, could be overcome via taxation. Just as taxation cannot be expected to fundamentally alter the class structure of capitalism, neither can it be expected to alter the course of environmental decline.

Could legislation do the job? Environmental laws backed by stiff sanctions might be variously effective.[44] However, if environmental laws were in harmony with natural laws, the results would be extremely deleterious for economic growth. Noneconomic considerations would have priority, and this is bound to counteract the interests of capital accumulation. Perhaps this is why in the five years after the U.S. National Environmental Policy Act was signed in 1970, the courts handed down only 200 decisions relating to suits filed under this law. In a case involving U.S. Steel and the Environmental Protection Agency, the company threatened to close down its plant rather than pay a daily air pollution fine. Shutdown in the face of environmental measures is a powerful weapon in the hands of private enterprise in an economy with chronically high unemployment.

The fact is that financial or legal pressures are not capable of decisively altering the course of environmental decline. So long as we live under the unflinching demands of economic growth, there can be no real solution to the ecological crisis. The growth system as such is responsible for the crisis and a solution can be spoken of only in terms of a revolutionary change in production and consumption values.

We should also keep in mind that the ecological crisis is a global one and must be dealt with on a global scale. Local penalties cannot hope to achieve global solutions. This should not be interpreted as a justification to avoid local environmental battles. After all, as of now the only world environmental agency, the United Nations Environment Program, has been able to move only sluggishly along, while another worldwide environmentally relevant conference, the Law of the Seas Conference, displayed little concern for pollution problems. Thus, local actions remain the chief means of fighting environmental degrada-

---

[44] Stuart S. Nagel, "Incentives for Compliance with Environmental Law," *American Behavioral Scientist* 17 (May–June 1974) :690–710.

tion. But when air masses, seas, waterways, drainage basins, and soil, for example, are involved, the environmental problems overextend local or even national boundaries.

These problems perforce become political problems and thus confront major political obstacles to their solution. National governments have been largely intransigent in compromising what they regard as national economic interests, however small, on behalf of regional or global environmental conservation. These realities raise the urgency of a cooperative world community all the more. Capitalist growth accentuates the world's national conflicts. Socialist growth is capable of integrating the world's people into a larger cooperative community, however long and arduous this task may be. The point to be stressed in this regard is that some sort of cooperative world society *must* be achieved, environmentally and otherwise, or the descent of humanity will not be long in coming.

8

Growth versus resources

How large a storehouse?

As the source of all wealth, nature resembles a storehouse of capital goods which society draws upon to meet its needs. Up until the period of industrialization, nature's gifts of material wealth were used rather sparingly or not at all. Suddenly, at least in historical terms, natural capital was being depleted with unprecedented speed, until today scientists are talking about the exhaustion of many key resources. The depletion of biological resources such as soil and water and forests has already been commented upon. The ruination of such renewable natural capital could be achieved only through the most ruthless and irresponsible exploitation of the environment and it would spell disaster to its inhabitants. Mineral resources, which at best can be recycled, represent a different kind of problem with respect to the depletion of nature's storehouse.

Prominent economists have contended that there is little reason to worry about the exhaustion of resources.[1] In economic calculating, the price of a potentially exhaustible resource will rise high enough to prevent its disappearance; moreover, as the prices of scarce resources rise, cheaper substitutes will become available. That irreplaceable resources

---

[1] See Walter W. Heller, "Coming to Terms with Growth and the Environment," in Sam H. Schurr, ed., *Energy, Economic Growth, and the Environment* (Baltimore: Johns Hopkins University Press, 1972), p. 9.

have been and are being wasted in the most specious kinds of endeavors, and that such waste will mean scarcity and costliness of basic materials for other societies and subsequent generations would not appear to bother these economists. Nor does the possibility that substitutes will be unattainable or environmentally degrading enter into the picture. An unwavering faith in the market mechanism and technology prevails. Where this faith has brought us today should be sufficient reason to look in other directions for a realistic assessment of future prospects.

An appeal not to worry about resources notwithstanding, we might note that the lifetime reserves of many strategic minerals are not particularly long. For example, current rates of consumption indicate that world reserves of lead, zinc, tin, and copper will be virtually exhausted by or before the end of the century.[2] Aluminum and nickel are given 125 years. Iron and chromium would last until the year 2500, but other iron-alloy metals less than to 2100. The future demands to be made upon mineral resources at current consumption rates, or increases in world industrial production of about 7 percent a year, amount in 50 years to a volume of resources extraction 32 times that of today.[3] In a century, the demand would be over 1000 times that of today. Even more striking is the fact that, if the *world* population of today (disregarding its own rapid growth) were consuming mineral resources at the American rate, years to depletion would drop to 11 for lead, zinc, tin and copper, 42 for chromium, 23 for nickel, 80 for aluminum, and only 80 for iron as well. The present annual output of all mines and smelters would have to increase 75 to 250 times, exceeding the quantity of all known or even inferred reserves of most minerals. Considering this would all have to be almost doubled by 2000 to compensate for population growth, we are able to catch a glimpse of what world economic growth in the American vein and magnitude implies for resources and environment. America's 6 percent of total world population consuming almost one third of the world energy and raw material total sets a depletion pace which the earth cannot possibly sustain for very long.

These depletion figures do not tell the whole story for the United States, for they give world resource reserves and not those for the

[2] John McHale, *World Facts and Trends* (New York: The Macmillan Company, 1972), pp. 75–79.

[3] Robert L. Heilbroner, *An Inquiry Into The Human Prospect* (New York: W. W. Norton & Company, Inc., 1974), p. 48.

United States alone. Depletion dates come much earlier for the United States, if the mineral is available at all. Optimists who believe that "the resource scarcity has decreased persistently for a long time" generously base a large part of their sanguine outlook upon the natural resources of other countries.[4] Their optimism also rests upon the continuation of an economic system which permits the United States open access to these resources—"a free international trading and investment system." However, the idea that the rest of the world is an American storehouse of resources cannot long be upheld in the face of rising nationalism in the developing countries, and the internal industrial needs of developed countries. Thus, the notion that Canada is a northern province of the United States cannot continue indefinitely, although this is the prevailing view. In sizing up American resources, Raymond Ewell writes that "the importance of Canada cannot be overemphasized. Canada is a vast storehouse of industrial raw materials that are virtually as accessible as if they were within our own borders. Without Canada our raw material position would be much more precarious that it is now."[5] Canada is neither the resource storehouse it is believed to be nor permanently as accessible as if it were another state.

There are, no doubt, various quantities of unproven reserves in remote regions of the globe, and as scarcities increase or the required technology becomes available, exploration will uncover them. Siberia clearly falls in this category. Yet, unproven reserves, especially those directly available to the West, are not going to substantially alter the depletion picture.

It is true also, as the optimists assert, that all minerals exist in limitless quantities as trace elements in such abundant sources as granite and sea water. However, the extractive technology doesn't exist, and even if it did, the energy requirements and consequences of mineral extraction as trace elements would be enormous. Geologist Preston Cloud points out that the question is not ultimately how much of the resources are available, but rather what are the limits to what can be extracted and kept in circulation without destroying the basis of the ecosystem.[6]

---

4 Joseph Fisher, "Impact of Population on Resources and Environment," *American Economic Review* 61(May 1971):392–98.

5 Raymond Ewell, "U.S. Will Lag USSR in Raw Materials," *Chemical and Engineering News* 48(August 24, 1970):42–46.

6 Preston Cloud, "Resources, Population, and Quality of Life," in Fred Singer, ed., *Is There an Optimum Level of Population?* (New York: McGraw-Hill Company, 1971), pp. 10–11.

The growth society cannot stop to raise such a question. Nor does it raise questions regarding the equity or political wisdom of gobbling up the remaining available resources while large masses of the under-developed world struggle for sheer physical survival. Even the needs of the growth society's own future generations are ignored in the mad rush of today's growth-sustaining production and consumption. However, there are limits to nature's storehouse and environmental support system; these limits are being rapidly approached.

Resources and population

Closely linked to the question of resource availability is that of population size and growth. The number of people living on the earth and the rate at which they are increasing has certain implications for the amount of resources available to each of them. The larger the population, at least given today's base, the fewer the resources the earth will be able to supply to each of its inhabitants. Unequal distribution may provide a minority with continued abundance despite a large and growing world population, but a revolution of rising expectations throughout the world is bound to put increasing pressure upon the existing resource distribution. The demand upon world resources is mounting from all sides and population growth is and shall be even more so contributing heavily to this pressure upon resources.

Nevertheless, population pressure upon resources is given short shrift by some observers. For example, one contention is that a doubling of the United States' population would obviously put some strain on our resources, but it will not overburden them.[7] Another viewpoint goes so far as to say that it is entirely possible enough wealth can be produced to support a population ten times the present one in even greater material comfort than today.[8] This would mean a population of near 40 billion, an unsustainable figure from an environmental standpoint, even if the resources could somehow be produced. The environment, however, is not often considered in the analysis; for example, one such analysis argues that a country's population growth is no prob-

---

[7] Willard Johnson, "Should The Poor Buy No Growth?" *Daedalus* 102(Fall 1973):166.

[8] E. A. Wrigley, *Population and History* (New York: McGraw-Hill, 1969), p. 228.

lem so long as production equals consumption.[9] And what happens when an existing large population is faced with declining resources production? To allow population to reach a magnitude which is sustainable only in the present is not very farsighted. We have previously pointed out the unsustainable pressures upon the earth's natural capital if even the existing population were all consuming as the advanced capitalist countries do. Since at least a doubling of population is certain, perhaps a trebling or even more, some major changes in world resource use and distribution will obviously have to take place in the relatively near future.

An intriguing proposition regarding population and resources is offered by demographic economist Richard Easterlin, who contends that fertility adjusts itself to environmental resources so that the optimal number of children are born in accordance with existing tastes, prices, and income.[10] Thus, humanity could never get itself into an environmental and resource bind, since population would begin to decline as soon as the earth's storehouse of natural treasures displayed signs of emptying. That population growth would begin to decline in response to mounting resource shortages and environmental deterioration is not hard to believe. This has happened before and may indeed be happening now. However, the optimal number of children for the moment at hand may be far too many 20 to 40 years hence. Rather than a population adjusting its birthrate to resources, resources force adjustments in population, and the adjustment process may be a difficult one. The worse the imbalance between population and the sustainable natural support system, the harder the adjustment when it comes. Even minor setbacks in production, not to mention major economic or natural catastrophes, may come down hard on an overpopulated society, since there is no margin to absorb the shock.

A more persuasive appraisal of the population-resource balance is given by Cloud: "We are, in fact, deluged with evidence that, for current conditions a world population of 3.5 billion already exceeds the optimum, while the more than 200 million inhabitants of the United States are also too many for its level of consumption, aspirations, and domestic resources."[11] Cloud suggests that the world population may

[9] Glen Cain, "Issues in the Economics of a Population Policy for the United States," *American Economic Review* 61(May 1971):408–17.

[10] Richard Easterlin, "Does Human Fertility Adjust to the Environment?" *American Economic Review* 61(May 1971):399–407.

[11] Cloud, "Resources, Population, and Quality of Life," p. 10.

level off at ten billion, and this could be supported temporarily, but this would be several billions more than could be sustained for very long. Three billion, according to Cloud, is closer to the sustainable number. Ehrlich and Ehrlich are of the opinion that "taking into account present population sizes, densities, and other factors involved in carrying capacity, we arrive at the inescapable conclusion that, in the context of man's present patterns of behavior and level of technology, the planet Earth, as a whole, is overpopulated."[12] The Ehrlichs concur with the estimation that only one billion persons could long be supported at American consumption levels.

To talk in terms of one or three billion is, of course, pure fantasy. The chance for a golden age has long gone by the boards. To talk in terms of a worldwide rate of consumption at American and European levels is also pure fantasy. The days of the growth society itself are numbered. The reality to confront in the foreseeable future is that of eight to ten billion persons living on a planet with an uncertain environment and a badly depleted stock of natural wealth. To think that, under these circumstances, anything but a revolution in productive and consumption patterns could avert large-scale social and environmental cataclysm is to engage in profound self-deception. We shall examine in part the kind of behavior which must be revolutionized in the last section of this chapter; just now we turn our attention to the most crucial and environmentally problematic resource—energy.

Energy consumption

Nothing grows faster in the growth society than energy consumption. In the United States, total energy consumption increased by almost two thirds between 1960 and 1970, while electric power consumption doubled.[13] Total energy consumption in America is expected to almost double again by the end of the century, with electricity consumption amounting to six times the 1970 level. Electricity consumption has been growing at almost 8 percent a year, or twice as fast as total energy consumption. The rate of oil consumption increase is

---

[12] Paul R. Ehrlich and Anne H. Ehrlich, *Population Resources Environment* (San Francisco: W. H. Freeman and Company, 1972), p. 258.

[13] Joel Darmstadter, "Energy Consumption: Trends and Patterns," in Schurr, ed., *Energy, Economic Growth, and the Environment*, pp. 155–223.

somewhat less, but a doubling of demand is expected by 2000 (delivery of this amount seems unlikely).

Owing to the rapid industrial development of the West, the world distribution of energy consumption is sharply skewed so that the growth societies account for the large portion of energy use. The United States alone accounts for about one third of world energy consumption and oil and natural gas consumption (1968), while 20 million Californians burn up more electricity than 800 million Chinese. The United States far overshadows other growth societies in energy consumption, burning up almost three times the per capita energy of Western Europe (1968). Underdeveloped regions use only a small fraction, say about $\frac{1}{30}$th to $\frac{1}{100}$th, of the American per capita energy consumption.

The United States is highly dependent upon petroleum as a basic energy source, deriving three fourths of its energy supply from it, compared to two thirds for Europe and Japan, and only two fifths for the Communist countries.[14] The shift away from coal to oil as the basic energy source, a shift engineered by American oil companies in the postwar period, has created serious energy problems and costs in Europe. Europe declined from 86 percent self-sufficiency in 1952 to 41 percent in 1972, and Japan declined from over 95 percent in 1952 to only 13 percent in 1972. American energy self-sufficiency dropped from near total to 85 percent in the same period. Meanwhile, the Communist countries increased their net export of energy. The Soviet Union has a per capita energy consumption rate about that of Western Europe, but has large petroleum reserves.

That the rate of energy consumption cannot be equated with the economic well-being of a country is attested to by the fact that in recent years the United States has had almost twice the per capita energy consumption of Sweden but only a slightly higher per capita GNP.[15] Canada has also had a considerably higher rate of energy consumption than Sweden, while having a lower per capita GNP. Whether the quality of life is any higher in the United States with its 310 million per capita Btu consumption (1968) than China with its 12 million per capita Btu consumption is a matter of opinion.

The chief energy consumer in the growth society is, of course, in-

---

[14] Michael Tanzer, The Energy Crisis (New York: Monthly Review Press, 1974), pp. 15–18.

[15] McHale, World Facts and Trends, p. 87.

dustry, which accounts for 40 percent.[16] Transport follows with 25 percent, residential 20 percent, and commercial 14 percent. A 4 percent annual increase in residential consumption may be accounted for by the rapid increase of electrical appliances and gadgets. Year-round air conditioning of new commercial and public buildings has greatly increased energy consumption in this area. Industrial increases stem from an expanding production base and the growth of more energy-intensive technology and products. Transport energy consumption gains derive from a constantly expanding volume of automobiles and trucks as opposed to rail travel and freight. To analyze the energy consumption of different sectors of society is not especially significant, since the logic of growth links them all together in a network of excessive waste. The logic of growth requires increasing production, and increasing production places heavier demands upon energy resources, the utilization of which raises the amount of environmental pollution and stress.

Growth is pursued with the greatest effort by precisely those countries where growth has long been the most extensive, placing extraordinarily large burdens upon energy supplies and the environment into which the spent energy is released. A 7 percent annual increase in United States electrical power demand, or a 4 percent increase in total energy demand, upon the presently enormous base means an exponential growth curve of immensely greater danger than that found in most other places in the world. At a time when long-range worldwide energy and environmental planning and foresight is a demand of survival, the growth society heaves forward on a burgeoning flotsam of electronic, motorized, and synthesized waste. The growth society is not given to reviewing the implications of the fact that, for the underdeveloped countries to attain its per capita level of affluence, a twenty- to thirtyfold increase in energy use would be required today, plus at least twice this for tomorrow's doubled population. Nor is the growth society given to reviewing the implications of further doublings of energy consumption for climatic conditions, which at a 4 percent world growth rate could within the foreseeable future raise or lower the earth's temperature sufficiently to produce disaster. Nor are the much more immediate and decisive pollution effects of increasing energy and resource con-

16 John C. Fisher, *Energy Crises in Perspective* (New York: John Wiley & Sons, 1973), pp. 5–7.

sumption given serious consideration in the growth society's calculations.

Much has been made of late over the energy crisis. Just where do we stand with regard to energy resources in terms of potential supply? We have briefly indicated the magnitude of demand predicted for energy resources. Can the earth meet this demand? Can the environment survive if the delivery could be made?

ENERGY SUPPLY

The predominant energy source of the growth society today is petroleum. Regardless of the varying estimates of world petroleum reserves, the use of oil as the major energy source will encompass but a wisp of human history, perhaps only about 150 years. Hundreds of billions of tons of oil will have been burned in this relatively brief time span, while it took 250 million years for nature to produce this oil. The exponential increase in oil consumption may be seen in the fact that from 1970 to 1980 the world will consume 200 billion barrels of oil, an amount equivalent to the total used prior to 1970.[17] The decade's consumption took 40 percent of all proven reserves. One estimate of the ultimate reserves of conventional crude oil is 200 billion tons or 70 years supply at present consumption rates.[18] This figure is greatly influenced by the huge Middle East supply. For the biggest consumer of them all, the United States (which was consuming 70 percent of the total world consumption as recently as 1952), conventional domestic oil has only a short lifetime left, depending upon how rapidly imports are increased and alternative energy sources, including other fossil fuels such as coal and oil shale, are expanded and developed. Proven reserves come to only ten years supply at present rates, but this figure could be doubled. However, with some 3,000 products produced from petroleum and 3,000 more from petrochemicals, the value of crude petroleum as a nonfuel commodity will increasingly reduce its use in energy production.

Even given the development of the world's oil shales and sands, which contain many times more oil than do conventional reserves, the heavy future energy demands are expected to substantially deplete all

---

[17] Philip Sykes, *Sellout* (Edmonton, Alberta: Hurtig Publishers, 1973), p. 21.
[18] Tanzer, *Energy Crisis*, p. 20.

forms of oil resources late in the next century. The most abundant of the fossil fuels, coal, is in several hundred years supply; and together with oil shale and atomic power, is expected to increasingly take over for conventional oil by the turn of this century.[19] Constituting almost 90 percent of fossil fuels, coal is expected to remain an important energy source for still another 200 years, gradually giving way to nuclear and solar energy. With natural gas supplies dwindling along with oil, coal gasification could figure prominently in future energy plans. However, as with shale development, American coal resources are heavily located in the water-short Western states, and shale development and coal gasification require large quantities of water. If coal resources were fully developed, however, they are considered so large as to raise the problem of waste heat prior to running out, and to raise even other limiting pollution problems even before the thermal pollution factor does.[20] Thus, given the technological and water resource capacity to develop all fossil fuels, and coal in particular, environmental limitations will present themselves before supply limitations. The practical evidence of this is very much at hand already.

If the world supply of conventional petroleum and natural gas is still good for several more decades, if there are oil shales to back these up for several more decades, and if there is enough coal to last for several hundred years, why was there, or still is, an energy crisis? The energy crisis as it originally emerged was essentially a contrived delivery shortfall created by those that control the bulk of international oil—the international oil companies and Middle East producers—in order to raise prices, royalties, and profits. An oil glut in the 1960s had driven down the wellhead or posted price of crude oil and with it the oil producing countries' (OPEC) revenue shares; the oil companies, however, managed to maintain their revenues as a result of very rapidly expanding demand.[21] As the producing countries moved toward full control of pricing and royalty percentages, raising both in the process, the oil companies had the rationale for raising their retail prices and realizing

---

[19] Earl Cook, "Energy Sources For a Steady-State Society," in Sylvan J. Kaplan and Evelyn Kivy-Rosenberg, eds., *Ecology and the Quality of Life* (Springfield, Ill.: Charles C. Thomas, Publisher, 1973), pp. 79–102.

[20] James Laxer, *Canada's Energy Crisis* (Toronto: James Lewis & Samuel, Publishers, 1974), pp. 4–5.

[21] See Robert Kronish, "The Coming of The Energy Crisis," *Socialist Revolution* 3(September–October 1973):9–43.

huge profit gains from sales on the already large and growing world market.

Thus, both OPEC and the oil companies were able to capitalize on oil-dependent world market by allowing burgeoning demand to close the supply gap, overtaking it in some areas, and forcing up the price of a barrel of oil to about four times its previous price. The shortage psychology permitted oil interests to greatly increase prices without arousing wide resentment among buyers and consumers. The oil companies, while not happy to lose control over production, had the ideal rationale for price rises and foisted the blame on the Arabs. The enormous profits which followed did not fail to stir public and congressional suspicion regarding the shortage or crisis situation. In addition to the price rationale, the energy crisis served as an ideal weapon to counterattack against environmentalists, especially those holding up the Alaskan pipeline development, but was also useful against offshore, shale, and coal-stripping opponents.[22] The shift of control of foreign production from the oil companies to the producing countries has required the companies to accordingly shift their profit-taking from the point of production to retail outlets, placing greater upward pressures on the price of petroleum products. The shift in foreign control has moved the oil companies toward forward integration of all sales operations and into mergers in a variety of petroleum-related industries.

With regard to the energy crisis, then, Michael Tanzer sums it up forcefully in saying that "There is no real energy crisis, in the sense of a physical shortage of energy resources; rather, there is an artificially contrived scarcity generated by various forces operating within the overall framework of the international capitalist economy. . . . The international energy crisis may be seen as a classic example of the irrationalities of the international capitalist system."[23] Tanzer stresses the basic irrationality is that production, including that involving energy, is based on profit calculations and not upon human needs and resource limitations. As long as the role of wealth and money prevail in economic organization, rather than the many basic needs of the people, Tanzer concludes that there can be no solution to the energy crisis.

The growth society has brought upon itself the conditions for an energy crisis. The tremendous expansion in the demand for oil revolu-

    [22] See Frank Ackerman and Arthur MacEwan, "Energy and Power," *Monthly Review* 25(January 1974):1–14.

    [23] Tanzer, *Energy Crisis*, p. 11.

tionized the control and pricing of foreign petroleum production. Given the continued rapid increase in oil and energy consumption, we may expect an indefinite prolongation of a crisis atmosphere. The crisis *is* real in the sense that the growth society has an insatiable appetite for energy and the production machine now is geared to run on oil and natural gas. The conventional supply of these fuels is, in fact, limited in the countries most dependent upon them today, including the United States—given its ravenous consumption rates. The crisis is *not* real in the sense that a rationally ordered society would not be blindly raising the demand for petroleum energy, but would rather be pursuing social growth and developing alternative energy technologies. As the consumption of readily available energy sources would slacken off, the lifetime of these sources would be greatly extended and allow time for the safe and certain development of long-range energy supplies. The actual course of events is quite otherwise, as large stocks of conventional oil and gas are burned up in the most wasteful profit-making ventures conceivable. The search for alternative energy sources goes on in the most haphazard way, if at all, the only thing being assured is a government sell-out of any promising new sources to the oil companies. A closer look at these companies and their profits is in order.

OIL POWER

The most important thing to keep in mind about the oil companies is that they represent the richest and most powerful sector of the economy. Since under capitalism the state is typically an instrument of the ruling economic groups,[24] it should come of no surprise that big oil has long played a highly influential, even decisive, role in government policy, especially foreign policy. Using the most powerful case of the Rockefeller interests to illustrate only the direct personnel aspect of oil and government links, we may note that the State Department in the postwar period has been completely dominated by such Rockefeller associated men as Dean Acheson, John Foster Dulles, Christian Herter, Dean Rusk, and Henry Kissinger.[25] The State Department has virtually been a government office of Standard Oil of New Jersey (Exxon) which had

---

[24] See G. William Domhoff, *The Higher Circles* (New York: Vintage Books, 1971).

[25] Barry Weisberg, *Beyond Repair* (Boston: Beacon Press, 1971), p. 137.

four fifths of its production outside of the United States in 1972. The close ties of oil to foreign policy may be observed in a quotation from *Petroleum Engineer* back in 1970:

> If and when the U.S. wins its objectives there (Vietnam), oil exploration could conceivably be successful enough to turn that part of the world into another South Louisiana-Texas-type producing area. This would be one of the biggest booms in the industry's history. It all depends on the Vietnam war, how long it takes to get the job done and how well the job is done.[26]

It can never be said that foreign policy chiefs Rusk and Kissinger didn't do their best to get the job done, and that Acheson and Dulles didn't create the atmosphere for them to work. Ironically, the disaster which took place in Vietnam laid the groundwork for a worldwide move against American military and financial presence, as in the oil-rich Middle East.

Oil profits went through the roof following the price revolution of 1973. With a handful of companies completely dominating the industry, oil profits in 1973 and again in 1974 soared over $6 billion; Exxon more than doubled its previous average annual profit take of $1 billion. In the third quarter of 1974, a mere 13 petroleum firms with a $1.7 billion after tax profit accounted for almost 18 percent of the total profit of 853 major corporations. The predominance of oil in the American economy is signified by the fact that roughly half of the largest 20 industrials are oil firms.

Greatly contributing to this oil giganticism is an extremely favorable tax position which has allowed major firms to escape paying but a few, if any, percentage points of their income in taxes.[27] The major tax concession has since 1913 been the depletion allowance of 26.5 percent, now reduced to 22 percent. This concession has saved the oil companies and cost the taxpayers approximately $150 billion since 1925, or $2.5 billion a year currently. Other tax favors extended to the oil companies is dollar for dollar write-off for foreign tax levies on domestic taxes rather than on taxable income and an investment tax credit for drilling and exploration amounting to 50 percent of costs.

The tax favors are supposedly designed to stimulate exploration and

[26] Cited in Martin Murray, "The United States' Continuing Economic Interests in Vietnam," *Socialist Revolution* 3(January–April 1973):11–68.

[27] Michael Harrington, "A New Crisis of Capitalism," *Dissent* (Winter 1975):7.

oil reserves; however, only one tenth of the depletion cost has been added to oil reserve values, or a 90 percent waste factor in this subsidy. Oil firms spent less on exploration for new reserves in the United States during the 1960s than they did for advertising, at a time when perhaps one half of reserves awaited to be discovered.[28] Appropriately enough, oil advertising has shifted from products to idea management and public image.[29] The money saved from tax concessions, however, has largely gone into other investments such as buying up other energy industries, chemical industries, highway construction industries, and a variety of others, including motels, Houston real estate, and Ringling Brothers Circus.[30]

The biggest government concession of all to the oil industries has been payment of the highway system, especially the interstate system which by 1970 had cost $32 billion. As late as this date the government was outspending mass transit for highways by 50 to 1. We have previously stressed the inefficiency of motor as opposed to rail transport; the oil and automobile firms have combined their power for over one half century to dismantle and abort alternative modes of transportation. The result has been a desecrated landscape and an energy crisis.

Despite their predominance in the corporate asset, revenue, and profit world, the oil companies are not especially significant in providing employment. This is due, of course, to the highly automated production and refining process. For example, Exxon with sales of $2.4 billion in 1973 employed only 137,000 people compared to Westinghouse Electric's 194,000 employees with a mere $162 million in sales.[31] LTV's $50 million in sales employed almost as many people as Texaco's $1.3 billion.

Destined to become one of the biggest government concessions to the oil industry, perhaps the biggest of all since the original sell-out of petroleum resources to private developers, is the oil shale deposits located in Wyoming, Colorado, and especially Utah. Fully 80 percent of American shale out of an estimated total of 1,400 billion barrels lie under public lands. The promise of *in situ* extraction of oil from the shale,

---

[28] Laxer, *Canada's Energy Crisis*, pp. 21–33.

[29] Desmond Smith, "Bonanza! The Petrodollar Publicity Blitz," *The Nation*, November 9, 1974, pp. 461–64.

[30] For data on oil companies' merger and ownership pattern, see James Ridgeway, *The Last Play* (New York: E. P. Dutton & Company, 1973).

[31] *Fortune*, August, 1974, p. 185.

that is, underground blasting followed by the pumping out of the melted oil, could avoid the more environmentally destructive stripping and the above ground separation process requiring huge amounts of scarce water. The *in situ* method would cost an estimated $1.18 a barrel, so with oil prices as they are now ($15 a barrel) the wealth to be had from shale oil is truly tremendous. Yet, the government is selling leases for as little as three cents a barrel. Gulf and Indiana Standard received a 5,120 acre tract at three cents a barrel; the public received $210 million for resources containing at least four billion barrels of oil or a current value of $60 billion.[32]

As a hedge against problems with the development of alternative fossil fuels such as oil shale and coal gasification (oil takeover of coal companies and lands has been going on for some time), the oil companies have moved into the nuclear field both in terms of technology and uranium reserves, of which they control 45 percent. The promise of atomic energy has thus far, however, proven largely false. Nearly one half of the nuclear power plant projects in the United States, at latest count 112 out of 236, have met with cancellations or major delays. Technological, environmental, and financial difficulties have resulted in a dubious outcome for one half the plants scheduled for completion by 1984. Considering that at the rate of growth of electricity demand in California during the early 1970s in 20 years' time that state alone would require 130 giant nuclear reactors spaced at eight-mile intervals along the entire coast,[33] we may be highly skeptical of the role which atomic energy will be capable of playing in the coming decades. Even more so than the case with coal, the issue to be dealt with is not one of supply, for there is enough uranium to equal the energy of one million times all fossil fuels, plus the possibility of the future development of the "breeder reactor" which manufactures its own fuel from uranium. There is also the ultimate possibility of power through fusion which can utilize elements from sea water for fuel. Certainly one may entertain doubts as to when, if ever, nuclear technology of the breeder and fusion type will be available, or even that today's atomic power development will meet the needs of the growth society before a large-scale return to coal is required. In view of the rapidly dwindling oil and gas supplies and the halting atomic energy start, it seems that the northern

[32] Peter Barnes, "Shale on Sale?" *The New Republic*, April 6, 1974, pp. 16–18.
[33] Sykes, *Sellout*, p. 43.

Rocky Mountain states will in a decade or so be in for an all-out assault on their underground supplies of coal and oil shale. The real limits to atomic power and coal are not those of supply but of environment. Both present inescapable problems of thermal pollution, while atomic power presents serious problems of radioactive waste, although fusion would almost eliminate it if based upon certain clean elements.

Clean and inexhaustible energy sources such as geothermal, hydrological (tidal), wind, temperature variations between lower ocean depths and surface water, and solar power are all being discussed as answers to the energy crisis. However, the energy czars in the corporate and government world are not much interested. Such projects are simply not "economically feasible" today. Innovation in these areas is being pursued largely by individual inventors and environmentalists. As is always the case, if anybody happens to come up with something interesting, the giants will no doubt take a look. However, at the rate the growth society consumes power, the size of investments required to develop these alternative sources are beyond those available to individuals. Nevertheless, for the individual inventor, the way is open for at least solar and wind experimentation.

The question which looms in the background of all the discussion about energy supply limitations and environment is why must we consume such incredible quantities of energy? Certainly, such outlandish levels of energy consumption are not necessary to live securely and creatively upon the earth. Indeed, the trail of pollution and destruction which such enormous energy consumption leaves in its wake has already lowered life quality in the areas where it has been most intensively used. What shall people in the growth society do with all this energy potential if and when it is realized? More of the same but in a bigger way of what they are doing today? Even if the environment could somehow withstand it, life would become intolerable or unlivable if such a course of energy consumption were followed.

All of this energy potential implies that there will be something to apply it to. Presumably once conventional mineral resources have been exhausted some of the energy could be used to extract more from sea water and granite. Yet, the question remains as to how the population of the growth society could continually expand its energy consumption into the indefinite future without ceasing to be human in the sense we know that concept today. Would not the psychological, social, and technological systems designed to bear such energy outputs eventually crumble under the demands of simply consuming it? In short, it seems inconceivable that a social revolution will not transform society in all of its manifestations long before even conventional energy supplies are exhausted. With such a social transformation, an entirely new energy demand situation will present itself. The foremost crisis, therefore, is not that of energy, but of the growth society.

The growth society thus has an unending appetite for more energy. But to grow requires more consumption as well as more energy. New needs must therefore continually be created, needs which then bite deeply into the stock of resources. A closer look into the mechanisms of consumption is in order.

Alienated consumption

"Production not only supplies the need with an object," wrote Marx, "but also supplies the object with a need."[34] Not even Marx, in all likelihood, could have imagined the lengths to which production has gone to supply the object with a need. The continuation of the existing economic and social system depends upon the sustaining and creating of needs. If people do not experience an unending series of new needs, there will not be the continually expanding consumption required to keep the growth society alive. Yet, for a great many people, the most basic needs go on; they trudge along in their jobs in a depressing circle of financial shortfalls and debt. Frequently, a need for the nonessential and useless is more strongly felt than that for the essential and useful. The growth society pushes the former the hardest, since the latter more or less takes care of itself. For other people, not only basic needs but the slightest whims can be largely satisfied.

Where basic needs leave off and extraneous ones begin is not clearly demarcated. The point may shift within a given range, depending upon the level of material and social development. However, we do know that the concept of unlimited needs developed alongside capitalism.[35]

---

[34] Cited in Weisberg, *Beyond Repair*, p. 55. On the economic determination of needs, see Melville J. Ulmer, "Human Values and Economic Science," *Journal of Economic Issues* 8(June 1974):255–66; and Herbert Gintis, "Consumer Behavior and the Concept of Sovereignty: Explanations of Social Decay," *American Economic Review* 62(May 1972):267–78.

[35] Walter A. Weisskopf, "Economic Growth Versus Existential Balance," in Herman E. Daly, ed., *Toward a Steady-State Economy* (San Francisco: W. H. Freeman and Company, 1973), pp. 240–51.

Capitalism overturned the wisdom of previous ages which stressed the pursuit of ideals above and beyond production and consumption. As Erich Fromm points out about modern society, "We as human beings have no aims except producing and consuming more and more."[36]

The citizen of the affluent society is easy prey for those pushing unlimited consumption. Work fails to hold the interest of the majority of people, so they become wide open to appeals for self-fulfilling consumption while off the job. With combinations of boredom, depression, and anxiety so widespread that 40 percent of the adult population uses some kind of pep up pills or tranquilizers,[37] it is easy to understand how self-realization might be avidly pursued through adventures in consuming. Indeed, the enterprise of altering human states of feeling and consciousness is itself a growing aspect of consumption, while at the same time relieving the problems which a life devoted to consuming raises.[38] Still, we are informed that individual consumption in 25 years will be almost twice what it is today. Gilven Slonim describes what some of this doubled consumption will involve: "Cities on and under the sea will follow. Under the ocean restaurants are being constructed in the Virgin Islands, the first indication of things to come spelling greater enjoyment—a more comfortable existence for future generations. . . ." And "with swifter ships to take us across the oceans on air bubbles at speeds in excess of 100 knots, our material wants can be satisfied more quickly and our strategic needs met more fully."[39]

At the top of the need-creating tools is television. Alienated work is matched by alienated leisure; watching TV is by far and away the leading leisure time use. The average child is exposed to 4,000 television hours even before starting school, much of it laced with violence. By the time youth is attained, E. J. Mishan argues that "nor poverty, nor filial bonds, nor church authority, nor tradition, nor idealism, nor inhibition of any sort stand between them and the realization of any freak of fancy that enters their TV-heated imaginations. . . . Using the magic pipe provided by Madison Avenue, private enterprise has taken on a new role of Pied Piper of Hamelin followed by hordes of youngsters

---

[36] Erich Fromm, *The Revolution of Hope* (New York: Harper & Row, Publishers, 1970), pp. 1–2.

[37] Louis Harris, *The Anguish of Change* (New York: W. W. Norton & Company, 1973), p. 4.

[38] Leon R. Kass, "The New Biology: What Price Relieving Man's Estate?" in Daly, *Toward a Steady-State Economy*, pp. 90–113.

[39] Gilven Slonim, "The Oceanic Contribution to Quality Living," in Kaplan and Kivy-Rosenberg, eds., *Ecology and the Quality of Life*, pp. 116–17.

jingling their money and tumbling over themselves to be 'with it,' without of course the faintest notion of what they are 'with' or where they are going."[40] Like boredom on the job, cynicism off the job nourishes the ideal consumer.

The ideal consumers in John Kenneth Galbraith's mind are women, a group with day-long TV exposure. Galbraith sees women as serving a crypto-servant function in household administration and maintenance involving goods, food, child care, social enjoyments, and social displays. "The servant role of women," observes Galbraith, "is critical for the expansion of consumption in the modern economy. . . . In few matters has the economic system been so successful in establishing values and moulding resulting behaviour to its needs as in the shaping of a womanly attitude and behaviour. . . . Thus it is women in their crypto-servant role of administrators who make an indefinitely increasing consumption possible."[41]

The role of youth and women in maintaining the consumption machine is evident enough in the manner in which advertising, promotion, and TV content are pitched. Youth and women are more likely than men to have the time to consume, and consumption does require large amounts of time. In particular, it is the youth and women of the affluent classes which have the leisure and the money to burn up in consumption. Consumption is an entire way of life for many of these people; it is the basis of their existence, self-image and reason-to-be. Men carry their fair share of the spending load, but women and youth tend to get much more attention from the sellers.

Since consumption requires time, leisure is an important ingredient to expanding sales. Yet, labor time is a prerequisite to capital for the realization of profits and to labor for the realization of purchasing power. Given today's high productivity rates, leisure seems to be too costly an alternative to work.[42] The necessity of labor time for the realization of profit and the necessity of leisure time for expanding consumption partially explains the tendency in the growth society for unusually expensive and programmed leisure time use. Expenditures for

---

[40] E. J. Mishan, *The Costs of Economic Growth* (London: Staples Press, 1967), pp. 150–51.

[41] John Kenneth Galbraith, *Economics and the Public Purpose* (Boston: Houghton Mifflin Company, 1973), pp. 33–37.

[42] Staffan B. Linder, *The Harried Leisure Class* (New York: Columbia University Press, 1970).

recreation exceeded $50 billion in 1973. Leisure time use calls for "escape" in a flashy car, summer homes, a trip abroad, a new wardrobe, exclusive restaurants, expensive sports equipment, the ultra in home decor—or at least as close as one's pocketbook will allow one to these things.

The result is an accentuation of alienation between a person's work and free time. Rather than viewing leisure as did the ancients, that is, as time for free and productive self-development and learning, leisure today serves narrow economic and escapist ends.[43] The ideal of an integrated life style in which one's work is as diverse and rewarding as leisure, in fact where work and leisure are substantially merged, has limited possibility and scope in the growth society. Work in the growth society means mass production, mass services, mass bureaucracy. Work means the sale of labor power for salary and wages, owners and workers, power and powerlessness. Leisure means escape and recuperation of strength so the job or household routine can be faced yet another day. Even further, Andre Gorz links the consumer society with violence: "Direct violence is the spontaneous response to a civilization which offers itself as something to be consumed, not something to be created."[44] The low level of creative interest during free time has been repeatedly documented by social research.[45] Equally well documented is the fact that many workers are too physically or psychologically exhausted from work to take up new pursuits; frequently, too, the financial means are unavailable.

The irony of leisure as escape is that with everybody escaping from where they live and work, there is a crowd wherever the escapists are headed. For example, tourism has increased so dramatically that few places of beauty remain serene. Mishan observes that:

> The phenomenal growth of tourism is the most potent factor in destruction of the earth's dwindling resources of natural beauty. In an attempt to cater for the growing millions of tourists by building hotels, villas, lidos, arcades, casinos, roads, airfields, once dreamy resorts and semi-tropical islands are transmogrified into neon-lit Meccas, agape with jostling crowds and swarming transistorized automobiles. Any

---

[43] Thomas Green, "Man's Work and Leisure," in Kaplan and Kivy-Rosenberg, eds., *Ecology and the Quality of Life*, pp. 139–46.

[44] Andre Gorz, *Socialism and Revolution* (Garden City, N.Y.: Anchor Books, 1973), p. 228.

[45] For example, Michael Young and Peter Willmott, *The Symmetrical Family* (London: Routledge and Kegan Paul Ltd., 1973).

hope of escape far from the maddening crowd is, for each of us, flick-
ering out.[46]

J. S. Mill was saved the pain of reading Mishan's words, and fortu-
nately enough, for Mill believed that:

> It is not good for man to be kept perforce at all times in the presence
> of his species. A world from which solitude is extirpated, is a very
> poor ideal. Solitude, in the sense of being often alone, is essential to
> any depth of meditation or of character; and solitude in the presence
> of natural beauty and grandeur, is the cradle of thoughts and aspira-
> tions which are not only good for the individual, but which society
> could ill do without.[47]

The growth society, of course, cannot tolerate such use of leisure, for
it does not raise the standard of living by increasing the GNP. In the
overpopulated, affluent society, where hordes of youth are able to become fulltime tourists, each seeking Mill's ideal, the most remote corners of the Rocky Mountains, indeed the world, have been abundantly
blessed with all the wonders of advanced technological society.

In contrast to the millions with nothing to do but consume, many
more find themselves on a grinding job year-around without a vacation.
A great many people moonlight in the evening or on weekends. The
large majority of American workers have only two weeks vacation or
less a year (Scandinavian and German workers have four weeks). Less
than 10 percent of the labor force take four weeks or more vacation.
This compares with precapitalist Europe when not much more than
190 days a year were worked, considerably fewer than even the straight
five-day week of the contemporary worker. Precapitalist Europeans
worked hard when required, but chose leisure when possible. As Ernest
Mandel points out, "As a rule, no community will voluntarily give up
a substantial part of its leisure to work and produce more if it is not
forced to by economic and social necessity."[48] Capitalist growth logic
was the force which altered medieval time use. Clearly, the 80-hour
work week of the early industrial period has been cut in half; but this
is an improvement only in terms of the growth society itself. Given the
vastly increased productivity and surplus wealth, the amount of work
had to be reduced to avoid glut and stagnation.

---

[46] Mishan, *The Costs of Economic Growth*, p. 135.

[47] J. S. Mill, *Principles of Political Economy*, vol. 2 (New York: D. Appleton &
Company, 1908), p. 339.

[48] Ernest Mandel, *Marxist Economic Theory*, vol. 1 (New York: Monthly Review Press, 1968), p. 59.

What happens to human personality under the conditions prevailing within the growth society, this society of technologism and consumerism? Most noticeable is the loss of the individual's ability to understand and control his own environment. People have become utterly dependent upon the operation of complex technological and social organizations which they can neither understand or control.[49] Generalized knowledge and practical problem-solving abilities are being undermined, leaving in their absence the specialists and experts with their set of instructions and push-button solutions. Samir Amin offers a description, perhaps extreme but nevertheless worthy of heeding, of the personality in the making: "These beings no longer speak—they have nothing to say, since they have nothing to think or feel. They no longer produce anything, neither objects nor emotions. No more arts. No more anything. The electronic machine produces—the word itself has lost all meaning—everything, these beings included."[50]

The growth society is living an illusory and self-deceptive existence, making every effort to escape and avoid reality. All of the artificiality which is equated with consumerist affluence and need creation is rendering modern society ill-equipped to cope with the survival challenges it has brought upon itself. This is not to say that these challenges cannot be met; it is only to say that the broad human ability required to adequately deal with these challenges must be fully cultivated rather than allowed to wilt away in an orgy of consumption. Neither human nor natural resources can long withstand the intensified onslaught of growth.

---

[49] See Tibor Scitovsky, *Papers on Welfare and Growth* (Stanford: Stanford University Press, 1964).

[50] Samir Amin, "In Praise of Socialism," *Monthly Review* 26(September 1974): 1–16.

9

Population growth

Overpopulation

The connection between overpopulation and the survival challenge is apparent: too many people threaten to overburden the earth's sustaining resources. Demands upon soil, minerals, energy, air, water, and even sheer livable space press more and more forcefully upon the earth's supply as the total volume of consumption and pollution steadily rises. Already overpopulation has taken its toll in human life and in environmental viability, not to mention all important declines in life quality.

A government commission in the early 70s learned that over 90 percent of Americans viewed United States population growth as a problem and 65 percent as a serious problem.[1] With only 8 percent thinking that the country should have more people, over one half favored government efforts to slow population growth and to promote population redistribution. There was widespread concern over the impact of population growth on resources, pollution, and social order. Thus, the impression received is that of concern over too many people, overpopulation. A current birth rate as low as that since the economically depressed 30s may well reflect the feeling that population pressures are mounting and opportunities are running out for additional children. The slowdown in population growth may also reflect a cultural change in the aspirations of women, a shift away from domestic to other types of

---

[1] *Population and the American Future* (New York: Signet Books, 1972), p. 196.

170

roles. As we shall note presently, the ideal or desired number of children has also greatly declined; this decline may be the result of several different social and economic downward pressures.

There are those, and their numbers are not at all small, who would discount the overpopulation concern. According to one such person, Robert Katz, the world is underpopulated from the standpoint of achieving a high living standard. Katz has the following to say about one projection of a stabilized world population of 15 billion: "This would appear to be below the 'proper and natural extent' of mankind, since the economies and synergistic benefits of high population densities probably could not be attained worldwide at such a level."[2] With regard to an estimate for the late twenty-first century of 36 billion, or a worldwide density of the United States' northeast coast, Western Europe, or Japan, Katz writes, "Whether this is the optimum, however, is debatable. It would seem wiser to prepare to accommodate a larger amount of people." Viewing the region between Boston and Washington as "an economically advanced zone with probably the highest standard of living in the world," Katz settles on a world population density of three times this or about 100 billion people.

Without questioning the old-fashionedness of his 19th century ethnocentrism, we might at least challenge the validity of Katz's assumption that 100 billion people could all maintain the living standard of the people living on the East Coast. In one short year the world adds over 70 million people, more than on the Eastern seaboard. Can anyone conceive of adding a new East Coast physical plant, resource consumption, and pollution output every year until the earth contained 100 billion people? Yet, Katz is not alone in his conceptions, for Colin Clark holds that the world's food potential today could support 47 billion persons at American standards and 157 billion at Japanese standards.[3] When one considers that food shortages are widespread and soil depletion moves forward with fewer than four billion earthly inhabitants, there would seem to be much room for doubt at such population figures. Clearly there is no excuse for four billion not being adequately fed, but 12 to 40 times that number stretches the imagination. (We shall take up the question of food supply in the next chapter.)

---

[2] Robert Katz, *A Giant in the Earth* (New York: Stein and Day Publishers, 1973), pp. 82–83.

[3] Colin Clark, *Population Growth and Land Use* (New York: Macmillan, 1968).

In the preceding chapter, we reviewed the resource, energy, and environmental limitations to population, and concluded that from this perspective—at least taking the growth society's living standards as a guide—the earth is already overpopulated. In this, leading demographer Kingsley Davis concurs when he writes that "it is now too late to 'solve' the world's population problem."[4] Davis contends that it would take centuries of *negative* growth to make population compatible with the way of life created by a scientific technology. In brief, Davis would more nearly agree with Preston Cloud's assessment of one billion or Paul Ehrlich's three billion as the sustainable number of people living in an advanced technological world. The gap between Cloud's one billion as optimum at Western standards and Katz's 100 billion optimum is so wide as to be ridiculous.

There is every reason to believe that Cloud is much closer to the truth. Writing at a time when the world's population was approximately one billion, J. S. Mill observed that:

> There is room in the world, no doubt, and even in old countries, for a great increase of population, supposing the arts of life to go on improving, and capital to increase. But even if innocuous, I confess I see very little reason for desiring it. The density of population necessary to enable mankind to obtain, in the greatest degree, all the advantages both of co-operation and of social intercourse, has, in all the most populous countries, been attained.[5]

Overpopulation may be viewed from entirely different perspectives than that of the earth's capacity to support population at a given level of production and consumption. Overpopulation may also be considered from the standpoint of the economy's ability to absorb and utilize labor. If an economy cannot effectively employ the existing labor force, regardless of its size, a surplus population may be said to exist in relation to employment opportunities. Marxist theory posits a direct relationship between capital development and surplus population; that is, the more advanced the productive machinery becomes, the greater is the number of potentially expendable laborers. As Marx puts it: "But in fact, it is capitalistic accumulation itself that constantly produces, and produces in direct ratio of its own energy and extent, a relatively

---

[4] Kingsley Davis, "Zero Population Growth: The Goal and the Means," *Daedalus* 102(Fall 1973):26.

[5] J. S. Mill, *Principles of Political Economy*, vol. 2 (New York: Appleton & Company, 1908), p. 339.

redundant population of laborers, i.e., a population of greater extent than suffices for the average needs of the self-expansion of capital, and therefore surplus population."[6] The surplus population however, is not thought of as a surplus in the sense of "too many" by the capitalist class, for the excess labor force holds the wage demands of the working labor force in check. The unemployed may be used as leverage against the demands of the employed. On the other hand, to the unemployed and employed alike, the surplus population is an onus; hence, the working class can usually be aroused to fight against the importation of foreign labor and immigration. To the worker seeking security through a strong bargaining position, a labor surplus is a dead counterweight.

Thus, the extent of overpopulation from an economic perspective varies greatly with the status of the economy and even more with the nature of the economy itself. The degree to which people sense or believe in the existence of population problems is in all likelihood importantly conditioned by the functioning of the economy. During economic upswings "population problems" recede, but during downturns "population problems" assert themselves. This is not to say that absolute population per se does not influence popular perceptions of the situation. Certainly the present concern with overpopulation goes beyond the existing high unemployment. Nevertheless, a fully occupied labor force would substantially reduce "population pressures" as popularly perceived. What could reduce population problems even more would be decentralization of both people and power, and the development of smaller-scale and locally sustainable production and technology.

A reduction of travel would also greatly alleviate the sense of overpopulation. With today's rapid physical movement, the same person can contribute to the feeling of overpopulation in a dozen different places the same day. The larger and more affluent the population, the more intense becomes the physical movement of people from one place to another. Thus, physical movement in a large and affluent society comes to be a different thing from that in a small and nonaffluent one. Increasingly, traveling about becomes an enormous privilege, since its impact is so much greater than in previous times.

The distinction between the economic and absolute senses of over-

---

[6] Ronald L. Meek, ed., *Marx and Engels on the Population Bomb* (Berkeley: The Ramparts Press, 1971), p. 92.

population may be illustrated by China and India. China's enormous population, although growing in absolute numbers, does not have the economically surplus population it had when its absolute size was considerably smaller. In effect, China has full employment and a greatly improved standard of living compared to 25 years ago. The result is at least an alleviation of population problems. India, on the other hand, stands out for many people as the classic case of overpopulation, in both economic and absolute senses. How much this situation could be altered with a social revolution is impossible to say, but the example of China suggests that India could still rid itself of the population disaster image which it now has.

While Asia's population density and enormity has already placed a great—though not yet insurmountable—strain on the potential of revolutionary change to alter overpopulation, much of the rest of the underdeveloped world has densities which could still permit a sharp reduction of their population problems with economic change. At the present rate of population growth, however, the period of demographic grace is shortening rapidly. To an examination of population growth rates we turn next.

How we grow

A world crude birth rate in 1970 of 33 per 1,000 population and crude death rate of 13 per 1,000 population produced a 2 percent rate of natural increase, some 70 million persons per year of which almost 90 percent were added to the population of the underdeveloped part of the world. At that time the world had 3.6 billion people, 2.5 in the underdeveloped part. The exponential aspect of population growth means that a 2 percent growth rate in the 60s yielded 650 million people during that decade but a 2 percent growth rate will produce 800 million in the 70s. With a growth rate now of slightly under 2 percent, the globe sustains in widely varying degrees of living standards something under four billion people.

The outstanding fact of world population growth, however, is that the regions with the highest per capita incomes have growth rates of about 0.5 to 1 percent, whereas those with the lowest per capita incomes have rates of 2.5 to 3 percent. The effect of this disparity will be to increase the underdeveloped world's share of population from the

69 percent of 1970 to almost 80 percent by 2000, or 5.2 out of 6.5 billion according to one projection.[7] At the basis of these figures is the fact that the underdeveloped world on the average counts slightly over two daughters for every woman compared to slightly over one per woman in the developed.

The history of population growth up until the 17th and 18th centuries was one of extremely slow growth marked off by periodic declines. The historical population declines, caused by such things as epidemics, famines, and war, were essential to holding population growth in relative check. Even if early societies grew only at a rate of 0.5 to 1.0 percent a year beginning at 8000 B.C., when the population stood at about five million, the earth's population would be "a solid mass of flesh many thousand light years in diameter expanding faster than the speed of light" had there not been recurrent peaks in the death rate often reaching levels of 150, 300, or even 500 per thousand population.[8] Agricultural societies tended to grow beyond their technical capacity to deal with crop failures or epidemics so that the probability of catastrophe continually increased until a crisis situation arose, and the death rates would rise dramatically. Infant mortality took 20 to 50 percent of births under the more normal circumstances and even higher losses during crisis periods.

Thus, population ebbed and flowed for thousands of years, not reaching 500 million until around 1650. Population doublings during the previous 9,000 years required on the average 1,500 years each. From then on the demographic story changes, and ever more dramatically with each century. The next doubling from 500 million to one billion required 200 years, the next to two billion required only 80 years (1850–1930), the next to four billion a mere 45 years (1930–75). In other words, it took all of one to two million years of human history up to 1850 to reach the first billion, but only 80 years to add the second, 30 years to add the third, and 15 years to add the fourth. The fifth billion is expected to be upon us in merely 11 years, and the sixth in less than a decade. Thus, unless some significant fertility declines or mortality increases occur, approximately 6.5 billion persons will usher in the new century. The exponential manner of growth is well illustrated

<hr/>

[7] Tomas Frejka, *The Future of Population Growth* (New York: John Wiley & Sons, 1973), p. 72.

[8] Carlo M. Cipolla, *The Economic History of World Population* (Harmondsworth, 1972), p. 81.

by the fact that about the same number of people were added to world population just during the 1960s as during the entire 19th century.

If things seemed to be changing fast during the 60s, they, in fact, were. The dynamics of population growth alone would see to that. Add to this the rapid technological developments of this period, as well as the economic accumulation on top of an already large base, and the pervasive instability of our society and precariousness of our planet are easy to understand. It is difficult to even so much as comprehend a billion net population increase in a decade's time, not to mention the physical accommodation of such a number. How the world withstands its next two billion people is going to tell us much more about the earth's carrying capacity than the previous two billion told us. All signs point to the approach of a critical juncture in the realm of population, specifically in the underdeveloped world. The continuation of existing Third World political and economic orders hardly seems possible under the weight of over 1.5 billion more people within such a short time as two decades.

In order for the underdeveloped world to attain replacement fertility, or a mean of slightly over two children per family, the number of children each woman has must be reduced by around one half. Even then, given the young age structure of the population, growth would continue for 70 years. If replacement fertility were reached by 2000, and this is about the best anyone really expects, the population of the underdeveloped world would still be 2.5 times larger in 2050 than it was in 1970. Mexico, with a population of 65 million in 1970 would, given a relatively rapid fertility drop to replacement level by 2000, still end up with over 140 million people by 2050. However, with a birth rate over four times the death rate, and fertility 150 percent over replacement level, the prospects of the Third World establishing no growth conditions by 2000 seem slim. A more plausible trend in the Third World birth rate would be gradual declines to zero fertility levels by 2050, at which time its population would be 3.5 to 4.5 times its present size, or approximately ten billion people.[9] Zero population growth could then follow in the twenty-second century.

The continuing high birth rates in the 70s, and no promise of rapid declines for the early 80s, assures large scale future growth as the waves of young mothers roll through their fertile periods later in this century

---

[9] Frejka, Future of Population Growth, pp. 55–76.

and on into the early part of the next. If the ten billion figure is reached in 2050, the Third World would then account for 85 percent of the world's population. One set of projections forecasts the possibility of 11.5 billion people in the Third World by 2050, compared to 1.4 billion people for the slowest conceivable growth pattern in the developed world, giving a 90 percent total for the former. On the other hand, a miraculously slow Third World growth to only 4.1 billion by 2050 compared to 1.4 in the developed would still result in an increase from today's Third World proportion of 70 percent to 74 percent in 2050. Unless death rates begin to rise, and recently they have only pushed further downward because of declines in infant mortality and the young age structure, the prospects for five billion in the Third World by 2000 and eight to ten billion for 2050 are considered realistic. The latter prospect is subject to much greater change than the former, the makings for which are already set in motion by recent fertility patterns.

Growth-reducing rises in death rates during upcoming decades cannot be ruled out. Malthusian positive checks on population have always, until recently, stalked the earth in a more or less effective manner. There is no historical guarantee that mankind's population will not once again push beyond the available technological and resource limits of support and survival. Despite what the technological optimists have to say, the plausibility of the planet supporting, say, even an optimistically small eight billion people by 2050 runs against the grain of practical assessment. How even the guaranteed 50 percent increase over the next 25 years is going to be accommodated is hard to grasp. These kinds of population increases, if catastrophes are to be averted, are of necessity going to require large-scale changes in economic and political organization throughout the world. If the catastrophes are not averted, large-scale social changes will take place anyway, albeit of a more desperate and undesirable kind than if planned in advance of a survival crisis.

Large-scale institutional changes in the world's most populous country, China, reversed what amounted to an ongoing population crisis and placed the country on a course which, before the end of the century, could eventuate in a replacement fertility level. From a birth rate of 43 prior to 1949, 38 was reached by the end of the 50s, and 32 at the end of the 60s—suggesting 26 could be attained by the end of the 70s. Leo Orleans asserts that "if the above estimates are anywhere close to being realistic, this drop in the birth rate represents a tremendous achievement for a country that, for all practical purposes is still under-developed."[10]

A 1975 estimated population of 825 million Chinese is growing at slightly over 1.5 percent annually, substantially less than most of the rest of the underdeveloped world, thus rendering China a declining proportion of the world's population. China's overall population density is only one third that of Great Britain, but one half of the country's land area contains only 4 percent of the population owing to its deserts, barren mountains, poor soils, short growing season, and inadequate rainfall.[11] The cultivated areas are already some of the most densely populated regions in the world. The population growth slowdown in China has for 20 years been a conscious government policy. A late age of marriage, birth control, and smaller family sizes have been emphasized. Decentralization from city to countryside has also been an aspect of official population policy, and while urban to rural migration has probably not significantly altered distribution, the fact that 85 percent of the population remains in places of under 2,000 suggests that a policy of decentralization has prevented the chaotic urbanization typical elsewhere in the Third World. In effect, China can no longer be considered as an underdeveloped country; in the strict sense it is a *developing* country and a rational population policy has been an important aspect of the development process.

United States growth

Until the 70s, and with the exception of the depressed 30s, U.S. population growth has been impressive—if one is impressed by population growth. From the late 40s to the early 60s, American growth rates more nearly resembled those of the underdeveloped world than those of an advanced industrial society. A 1960 survey revealed that 40 percent of the population desired four or more children. The number of children per woman at this time was about 3.5. The result was a 2 percent annual growth rate, or just above the world average of today. Since that time, U.S. fertility has declined significantly, and in recent

---

[10] Leo A. Orleans, *Every Fifth Child* (London: Eyre Methuen, 1973), p. 49; also, H. Yuan Tien, *China's Population Struggle* (Columbus: Ohio State University Press, 1973).

[11] Orleans, *Every Fifth Child*, p. 75.

years it has approximated replacement levels. The percentage of people desiring four or more children has declined to under 20 percent, and one half regard two or less children as ideal. A desired mean of slightly over two children, combined with a falling number of unwanted births because of increased contraception and abortion, has pushed actual mean family size to around the replacement level. Nevertheless, even at this level the country will inevitably experience a 36 percent population increase, or 250 million by 2000 and 280 million by 2050.[12]

Thus, shortly after having century-high fertility rates, the population growth rate has slipped beneath 1 percent a year. Yet, the baby boom of the postwar period is a potential boom 20 to 30 years later, thus placing upward pressure on the birth rate in the coming years. Reaching a zero growth society will be a harder and longer task as a result of the younger age structure created by the boom, and will require women to have fewer children than would otherwise have been the case if zero growth is to arrive in the middle of the next century. This is not an impossibility, since countries such as Sweden and Finland were at 1.9 and 1.8 sub-replacement rates in 1970.[13] At these low family size levels, these slow growers face less than a 10 percent population increase before reaching a stationary population prior to the middle of the next century. Denmark, Germany, Austria, and Hungary are headed for zero growth at about the same time. With a birth rate of 14.5 and death rate of 12.2, Belgium's growth has slowed to a 0.2 percent crawl. Although European countries should be the first to attain zero population growth, many of their densities are already such as to require vast amounts of non-European agricultural products and other resources to support the existing living standard.

The ramifications of the baby boom in the United States, and in Canada where the fertility boom was even greater than in the United States, will be felt for a long time to come. An upward pressure on the birth rate will be exerted every time the generations set off by the baby boom reach reproductive age. The 2.4 million babies born in 1937 during the lowest fertility period in U.S. history were, ironically enough, partially responsible for producing a huge crop of 4.3 million newborns in 1962. These 4.3 million will be entering the prime child-bearing period in the

---

[12] Frejka, *Future of Population Growth*, p. 165.

[13] Charles F. Westoff et al., *Toward the End of Growth: Population in America* (Englewood Cliffs, N.J.: Prentice-Hall, Inc., 1973), pp. 70–73.

1980s, and will have to show much greater restraint in family size than did their parents if conditions for another fertility crest are to be minimized after the turn of the century. The precariousness of the American growth slowdown is in evidence by the fact that even at a recent low point in the birth rate, 1972, 3.2 million births were recorded. There is reason to believe that the low fertility of the early 1970s could be the result of postponed births and the late 1970s will reap this pent up fertility pressure.

The potential for upward spurts in fertility and the growth rates will be great until the age structure and births and deaths evens out. Even then, we should keep in mind that demographic variables, especially fertility, are always capable of significant fluctuations. While not likely, it is also not inconceivable that fertility will take an unprecedented turn downward closer to one child per woman and zero growth will be upon us sooner than expected. (One child per family would mean zero growth immediately.) While this would go a long way to counteract the pressures created by the baby boom, the prospects for these same babies to produce, in turn, such an unprecedentedly low birth rate are not all that good. Interestingly enough, the peak year of the boom, 1957, has in 1975 seen its babies turn into high school graduates. Unfortunately, the unemployment rate is at a post-Depression high. With growing numbers of college graduates out of work, the prospects of four more years education are not entirely promising either. Had 1957 been less fertile, the class of '75 would undoubtedly feel much less futile. Perhaps the class of '75 will go on and help to undercompensate for the demographic bonanza of the 50s.

Growth momentum

Talk of reaching global replacement fertility sometime in the future comes easily. The declining growth rates of advanced industrial societies offers encouragement, as do certain countries in other parts of the world. Nevertheless, the reality of replacement fertility and eventually a stationary population, particularly in the underdeveloped world, seems frustratingly difficult and distant. Latin American birth rates have in general been maintaining a torrid pace, with Africa not too far behind. Asia maintains a traditionally high growth rate which adds even larger absolute numbers each year. Rural areas, where the overwhelming majority of people live, have evinced particularly strong resistance to any major fertility slowdown. Urban areas where literacy and occupational mobility have entered on a larger scale have in some cases turned birth rates downward to a significant extent. Overall, however, the social and economic situations prevailing in the Third World offer little encouragement to back up some of the optimism underlying no-growth dates for world population. The social conditions which set off rapid population growth remain unchanged, and there is slight hope that population stability can be attained so long as the original growth-producing conditions remain unaltered.

The poor countries of the world have always had a high birth rate; indeed, most if not all pre-industrial societies have had high birth rates. The key to slow population growth has been a high death rate, particularly infant mortality. Improved sanitation and the reduction of disease brought about gradual declines in death rates very early in the developed countries, and much later on, rapid declines in the underdeveloped countries. And over about a century's time, the developed countries slowly lowered their birth rates, while the underdeveloped countries are equally as slowly lowering their birth rates. Given the world's population situation of today, however, the length of time or grace period the underdeveloped world has to reduce fertility, if it is to avoid a compounded disaster, is much shorter than that the developed countries enjoyed.

Behind the momentum of high fertility and population growth is the continuation of a peasant agricultural society in which large families are an economic asset. Among the benefits of children in a peasant society are labor supply, economic security, old age security, protection against premature death of other children, and physical security.[14] There exists strong pressures upon the female to bear children, especially sons, since her status within the family is largely decided by her fertility. A barren or female-bearing woman will suffer socially. As long as security is set by the family alone, and the status of women is set by their child-bearing, the main forces behind high fertility remain.

India, a nation of approximately 615 million and now growing at a 25- to 30-year doubling rate, is a prime case in point. The reckoning

---

[14] Laila Shukry El-Hamamsy, "Belief Systems and Family Planning in Peasant Societies," in Harrison Brown and Edward Hutchings, Jr., eds., *Are Our Descendants Doomed? Technological Change and Population Growth* (New York: The Viking Press, 1972), pp. 335–57.

here is that each additional child is less costly, since their economic contribution exceeds their marginal cost. With the vast majority of people on acreages too small to mechanize even if it could be afforded, or totally landless, well-being hinges on the number of workers a family can put in the field. A retired Indian farmer reported, "You were trying to convince me in 1960 that I shouldn't have any more sons. Now, you see, I have six sons and two daughters and I sit at home in leisure. They are grown up and they bring me money." Another said, "A rich man invests in his machines, we must invest in our children."[15]

Thus, Mahmood Mamdani observes that "people are not poor because they have large families. Quite the contrary: they have large families because they are poor."[16] Hans Schenk's studies lead him to similar conclusions: "At the very least, therefore, it seems doubtful whether families in situations of great poverty can benefit economically by having fewer children. It is more likely that this group will consider the conception of children as an investment that will supply middle- and long-term interest far in excess of the short-term expenditure."[17] As it turns out, the better-off farmers tend to have larger families than the poorer ones, thus confirming the belief in the value of large families. Even families with tractors and other machinery persist in the large family norm, as the momentum of traditional society holds on.

The catch to all of this is that with everybody seeing greater benefit than cost in an additional child, everybody has additional children, with the result of ever intensifying pressure upon the land. A rural overflow floods into the cities, while the numbers of rural landless laborers bound upward. Also at work is what Garrett Hardin terms "the tragedy of the commons."[18] Each person stands to gain more than lose in putting an additional cow to graze on the commons, but as each person adds additional cows to take advantage of the immediate personal benefits, the pasture itself is being destroyed by overgrazing. Peasant agricultural society, whether Indian, Arab, African, or Latin American, represents a similar situation with regard to children. The individual

---

15 Mahmood Mamdani, *The Myth of Population Control* (New York: Monthly Review Press, 1972), pp. 109, 113.

16 Ibid., p. 14.

17 Hans Schenk, "India: Poverty and Sterilisation," *Development and Change*, vol. 5, No. 1, pp. 73–74.

18 Garrett Hardin, "The Tragedy of the Commons," in Herman E. Daly, ed., *Toward a Steady-State Economy* (San Francisco: W. H. Freeman and Company, 1973), pp. 133–48.

families may benefit by additional children, but the land and resources of a society eventually become overburdened by the sum of all the individual actions. Soils are depleted, water supplies reduced, pastures overgrazed, forests cut, and land eroded.

The prospects for individual families each acquiring acreage large enough to support mechanization dwindles as new generations of sons and their families attempt to carve out an existence on the small land inheritance. More successful farmers push the failing cultivators off their shrunken holdings and landlord power is strengthened. To shift a society from individual working against individual to one of cooperation and merging of resources and assets would also be to shift away from family-based security systems and thus away from women as subordinate child-bearers. If well-being and security were tied up with the larger community, and women were free to pursue alternative roles in production, the foundations of peasant society would crumble and with them the strongest motive force behind high fertility. This constitutes nothing less than social revolution. China is a country which laid to rest the self-defeating backwardness of peasant society, and joined rural peoples together in joint undertakings and cooperative agricultural production. The results have been impressive both in terms of the ability to feed the population and to reduce the rate of population growth. Still, the margin to absorb natural catastrophes is not large, and a steadfast program of population control and agricultural productivity is an essential component of continued Chinese success.

Controlling growth

The developed world has over a long period of time slowly reduced birth rates to a point where population growth has declined to less than 1 percent a year. After a history of what amounted to pro-natalist policies, including bans against the dissemination of birth control information and contraceptives, the laws affecting family planning in the industrialized countries began taking a more liberal course. Actually, the slowdown in population growth had proceeded quite far before official policy began to shift. Nevertheless, the newly liberalized family planning and contraceptive context, including the practice of abortion, greatly assisted in holding down growth at a time when the age structure was exerting an upward pressure on fertility rates. While government policy is far from omnipotent in the realm of population, it has the potential of significantly influencing the birth rate by its economic and legal policies.

Just how much official policy can alter the demographic picture might be illustrated by Rumania. Rumanian officials were concerned over what they considered to be too low a birth rate. Despite our discussion of the problems of overpopulation, the governments of some countries fear slow or no population growth. As noted demographer Charles Westoff has remarked, "In some quarters of the Western world . . . , people are expressing concern about the end of population growth and the possibilities of future declines in numbers."[19] In particular, France, Israel, Argentina, Japan, Greece, Hungary, Bulgaria, Poland, and Rumania have been cited as being concerned about declining population growth. The Rumanian case is especially informative and raises the spectre of politicians dealing a blow against zero growth. After witnessing a sub-replacement level of fertility in 1962 due to legalized abortion and contraception, the Rumanian government in 1966 shifted to a policy of limited abortion, banned the importation of contraceptives, increased taxes 10 to 20 percent on unmarried and childless persons, reduced taxes 30 percent on persons with three or more children, granted large birth premiums after the second child, provided free health resorts for children of large families, and offered early retirement for mothers of large families. The result was an incredible leap in the crude birth rate from 14.3 in 1966 to 27.4 in 1967. In September of 1967 the monthly rate soared to Latin American levels of 40. The terrific increase was, according to Michael Teitelbaum, "the sharpest increase in fertility of a large population in the history of the human species."[20]

In contrast, the New York state abortion law was highly instrumental in lowering the New York City birth rate by 23 percent between 1970 and 1972, three times the nation's rate of decline as a whole.[21] The incidence of legal abortion in 1971 in New York City was 508 per 1,000 live births, or one in three pregnancies. Accompanying the sharp upswing in legal abortions, almost three fourths of which were drawn from the previously illegal market, was a decline in the maternal mor-

---

[19] Westoff et al., *Toward the End of Growth*, p. 1.
[20] Ibid., p. 81.
[21] Ibid., pp. 43–44.

tality rate to an all time low in 1971 of 29 per 100,000 live births compared to 53 two years earlier. Illegitimate births also declined for the first time since 1954.

Still, the fight against abortion goes on, and in some places shows signs of increasing rather than decreasing in intensity. Montreal, Quebec, has recently been the site of an especially strong state move against abortion, focused on the prosecution of a 51-year-old doctor who had performed many abortions. Although twice acquitted by a jury of his peers in two separate cases, a higher court overturned the verdicts and the doctor has been held in jail. He faces further abortion charges, despite ailing health. Such is the status of a physician who practiced abortion in Canada's largest city.

Contraceptive information and means have long faced legal obstacles in the Western world outside of England and Scandinavia. Italy, France, Belgium, Spain, Portugal, and Ireland have been especially adamant on family planning, although Italy and France have made liberalization moves in the 70s. Yet, such official opposition has not prevented these very countries from having some of the world's lowest growth rates. The European communist states, with an early liberalized contraception and abortion program, also rank low in growth. Despite the continuation of some antiquated family planning and contraception laws in many states, the percentage of the American population knowing about birth control techniques and practicing contraception steadily increases. Most people facing the possibility of conception take some sort of preventive measures, increasingly the pill. This includes Catholics as well as Protestants, blacks as well as whites.

Government economic policy, however, remains essentially pro-natalist in that income tax deductions are allowed for all children, while taxes on single persons are higher than on married couples. A neutralist natalist policy would have to include, at the very least, tax equity for single and married persons and tax deductions limited to two children. Tax penalties for more than two children have been advised by some, while others would go further in the drive toward zero growth by limiting by law the number of children per couple to two.[22] A third would be aborted or given to a sterile couple. License systems have been proposed which would allow one child per person, and this license could be bought and sold by those who either wanted fewer than the law per-

---

[22] See, for example, Davis, "Zero Population Growth: The Goal and the Means."

mitted or more. Those who argue these positions, leading demographers among them, contend that there is no more right for people to have as many children as they please as for them to murder, rape, and rob.

The role of the state in controlling population growth has received considerable attention in such places as Japan, Hong Kong, Taiwan, and South Korea. Birth rates have fallen significantly in all of these places, especially Japan where below replacement fertility has been maintained for some time. How much of the decline can be attributed to state action is not clear, but the overall evidence suggests that government can at most play a catalyst or supportive role. Unless the objective social conditions are conducive to lower fertility, the government cannot do a lot to alter the growth rate. These social conditions are predominantly those which alter an individual's economic situation and decision-making, and become evident during both industrialization and major political change.

Declines in growth rates in the aforesaid Westernized countries may be largely traced to urban industrialization, whereas structural political and economic changes in revolutionary societies such as China and Cuba alter incentives for large families. As Harrison Brown and Edward Hutchings observe, "To be effective a policy must do more than furnish technological devices and services; it must make social and economic changes that affect individual reproductive decisions."[23] In other words, the conditions of a traditional peasant economy must be altered toward those of urban industrial or revolutionary socialist society.

India is not either of these. Despite 180,000 people working in family planning programs, a department within the Indian government larger than any other except the postal service and railway, only 6 percent of couples of reproductive age practice contraception. An official policy of population control has not made a significant dent in India's growth rate. Elsewhere in the fast-growing and frequently hungry, Third World, only 25 countries had, by 1970, taken an official position in favor of family planning. Many of these are only token positions and little is done to implement policy. Admittedly, even a government tour de force against population growth would soon run up against limits without real changes in the economic and social conditions of the people. But a favorable ideological atmosphere for family planning could at least be stimulated through a variety of media and agencies.

---

[23] Brown and Hutchings, *Are Our Descendants Doomed?* p. 26.

The cultural, religious, and economic obstacles to birth control could be formally challenged.

Urban growth

Along with population growth has come urban growth. In fact, urban growth rates have far outstripped those of general population growth. The growth society has, in effect, been an urban growth society. Prior to the emergence of capitalism, cities were relatively integrated and stable communities within which craftsmen pursued their arts and engaged in simple production and trade.[24] The size of cities was compelled to remain within the limits of agricultural productivity in the surrounding regions. Cities were extensions of and in balance with their environs. Whenever urban concentrations overextended themselves and abused their relation to the countryside, their demise soon followed. Rome stands as the classic case of urban parasitism upon nearby lands as well as those more distant. Roman living standards were out of proportion to the productivity of the city and its rural environs, and thus the land was greatly abused and devastated at the time the city declined and fell.

With the emergence of capitalism the nature of the city was fundamentally altered from that associated with the medieval period. In England, the rural population was widely dispossessed by the land enclosure movement, sending millions of uprooted peasants into the cities, overwhelming the guild and communal nature of the traditional city, and turning the city into an anonymous mass of wage laborers and paupers. The rural to urban drift had been going on for some time prior to industrialization, but it was greatly accentuated around 1800 as land enclosures reached a high point and industrial development absorbed the rural cast-offs. London grew from one to four million during the 19th century, not an impressive figure by today's world standards, but unprecedented in previous history. Murray Bookchin declares that "barely manageable in 1800, the capital of England had turned into a monstrous urban cancer in a single century."[25]

In America, the population was only 6 percent urban in 1800, while

---

[24] See Murray Bookchin, *Post-Scarcity Anarchism* (Berkeley: The Ramparts Press, 1971).

[25] Ibid., pp. 58–59.

by 1900 the percentage of urban dwellers had jumped to 40. Today the figure is around 75 percent. A large percentage of these people are concentrated in urban areas along the East Coast, branching out along the Great Lakes, and along the California coast. These urban conglomerates, the central cities of which are up to 60 percent consumed by parking lots, roads, and garages, have smothered hundreds of thousands of square miles of prime agricultural land.

The engine of urbanization in the growth society is economic accumulation. Heavy agricultural capitalization means fewer farms, farmers, and small towns; it means centralization of population into urban sprawls of industrial, commercial, and residential development. The process of urbanization is pushed ahead as blindly by the forces of economic growth as is environmental degradation, itself closely linked to rampant urbanization. Bookchin phrases the situation succinctly: "All pretensions aside, it matters little whether the city is ugly, whether it debases its inhabitants, whether it is esthetically, spiritually, or physically tolerable. What counts is that economic operations occur on a scale and with effectiveness to meet the only criterion of bourgeois survival: economic growth."[26]

We need not enter into an extensive discussion of why economic growth in bourgeois society is inevitably accompanied by rapid and uncontrolled urbanization. It is evident enough that profit maximization is centered around labor availability, market size, and transport costs. All the mechanisms of economic growth functioning within capitalism propel people off the farm, out of small towns, and into urban areas. Industrialization via any economic structure brings strong pressures to bear toward urbanization, and the two are closely associated throughout the world. However, industrialization *can* occur without rapid and uncontrolled urbanization; it can conceivably occur without extensive urbanization at all. China is making a remarkably successful effort to control and limit urban growth and at the same time to pursue a course of industrialization. On the other hand, rampant urbanization is taking place throughout the underdeveloped world without much industrialization to accompany it. As Joao Quartim points out about urbanization in Brazil, it "means the flight to the cities from famine in the countryside."[27] This obviously has little to do with industrialization.

[26] Ibid., pp. 63–64.

[27] Joao Quartim, *Dictatorship and Armed Struggle in Brazil* (New York: Monthly Review Press, 1971), p. 150.

In the face of all previous experience with urban concentration and growth, a blue-ribbon task force studying urban growth concludes that "no urban growth is simply not a viable option for the country in the remainder of this century." "The needs of the American population, existing and projected, can be met only through continuing development."[28] So from today's 350,000 square miles of urban land area, look forward to 500,000 in the year 2000, or one sixth of the land area of the entire country—wasteland included. San Jose, California, a city of 95,000 covering 17 square miles in 1950, and 450,000 covering 136 square miles in 1970, can look forward to continued development over the next quarter century. Around every one of the some 20 major urban regions of the country, sprawl will continue to eat up large chunks of land.

The prospects for the year 2000, then, are for over four fifths of the population to be concentrated on less than one fifth of the nation's land area. No one can prove, argues one observer, that this is good or bad.[29] What the nature of the proof might be that such imbalance is, in fact, bad would itself be a slippery question. Aside from the increasingly unwieldy, and in some respects chaotic and uncontrollable, situations found within the major urban centers, and the obviously intensified environmental impact of such concentrations in an advanced industrial society, one might look at individual preferences regarding living location. Past survey evidence is fairly consistent in finding that preferences tend to run toward low density areas as in small towns, open country, and farms more than toward large cities and their suburbs.[30] The catch is that the preference is also to be within a relatively close distance to a larger city. Americans want the tranquility of rural living combined with the conveniences and attractions of metropolitan areas. The manner in which central cities began to empty out into the suburbs early in the postwar period, and then the continual pushing out into the surrounding countryside and small towns, is a phenomenon closely associated with this schizoid rural-urban personality. The result is longer and longer commuting distances and higher and higher levels of energy

[28] William K. Reilly, *The Use of Land* (New York: Thomas Y. Crowell Company, 1973), pp. 18, 13–14.

[29] James Sundquist, "Population Dispersal: Europe Stops the Urban Swarm," *The Nation*, July 20, 1974, pp. 39–42.

[30] Reilly, *Use of Land*, p. 86; *Population and the American Future*, p. 36; and Leonard Downie, Jr., *Mortgage on America* (New York: Praeger Publishers, 1974), p. 209.

consumption to accomplish it. Quite a number of people, especially in the younger age brackets, have given up on this struggle entirely and packed off to more remote rural areas, particularly to woodlands and mountains where living and recreation can be more easily mixed. However, this "ruralization" move pales up against the continued growth of metropolitan America.

If the big city repels the majority of people as a place to live, and that this should be so is a sad commentary on the state of civilization, why do they insist on crowding in and around it? The answer is fairly obvious: the growth society centers all of its opportunities in the city. Industry, finance, commerce, administration, technology, science, education, medicine, culture, entertainment, and most other foundations of growth and accumulation move toward the city in magnetic fashion. Decentralization, outside of urban sprawl, is not profitable. Urban overkill is another of the irrationalities of the growth society which moves according to the laws of its economic development. Urbanization is not a matter of choice; it is a regularity dictated by the logic of economic growth. People are free to live where they please only in the most abstract sense; in reality, the labor market decides where people live. Urbanization, like the manner in which the society behaves economically, is a manifestation of human alienation, of the powerlessness of people over their own lives.

Urbanization in the underdeveloped countries is proceeding at a pace equal to or greater than the most outstanding examples of Western urban growth. Although still overwhelmingly rural societies, the sheer growth of absolute numbers of people and the flow of surplus rural population into the cities have assured enormous urban growth. Every decade hundreds of millions of people leave the countryside of the underdeveloped world for the cities. Some return, but many more stay. By 2000 the cities of the Third World will perhaps contain some 3 billion people compared to the 600 million of 1970. "By future standards," writes Lester Brown, "the Calcutta of today may be a model city."[31] With perhaps 600,000 persons sleeping in the streets of Calcutta every night, and over one half of the population of Ankara, Turkey, living as squatters, it is difficult to imagine the horrors of the year 2000 should Brown's estimation be correct. However, the trend is unmistakable.

---

[31] Lester R. Brown, *World Without Borders* (New York: Random House, 1972), p. 73.

Mexico City's slum population grew from 330,000 and 14 percent of the city's population in 1952 to 1.5 million and 46 percent in 1966; slums and uncontrolled settlements in Lima, Peru, jumped upward from 114,000 and 9 percent of the city in 1957 to 1 million and 36 percent in 1969.[32] These examples could be multiplied throughout the Third World where it is commonplace to have one quarter to one third of the major cities' populations living as squatters in uncontrolled slum settlements. If the population without water or sewage connections were included, the figure would be higher still.

In the previous century, Frederick Engels pointed out that the big cities of the capitalist era will be abolished only with the abolition of the capitalist mode of production itself.[33] This is virtually self-evident inasmuch as the modern city came into being with capitalism and will continue on its present course of growth until the logic of the growth society is reconstructed. The pace of modern urbanization is understandable only within the framework of capitalist growth; growth of the latter means growth for the former. Every economic boom is also an urbanization boom. A change in the economic structure, and therewith the technological structure, must precede a change in the distribution of population. This redistribution is furthermore a necessary forerunner to a solution of the environmental crisis.

We have posited a relationship between capitalist and urban growth. What are the ties between economic growth and population growth? Does economic growth stimulate population growth as it does urbanization? Does population growth act as a catalyst for economic growth? To an examination of these questions we turn next.

Population and economic growth

The relationship between population and economic growth is a rather complex one, and we shall only probe some of the most fundamental aspects of the linkage. It is evident that in order for a society to develop the differentiations and divisions which have accompanied economic growth the society must have attained sufficient numerical size to en-

---

[32] John A. Loraine, *The Death of Tomorrow* (Philadelphia: J. B. Lippincott Company, 1972), pp. 171–74; and *Development and Environment* (Mouton: The Hague, 1972), p. 156.

[33] Engels, *The Housing Question* (Moscow: Progress Publishers, 1970), p. 49.

able such a variegated structure in the first place. A certain density threshold is thus necessary to the initiation of economic growth. What this density is cannot be precisely stated, although it evidently is not very great considering that 19th century America had the population to industrialize quite rapidly. Countries such as the United States, Canada, and Australia have in the past strongly encouraged both immigration and a high natural rate of growth. Today, however, there are few if any countries in the world that lack the densities requisite for economic development. The situation is, in fact, much the opposite; that is, there are a great many countries whose population and population growth rate is a handicap to industrialization.

Yet, Latin American countries with crushing birth rates, such as Brazil and Mexico, may seek economic strength through high fertility. The outcome has expectedly been more poverty, even though economic growth rates have sometimes been high. Data reveal that countries with the most rapid population growth, such as Mexico, Ceylon, and the Philippines, have experienced the greatest worsening of the income distribution.[34] An economy, such as that of Brazil, can show an impressive rate of growth, but still find larger and larger numbers of people living in poverty. High fertility means a larger proportion of the population in the dependency ages, consuming the rudiments of survival. Instead of supporting excessive numbers of infants and children, an economy could be investing in the machinery of industrialization which could raise individual productivity. Fewer children combined with higher productivity provides the impetus toward higher per capita wealth, which, in turn, raises the level of demand or purchasing power.[35] The higher demand encourages further investment, and the momentum of growth continues. Without the drain on production of rapid population growth, savings and investment can be maximized. Without population or labor surplus, cheap labor cannot be substituted for capital investment; the result is more capital investment, higher productivity and per capita wealth. The ideal for the capitalist is labor immigration without a high birth rate, thus reducing the need for expensive capital investment while

---

[34] Brown, World Without Borders, p. 47.

[35] Joseph J. Spengler, "Demographic Factors and Early Economic Development," in D. V. Glass and Roger Revelle, eds., Population and Social Change (London: Edward Arnold, 1972), pp. 87–98; and Stephen Enke, "The Impact of Population Growth on the National Economy," in Westoff et al., Toward the End of Growth, pp. 97–108.

minimizing the proportion of nonproductive population. The ideal for the worker is minimizing population growth from any source, thus bidding up the price of labor and encouraging income-raising capital investment. The worker also benefits from fewer people competing for, and bidding up, the price of goods and services. Slow population growth also provides for more opportunity for technological and productivity advances in relation to labor force increments, again improving the prospects for gains in individual well-being.

In agricultural societies, gains in individual well-being frequently result in lower age of marriage and more children; however, more children subsequently reduce the size of land holdings which again reduces well-being, raises marriage age, and lowers the birth rate.[36] Urban society does not usually respond to greater prosperity with a higher birth rate, although the postwar baby boom was certainly buoyed to some extent by the ability to pay for additional children. The reaction to this, however, will be a hard pressed job market for the rest of the century, with 35 million new labor force entrants each decade. All of these new entrants will in all likelihood push the gross national product on up to new highs, but American per capita income will probably decline in relation to those of other industrialized countries who practiced more demographic restraint in the recent past.

It is significant to note that population growth at a given level tends to require economic growth at some higher level just to maintain a constant per capita income. This is so owing to the fact that additional population requires additional production, each production addition being, after the point of diminishing returns is reached, more costly than the previous one. Each bushel of corn produced in America today costs more than the previous bushel and each ton of copper mined costs more than the previous ton. As the storehouse of nature, the ultimate source of all wealth, is depleted, the rich original yields become more and more difficult to maintain without increasingly heavy inputs of capital and labor. Once beyond the point of prime yield or efficient production, diminishing returns set in and the economy must grow more rapidly than population in order to maintain the previous living standards.

The physical plant or capital commitment required to maintain and reproduce a large population must be continually recreated at the same

---

[36] See E. A. Wrigley, *Population and History* (New York: McGraw-Hill, 1969), pp. 108–43.

scale as before, if living standards are not to decline.[37] The result is an unnecessarily heavy burden upon resources and the environment. More people may be buying and consuming, but they may individually spend relatively less and less. Fewer people with more to spend could yield the same or a higher level of demand as more people with less to spend, but the kinds of things purchased—say, baby food instead of French wine—would certainly be different.

Certain sectors of the economy may benefit from population growth, whereas other sectors may suffer. However, the goods and services which have come to be equated with a high standard of living are obviously more plentiful in a society with fewer people to consume them than in one with more. The intangible goods associated with privacy, accessibility, and open space are also more plentiful in a less densely populated society. So, too, does the provision of services enjoy a greater amount of time to be delivered and consumed with fewer people pressing their demands for them.

Towering above the whole issue of population and economic growth is the point stressed throughout this study: the needs and interests of the people should have priority over the needs and interests of the economy. Even if the economy did require more population, should a society submit itself to intolerable densities in order to keep the economic machine running? The question to be answered is not whether the economy is better off or not with a large or small population, but how many people should live in a given area if the benefits of that area are to be enjoyed to the maximum by all the people living in it. The population should be adjusted to resources and environment, not to the laws of economic growth. As it stands today, whether the country be rich or poor, the shape of the economy sets the conditions for population. In the Third World, population grows virtually out of control because of the underdeveloped economic structure. In the developed countries, population has slowed down because of the success of industrialization and the establishment of urban living standards and security systems. In both cases, population is adjusting to economic conditions.

One final point should be stressed with regard to population and economic growth. This is that Europe cannot be used as a universal

---

[37] Simon Kuznets, *Population, Capital, and Growth* (New York: W. W. Norton & Company, Inc., 1973).

example of the compatibility of high density and economic abundance. To do so is to oversimplify the more complicated situation and overlook a number of qualifying facts. As we shall discuss in the next chapter, the riches of Europe have depended to a significant extent upon the support and assistance of the rest of the world. The rest of the world has supported and assisted in European affluence in two main ways: first, raw materials and agricultural products have been imported from abroad in large quantities, and second, population surpluses have been drained off through emigration, especially to North America but also to the other continents as well. This siphoning of population was especially marked during a time of rapid population growth from about 1830 to 1930. Contemporary European affluence depends heavily upon huge inputs of raw materials, energy, and agricultural products from around the world.

Japan is the other example of high density and economic riches, but there, too, we have a case of heavy borrowing of external resources, including the sea. Within the overall low density affluent societies, such as the United States and Canada, the denser and richer regions are deeply indebted to external resources coming both from outside and inside the country. In other words, high density, affluent countries and regions can maintain economic prosperity only by constantly drawing upon outside resources. If "the outside" were equally as dense as "the inside," something would clearly have to give in a big way.

The dense regions of the underdeveloped world will obviously not become rich simply because they are dense; quite to the contrary, their development is hampered by the pressures of surplus population. Even China, whose entire agricultural area is extremely dense, but who is utilizing its massive manpower as rationally as possible in the development struggle, is hampered by too many people. As Jan Deleyne points out in this regard, "For the moment, the vast size of its population is simply a handicap."[38] At least China has an economic structure which has been conducive to significantly lowering fertility within the context of an essentially agricultural society; most of the Third World finds itself in the throes of an underdeveloped economic structure which, if anything, encourages large families.

In brief, the path to economic development is much easier if it is not

---

[38] Jan Deleyne, *The Chinese Economy* (London: Andre Deutsch Ltd., 1973), p. 186.

cluttered with demographic obstacles. Once development is achieved, it is much easier to preserve under conditions of lower density and slower population growth. For much of the world's population, it is already too late to avoid the demographic obstacles; a permanently lower than necessary living standard, even given substantial development, has been set for the future. Another part of the world's population is busily erecting demographic obstacles to economic development where they do not clearly exist already. Still another part is faced with a gradually declining living standard due in part to excessive population burdens. Finally, there are the fortunate few who have achieved a high level of economic development without any excessive population pressures. These people are in a unique position and have not experienced the harsh dynamics of population and economy. They would do well to contain population and cut to a minimum any net drain they might be making upon the rest of the world.

10

Growth and food supply

Agriculture and economic growth

That agriculture is the basis of the growth society, indeed of all societies, is easily forgotten in the midst of urban industrial life. Yet urban industrial society was made possible by developments and changes in agriculture, and no less does the continuation of this society depend upon successful agriculture. Ernest Mandel correctly observes that "agricultural surplus product is the basis of all surplus product and thereby of all civilization."[1] Thus, after about 500,000 years of hunting and gathering subsistence, Homo sapien took up agriculture during the eighth millenium B.C. around the hills of Asia Minor and the floodplains of the Tigris and Euphrates. The eventual surplus produced by agriculture permitted the emergence of cities with their specializations in craft and trade.

The establishment of agriculture by no means set in motion a rapid urbanization process. As late as 1750, four fifths of the world's population remained agricultural; from that time on, however, urbanization moved ahead with accelerating speed until today world population is almost equally distributed between urban and rural locales. As previously, urbanization is founded upon agricultural surplus. The most highly urbanized countries are also those with the highest agricultural

---

[1] Ernest Mandel, *Marxist Economic Theory*, vol. 1 (New York: Monthly Review Press, 1968), pp. 271–304.

productivity, while predominantly rural countries have the lowest agricultural productivity. Thus, an American farmer can produce 100 pounds of grain in five minutes' work compared to five days' work for an Asian farmer. Or, the farmer in the more highly urbanized United States can support 46 people compared to the farmer who in the less urbanized U.S.S.R. can support only six. The greater the capital investment in agriculture, the higher the productivity and the greater the possibility for urbanization.

The reason behind the accelerated urbanization of the past 200 years is the same as that which lies behind the acceleration of economic growth—the rise and development of capitalism. Now, we must be careful to avoid the mistake of linking capitalism solely with urban industrial society and agriculture with precapitalist or traditional society. As Marx made clear, the roots of capitalist development are to be found in changes in agricultural production. In a seminal research paper, William Lazonick points out that the "Marxist approach locates the key to the rise of capitalism in the transformation of the production relations in the agricultural sector itself. Only then does the 'industrial revolution' in the manufacturing sector become possible."[2] Lazonick goes on to clarify that "as long as the mass of people have direct ties to the soil and hence to their means of subsistence, capitalist production cannot become widespread, for the essential element of capitalist production is the existence of a mass of laborers who are forced to sell their labor power to capital in order to subsist."

The essential lever to capitalist development becomes the elimination of peasant or free agriculture so that the bulk of the population can no longer rely upon subsistence production to meet their needs, and must gravitate toward the points of capitalist production instead. This expropriation of the means of agricultural existence had been going on for centuries prior to the onset of industrialization, and the cities had been growing accordingly. However, the displacement of rural population through the enclosure movement in England, the forcible expropriation of people from the land by means of eliminating communal and semicommunal property in favor of commercial farming and sheep raising, reached its height from about 1750 to 1850. This coincided with the industrialization of capitalism, and the conditions for urban indus-

---

[2] William Lazonick, "Karl Marx and Enclosures in England," *The Review of Radical Political Economics* 6(Summer 1974):3–5.

trial society had been set. A new proletariat to work in the factories had been created by the destruction of peasant economy and society. A new market for industrial goods had arisen in agriculture as the drive for increased productivity and profit gained momentum in the country-side; both rural and urban wage earners with their complete depen-dency upon money, added to the drift toward a fully capitalist econ-omy. Turning the prosperous and independent peasant of the 15th cen-tury into the degraded and dependent wage laborer of the 18th had not been an easy task. It took 300 years of social turmoil and breakdown for the free peasant to succumb to the enslavement of the factory. But the wheels of economic history ground forward, crushing the most staunch resisters under its irreversible weight.

The establishment of urban industrial society by no means rendered agriculture obsolete. Agricultural surplus remains as essential as ever to the support of the urban labor force and the society which grows around it. Agricultural raw materials remain essential to a variety of industries. Agricultural demand for industrial products, in turn, plays an important role in the growth society; indeed, agricultural demand provided the crucial market for the growth of 19th century industrial capitalism. The industrialization of agriculture continues to absorb an important part of urban output. Finally, agricultural surplus plays an important role in the profitable operation of the overall economy, both as a source of profit in itself and as a means to pay for a nation's im-ports. The latter role of agricultural surplus has historically been espe-cially important to the United States, and has recently been crucial to rectifying a deteriorating balance of payments situation and helping with mounting costs of oil imports.

Regardless of the type of economy considered and the course of in-dustrialization followed, agriculture and agricultural surplus remain as the most basic aspect of the modernization process. A failure in the agricultural sector dooms to failure a country in its struggle for devel-opment. Agriculture is in too many ways functionally linked to indus-trial development to receive anything but the highest priority. A revo-lution in agricultural production laid the foundations for the rise of industrial capitalism, and a revolution in agricultural production will inevitably accompany the emergence of a new society. A revolution in agricultural production accompanied the emergence of the world's non-capitalist, state-planned societies. An agricultural revolution must also accompany the successful development of all Third World countries.

As we shall discuss presently, a world agricultural revolution will be required if the threat to survival posed by overpopulation and food shortages is to be surmounted.

Food and politics

Prior to an examination of the contemporary state of agriculture and food supply we might take note of a sensitive political issue in this area. The charge that concern with overpopulation diverts attention away from economic and class exploitation has previously been noted. There exists a related charge that concern with agricultural production and supply, or with food shortages, is also a diversion from the hard stuff of economic oppression and class conflict. However, both the population surplus and food shortage are integral aspects of precisely this economic oppression and class conflict. To charge that concern with the former detracts from the latter is to undercut the investigation of important manifestations of this economic oppression and class conflict whether on the national or international level. Certainly economic development is a prerequisite to the reduction of population problems and the expansion of efficient agriculture. As Paul Baran argued in his classic study of growth, "For economic development, and only economic development, can solve both aspects of the so-called overpopulation problem. It increases the supply of food and at the same time reduces the growth of population."[3] The urgency of development cannot be fully appreciated without an understanding of the population and food crisis. And the population and food crisis cannot be understood without an understanding of underdevelopment.

The writings of Marx and Engels suggest that they, among others, recognized the error in Thomas Malthus's notion that the growth of food supply cannot remain abreast with growth of population. Food supply, through the aid of science and industry, can be expanded at least if not more rapidly than population—at least up to a point. This has, in fact, been demonstrated to be the case over and over again, dramatically so in the industrialized regions of the world. Elsewhere, the

---

[3] Paul Baran, *The Political Economy of Growth* (New York: Monthly Review Press, 1957), p. 243.

picture is increasingly becoming more similar to the one drawn by Malthus—population growth outstripping food supply.

Yet it is not a failure of food supply to keep up with population so much as it is a failure of economic development in general. Given development, food increases could match or even surpass population growth in the large majority of countries in the world, even the large and critical ones—as the case of China attests to. But development requires political revolution. This is where food and politics clash. The old order is one which perpetuates the social conditions responsible for excess population growth and inefficient agriculture. A new political and economic order must be established which sets in motion forces against large families and against inefficient uses of farmland. In England, the peasant economy was torn asunder by the forces of capitalist development. Today this peasant economy, combined with the underdevelopment of the urban economy, stands in the way of positive change in the Third World. Underdevelopment, marked in the rural sector by extremely unequal distribution of land and a highly inefficient agriculture, blocks progress on both the human fertility and food fronts. Birth control clinics and government agricultural research stations can make but a small dent in the immovable structure of underdevelopment, however important such clinics and research stations will certainly be in a revolutionary society.

It is up to the developed countries to see that their own political and economic actions become stimulative rather than obstructive to development. It is in their own vital interest to do so. So far we have seen relatively limited amounts of direct economic aid from developed to underdeveloped countries, and for the most part this aid assists in the perpetuation of dependence and underdevelopment. Most developed countries are not willing even to stand aside and allow the course of events in the Third World to work themselves out alone. It is thus too late for quick and easy solutions to the clash of interests between food and politics. The forces of reaction in the Third World have been bolstered by those in the developed world. The latter tries to make advances with contraceptives and miracle grains, but these palliatives won't go very far against the bulwark of underdevelopment. Stronger political and economic measures are required for the kinds of changes which must be wrought if the Third World is to rise from its food and population crisis into a condition of economic and demographic stability.

Food and population

A deadly serious race is being run today between food supply and population growth. This fact should not be allowed distortion or misrepresentation. This is not, however, a new competition; it has to greater or lesser extent been going on from the beginning. The amount of food which *can* be produced varies greatly with the kind of technology applied to the land and the fertility of the land itself. The amount of food which *must* be produced varies with the number of people to be fed. The most advanced agricultural technology applied to the most fertile land can still fall short of food requirements if the numbers of people which must be fed are simply too great. Conversely, very primitive techniques applied to relatively infertile soil can sustain a society which keeps its population size within the required limits. Today we may find examples of all types of food and population combinations.

The most prevalent combination, however, is that of inefficient agriculture amidst surplus population. The result is increasingly widespread hunger and malnutrition. Setbacks from the weather, as in Bangladesh and sub-Sahara Africa, can now trigger starvation in many areas, and as population growth presses ahead, the chances for regional starvation on a larger and larger scale increase. Given the existing mode of world agricultural production and consumption, the ability of the world agricultural storehouse to respond to regional famine weakens. Just a decade ago the United States was confronted with a problem of grain surpluses and storage costs; this surplus has all but vanished, and the world's food reserves have shrunk to a mere 27 day's supply. The race between food and population has not gone at all well in the 70s. The previous two decades witnessed a standoff; at the present moment, however, it appears that population is going to pull ahead in broader regions of the globe. Various bad weather in certain recent years exacerbated the current general food crisis, but this only served to demonstrate how narrow the food margin really has come to be.

The most familiar food-population situation to North Americans is high agricultural productivity which exceeds the ability of the population to consume it. The United States has long been the world's major agricultural exporter and is destined to play a critical role in the fate of the world food-population race. This is so for two reasons: first, the direction North American agricultural surpluses are shipped will decide for many millions of people who will eat and who won't; second, the kinds of crops grown and the uses these are put to will decide how many more people can be fed from the world's major surplus grainery. We shall explore this point presently.

In rough terms, one third of the world's population faces various degrees of undernourishment, ranging from outright starvation for many millions to inadequate caloric intake. For the remaining two thirds of the world's people, food is presently in adequate supply, even superabundance for many. Developed countries in particular have high agricultural productivity, *and more importantly*, the wealth to purchase what agricultural products they don't produce themselves. The rich have the ability to pay for what they don't produce themselves; the poor must watch surpluses stand in storage or even be destroyed.

Population growth in a traditional technological context forces increasingly more intensive use of land and labor. As the number of mouths to feed increases, fields can be allowed shorter and shorter fallow periods, and the soil is depleted more rapidly. Then annual cropping is required, and finally multi-cropping becomes necessary to keep up with new population growth.[4] Concurrently, the hours of labor grow longer, from a few hours a day seasonally to almost all daylight hours the year around. The impact upon the land becomes heavier and the demand for fertilization increases, as does the pollution impact which chemical fertilizers entail. Forests are cut, hillsides are terraced, and irrigation systems are extended to arid land. The environmental consequences may be negative if the thin topsoil of marginal land and forest areas erodes with rain and vanishes with the wind. Nutrients may be leached away and in some areas the land is scarred or hardened to brick-like consistency (lateritic soil). Overgrazing accomplishes similar self-destructive ends. Intensive land use, if it is to avoid such ends, must be accompanied by equally intensive soil conservation practices. In some areas of the world, soils have seen much of the necessary care; in far too many areas, however, there has been continuous decline of soil productivity.

This raises the question as to how much land the world's population has available for agricultural expansion. If population is expanding, can farmland be expanded as well? There are obviously enough people to work the land should it be available. The answer to the question of

---

[4] Ester Boserup, *The Conditions of Agricultural Growth* (London: George Allen & Unwin Ltd., 1965), pp. 43–56.

how much unused cultivatable land there is left in the world is a tricky one to deal with. However, it may be stated that, in broad terms, almost all of the world's good agricultural land is now under cultivation. This does not mean that all good farmland is being used efficiently or as intensively as is possible. Indeed, the future of the food versus population race will ultimately be decided by how much more food can be grown upon land already claimed for agriculture. Bringing new land under cultivation will undoubtedly play a role of some importance, but it will not be decisive. Such new land, which represents perhaps as much as one half of the world's *potentially* cultivatable land, will prove productive only with immense investments—predominantly involving irrigation. It has been estimated that $28 billion a year would have to be invested in new land development just to feed the globe's annual newcomers.[5] In this connection, the cost of new land development is so high that to intensify current land use is much more economical. Hence, we see the decisiveness of the efficient use of existing farmland.

The new lands scheme has been tried unsuccessfully throughout the world, from the semiarid Soviet plains to the humid Brazilian rain forests. Climatic and soil conditions are variously at odds with most new land development. Irrigation of semiarid land holds the most potential, but irrigation can be enormously expensive and raises numerous related environmental problems, not the least of which is the water-logging and salinization of the irrigated soil itself. The world's most irrigable land areas have already been developed. Indeed, agriculture originated on irrigated land and has always been conducted in large part upon irrigated soils in the equatorial zones. It is in these areas that civilizations rose and fell as irrigated lands salinated and dams and ditches silted over.

As we shall document presently, there is a considerable amount of good farmland not being efficiently used, especially in Latin America. Productivity can also be greatly increased elsewhere in the Third World. Yet there are a number of conditions attached to increased productivity, such as the availability of fertilizers, machinery, and water. More important, the social and economic structure of underdevelopment must be greatly transformed before agricultural productivity can be sufficiently increased and population growth can be curbed. For the mo-

---

[5] Paul R. Ehrlich and Anne H. Ehrlich, *Population Resources Environment* (San Francisco: W. H. Freeman and Company, 1973).

ment, then, it may be asserted that most economically feasible farmland is already being used, in many cases already too intensively for sound long-term soil practices. The fertility of the American grain belt, for example, has been substantially reduced, and with this reduction a decline of the nutrient quality of the food yield.

On a worldwide basis, only 11 percent of land is permanent cropland, 19 percent meadow and permanent pasture, 40 percent wasteland, and 30 percent forestland.[6] Most of the forestland is tropical or subarctic, meaning that little is available for successful cultivation. Some of the meadow and pasture area has grain potential, while wasteland is precisely that—unless the desert can be made to bloom. Best off in terms of percentage of cropland is Europe with three times the world average, followed by South Asia with twice the average cropland. These are also two of the most densely settled regions of the globe. North America and East Asia have about the world average, though the United States is by itself over twice as well endowed with good farmland than the world average. Africa has slightly less than the average, and South America has only one half the average cropland. South America, thus, cannot long afford the luxury of uncontrolled population growth, despite its relatively low overall density. Africa and especially Australia have a somewhat similar situation of a deceptively small overall density facing limited amounts of good cropland. Canada and the Soviet Union are the northern hemisphere's low density, large land mass areas with only average amounts of cropland. While Canada with its small 22 million population is a surplus grain producer, the Soviet Uion has on recent occasions made large purchases of foreign grain, owing mainly to poor climatic conditions and subsequent crop failures.

The irony of the world's land situation is that, in an era of pressing food needs, urbanization is gobbling up large chunks of prime farmland, especially in the most highly developed areas of the world. The United States has been the most careless in regard to giving up farmland for urbanization and attendant highway development. With powerful real estate developers and highway construction companies in the forefront, urban sprawl eats up 2.2 million acres of good farmland every year, a rate 50 percent higher than a decade ago even though population growth has been halved. The interstate highway system alone,

---

[6] John McHale, *World Facts and Trends* (New York: The Macmillan Company, 1972), p. 19.

much of which crisscrosses the most fertile land in the world, covers an area the size of the state of Delaware; to this must be added the entire overgrown network of state and county highways.

Since 1945, 30 million acres, much of which is prime agricultural land, has been buried under concrete and steel. California is a leading example of cropland burial, a continuation of which will lead to the loss of one third of the state's best farmland by 1980. By 2020 the projection is for 13 million acres of California's arable land to be lost, one half of the total tillable acreage.[7] Santa Clara County, with loam soil 30 feet deep, experienced a population jump from 150,000 in the 1930s to one million in 1970. A county planner said, "Wild urban growth attacked the valley much as cancer attacks the human body. What so recently had been a beautiful productive garden was suddenly transformed into an urban anthill."[8] The majority of orchards are gone, the water supply is short, flooding threatens because of so much paving and ground cover, land is sinking with the falling water table, and air pollution damages remaining crops. As agricultural production declines, urban social problems increase. "Only real estate speculators," writes Leonard Downie, "can win in this situation."[9] The price of farmland soars as urbanization approaches. Rising property taxes and a host of difficulties arising from farming in urban regions—such as theft of crops, damage to crops by intruders on jeeps and motorcycles, flat tires on farm machinery because of broken glass and trash dumped in fields—force even the most reluctant farmer to sell out.[10] Such has been the fate of one of the world's most fertile soil areas.

A closer look

The world demand for food grows at least as fast as does population, *faster* if one adds the extra demand created by rising affluence. The developed countries as a whole have in recent decades increased food production at a faster rate than their populations grew, whereas

[7] Paul R. Ehrlich, Anne H. Ehrlich, and John P. Holdren, *Human Ecology* (San Francisco: W. H. Freeman and Company, 1973), p. 83.

[8] Leonard Downie, Jr., *Mortgage on America* (New York: Praeger Publishers, 1974), p. 107.

[9] Ibid., p. 104.

[10] "Paved Fields," *The Wall Street Journal*, Friday, October 17, 1975, p. 1.

the underdeveloped countries have just barely managed to break even. Projections to 1985 suggest a 3.7 percent increase in food demand for the underdeveloped countries compared to 1.6 for the developed, or a 2.5 percent global increase. This means the world's food supply by 1985 will have to be increased by one third again from its present size if today's dietary standards are to be maintained. In terms of specific foods, the next ten years must witness an increased production of 30 percent for wheat and rice, 48 percent for vegetables, 58 percent for meat, and 64 percent for fish.[11] In terms of cereal grains, the developed world's demand will amount to an increase of about 25 percent, or 619 million to 781 million tons; the underdeveloped world's demand will increase by over 50 percent, or from 592 to 902 million tons. Fully 42 million new tons must be added each year in order to meet additional food requirements for new population. But already a 50 million ton deficit for the Third World in 1985 is projected.

During the past quarter century the slowest growing areas of the world have increased their per capita food production the most. Eastern Europe, the Soviet Union, and Western Europe led the world in per capita food production increases. At the other end, Latin America has seen its per capita food production slightly decline. Up until recently, the global population versus food contest had not revealed any definite trend. The large and rapid increases in population which lie ahead in the coming decades, however, will place unprecedented strains upon food supply. Food analysts William and Paul Paddock predicted in 1966 that the United States could not fill the food gap by 1974.[12] With some help from bad weather in 1972, their prediction turned out to be quite exact, as a storage glut of 20 years earlier had all but disappeared. They predicted increasing famine for 1975, and we have seen it in both Africa and Asia. The United States Department of Agriculture expects that by the mid-1980s world population will have clearly outstripped world food supply. To pinpoint an exact time of widespread famine is not really possible, although most serious observers agree that what we have seen in parts of Africa and Asia may only be harbingers of things to come on a much wider scale in the near future. The distinction be-

---

[11] Harold Jackson, "To have . . . and have not," *Calgary Herald Magazine*, Friday, November 15, 1974, p. 6.

[12] William Paddock and Paul Paddock, *Famine 1975!* (Boston: Little, Brown and Company, 1967), p. 140. For a relatively sanguine overview of the world food situation, see the May 1975 issue of *Science*.

tween undernourishment and famine is not precise, since starvation can be and usually is a slow and insidious process. Before the end of the century, food scientists will perhaps have been forced to construct more precise indicators of starvation, much as social scientists have constructed measures of economic growth and fertility.

Rising above all other nations in scope of potential disaster is India with its over 600 million people. India adds almost one million new people each month with the average woman having between five and six children by age 46. By 1990 India will have double the present number of women in childbearing age. India's population growth rate has declined from 2.5 to 2.1 percent a year owing as much to a rising death rate as decline in the birth rate. This is the demographic situation in a country which 200 years ago when the English came had 60 million people of which 10 million were inadequately fed. Out of today's 600 million a reversed food situation exists with only 10 million adequately fed.[13]

During the 1960s India's per capita food production declined despite some record harvests. A similar decline in the consumption of food grains per capita in rural Pakistan also occurred in this decade, again despite some record harvests.[14] India was the prime recipient of surplus American grain during these years as well, receiving up to one fourth of the entire U.S. wheat crop. The magnitude of India's food needs is further suggested by the fact that the entire world's fish catch would provide each Indian with the equivalent of only one half herring a day. Just to meet its existing food gap India requires at least 50 percent more food than is now available. That this could be produced with higher productivity is suggested by the fact that India and the United States have about the same amount of cropland, but India realized only a fraction of what the American acreage yields, despite India's 60 million farmers and America's three million. The difference lies, of course, in the level of technological development. India has only a single agricultural research worker per 100,000 active agricultural population compared to the Netherlands' 133 and Japan's 60. However, there is little agricultural research can ultimately accomplish if the possibility for

[13] Georg Borgstrom, *The Hungry Planet* (New York: Collier Books, 1972), p. 137.

[14] Naved Hamid, "Alternative Development Strategies," *Monthly Review* 26 (October 1974):31–52.

application is not present, and in the context of much Indian agriculture, modern farming practices are difficult or impossible to apply. Neither the available capital nor the size of most land holdings permit modern techniques on the necessary scale. A pooling of capital, land, and labor is required, but this means a revolution in rural society.

India's food problems include such competitors as hordes of rats, monkeys, and cattle. Rats alone consume the grain equivalent of that contained in a 3,000 mile long train, or 10 percent of India's grain production. In this area, too, much technological research and capital financing for transit and storage, where food losses to moisture ruin another 10 percent, is urgently needed. But with grain import prices at record highs, and an oil import bill several times higher than previously, India is hard pressed for financing of technological research and development.

At the other end of the financing scale is Europe, which is able to purchase its unmet agricultural needs from abroad. Europe is by far and away the world's leading net food importer, accounting for almost one half of world food imports. Georg Borgstrom refers to the "European octopus operation."[15] Europe is an especially heavy importer of feed grains and soybeans to bolster its livestock production. Over one half of U.S. soybean exports goes to Europe and one quarter to Japan, also a heavy food importer. Denmark is the world's leading importer of protein, mainly in the form of feed grains, soybeans, and oilseed cakes; the Netherlands ranks second in protein imports. The Netherlands imports the equivalent of 1.5 times the agricultural production of its own farmland; from the seas this crowded little country takes the food equivalent of 2.5 times its own agricultural production.[16] Japan must go further to feed itself, requiring 1.8 times its own agricultural acreage in food imports and 3.8 times its own acreage in equivalent fish take. In other words, Japan is able to produce only 17 percent of its food on its own land. Furthermore, because of intensive agriculture and double-cropping, Japanese rice has a low protein content. Interestingly enough, the Japanese are getting fatter and encountering health problems associated with overeating. England is another crowded country which must draw heavily from outside agricultural resources, import-

---

[15] Georg Borgstrom, *Focal Points: A Global Food Strategy* (New York: Macmillan Publishing Company, 1973), p. 5.
[16] Borgstrom, *Hungry Planet*, p. 79.

ing one half of its food and feed. Unlike Europe and Japan, hungry India cannot pay the food import bill and is ordinarily a relatively small net importer of food products.

An important point to remember in the matter of food and population is that, so long as a nation is affluent, it can overcome any food deficit through importation from the world market. This also includes the importation of fertilizer with which to expand its own production. The economic factor intervenes between food and population so that self-sufficiency considerations become obscured without further analysis. Europe and Japan are populated and eating well beyond the limits of their land, borrowing heavily upon acreage from other continents and from the seas. A similar point may be made with regard to a wide spectrum of nonagricultural resources. Americans have not yet lived so much beyond their immediate means as they have borrowed heavily from the future; soils have been depleted and resources rapidly consumed. The future will accordingly become ever more costly.

The manner in which the food versus population contest is played out on a global scale is replete with irrationalities and inequities. The rich eat too much and too inefficiently. The poor charge greed and gluttony. The poor continue to have rapid population growth directly in the face of a mounting food crisis. The rich charge irresponsibility. In the end, both rich and poor are losers, for no one can live at peace in a world beset by hunger and want on a massive scale.

Food: Actual and potential

The kinds of food people eat determine to a significant extent how much food is available. This can best be illustrated by meat over against vegetable consumption. An acre of land used for rice growing can feed four to six people, but an acre used as pasture to produce meat cannot quite sustain one person. Viewed from another perspective, up to ten times as much land is required to produce a given number of beef calories as corn calories; that is, the efficiency of cattle in converting corn to meat is only about 10 percent.[17] A pound of beef requires at least seven pounds of grain; pork requires four pounds and fowl three

---

[17] Carlo M. Cipolla, The Economic History of World Population (Harmondsworth, 1972), p. 38.

pounds. The amount of food, in terms of both calories and protein, would be greatly expanded if nutrition were more often taken directly from plants rather than animals.

The average American consumes 11,000 primary calories a day, primary calories being original plant calories derived from both plants and animals feeding from plants. Because one calorie of animal foodstuff requires from five to ten times the amount of plant produce, big meat eaters will consume much greater quantities of primary calories than those who eat limited quantities of meat. Thus, a black African living primarily on plant produce will consume only 2,400 primary calories compared to a New Zealander's 14,000. The average American consumed 114 pounds of beef in 1970, and the Secretary of Agriculture projects 140 pounds by 1985. This could well be so inasmuch as beef consumption doubled between 1940 and 1970. The average Tanzanian, by contrast, eats only one half of one ounce a week or less than two pounds a year. A Tanzanian also eats only one egg a month and drinks one pint of milk per week.[18] Because of their heavy animal-based diet, Americans consume on the average almost 2,000 pounds of grain annually—only 150 pounds of which is direct grain—compared to 400 pounds for the average Indian—most of which is eaten directly as grain. Fully 85 percent of the gigantic U.S. corn crop is fed to livestock, and the same holds true for barley, oats, and sorghum—all excellent nutrient sources for the human diet. The most protein and nutrient rich plant product of them all, the soybean, is also fed primarily to livestock, although much of the oil is pressed out for margarine and salad oils. As with corn, the United States leads the world in soybean production.

Livestock in the Western world eat extremely well. They eat such protein rich diets that they consume the equivalent amount of protein to feed another 1.2 billion Americans.[19] The increased pressure upon the land from heavy meat diets is enormous, say at least five times the amount than would be required for a predominantly non-meat diet. Very little of what people see as they travel across the expanses of American farmland goes directly to their table. These endless fields of corn, soybeans, alfalfa, and oats are the staples of livestock. On the Great Plains, wheat production is closer to the human diet, but not be-

18 Clive Y. Thomas, *Dependence and Transformation* (New York: *Monthly Review Press*, 1974), p. 147.

19 Borgstrom, *Hungry Planet*, pp. 7–14.

fore the better part of the grain has been milled out to leave white flour.

The pressure of livestock feeding upon the land may be illustrated by the fact that China has approximately six times the amount of population per tilled acre as the United States, but only 2.5 times the amount of population *plus livestock* (translated to human weight equivalent) per tilled acre.[20] India, with its enormous number of cattle, is worse than the United States when it comes to animal pressure upon the land. Indeed, India is *much* worse off insofar as the United States uses livestock efficiently whereas India mainly uses only the dung. India is one of the main reasons why the underdeveloped world has had a majority of the world's cattle (1964) but produced only one fifth of the world's meat supply, although animal husbandry throughout the Third World is backward.

Despite the fact that the richest one third of the world's population gets the large majority of the animal protein produced, that same richest one third imports 40 percent more tonnage of gross protein from the poor countries than it exports to these countries in return. The imported protein goes mostly to livestock in the form of fish meal, presscakes from oilseeds, and soybeans. Among the terrible ironies of this unequal protein exchange is that a beef glut had materialized in the West by early 1975. The United States and Canada carried on a diplomatic war over beef exports and quotas, while European Common Market governments had bought up 260,000 tons of surplus beef to support sagging prices. In another instance of protein glut, at least 30 million eggs rotted in Canada after being in storage too long in an attempt to maintain high prices. More irony still lies in the fact that, while the Third World is protein deficient, the protein rich United States spent $3 billion on advertisement and $3 billion on promotional gimmicks for largely low nutrition food and drink such as soft drinks and liquor, snacks, candy, and cold cereals.[21]

Not only are plant foods more efficient resource users than livestock, but certain kinds of plant crops are more efficient than others. Most importantly, legumes for example—all varieties of beans, peas, and lentils—are two to four times higher in protein content than are grains such as wheat and rye. Legumes have also been referred to as "green

---

[20] Ibid.

[21] Jennifer Cross, "The Politics of Food," *The Nation*, August 17, 1974, pp. 114–17.

manure" inasmuch as the roots have the ability to fix gaseous nitrogen from the atmosphere and convert it to usable plant food. Thus, legumes are both more efficient protein producers and more efficient fertilizing agents than are grains. A better balance could be struck between legumes and grains in the human diet. The soybean in particular could be processed into a variety of food forms suitable even to pampered Western tastes. Alfalfa, 60 million acres of which are now planted for livestock, is another variety of legume with high nutritional content. The leaves of alfalfa are particularly high in nutrition and could be processed for human consumption. Peanuts, another legume, could be more widely grown and processed to meet protein deficiencies in many regions of the globe.

The pressure on American farmland to feed livestock has resulted in a heavy drain of soil nutrients. Soil fertility has been significantly reduced, thus reducing the protein and mineral content of crops. Chemical fertilizer is only a partial fertilizer and cannot replace the complex soil structure produced by organic and natural processes. Chemical fertilizer also damages the soil's natural ability to restore itself, rendering the soil more and more dependent upon artificial sustenance. On top of the soil depletion stemming from the heavy livestock food demands comes the environmental pollution from fertilizer runoff and from feedlots.

If a dietary change in connection with foods produced on the land could substantially increase the amount of available calories and protein, what sort of potential expansion of food products might be expected from the sea? The first point to be made regarding the ocean as a food producer is that most marine life is concentrated in that 10 percent of total sea area which constitutes continental shelves and relatively shallow water depths. Most of the ocean is not amenable to marine life production and sustenance usable to man. As it stands, about 90 percent of the ocean's living products are not directly usable.[22] The 10 percent that is usable, including fish meal for animals, is largely concentrated in waters which are most subject to pollution. The loss of marine life to pollution is already large, and the situation continues to deteriorate. The point is that the ocean is not the infinite reservoir of food it may appear to be.

Nevertheless, the ocean plays a prominent and crucial role in the

---

[22] Borgstrom, *Hungry Planet*, pp. 442–43.

world's food equation. While providing only a few percent of the world's caloric intake, fish provide one fifth of animal protein consumed and two fifths exclusive of milk and eggs.[23] An annual catch of 70 million metric tons represents 70 percent of the 100 million tons available to man on a sustained yield basis out of a total annual production of 240 million tons. Approximately one half of the catch ends up as fish meal for animals, especially pigs and chickens in the developed countries. In order to support this oceanic yield, 20 percent of total ocean photosynthesis is utilized; this fish yield requires plankton and seaweed protein equal to 63 world wheat crops or 119 rice crops.[24] Such is the magnitude of the food task already performed by the ocean.

The point of diminishing return in fish yield has long passed for most of the basic table varieties of fish such as cod, haddock, halibut, herring and ocean perch. Advanced techniques and intensive fishing practices have already overexploited the seas so that more and more input is required to obtain previous yields that had been brought in more cheaply. Even if the maximum 100 million ton catch is eventually reached in the next 25 years at the required cost, the world's population is growing more rapidly than this optimistic increase in fish yield. In brief, while fish will continue to play an important role in holding down the hunger gap (or help maintain the surplus in the affluent countries), the seas cannot be expected to do much in closing that gap. The richer countries have the fishing fleets and technology to roam the world's seas in search of the catch, Japan and the Soviet Union doing the most in this regard. Soviet trawlers have been brought into Canadian ports for encroaching too closely on coastal waters. Both Soviets and Japanese have the utmost in whaling technology and pursue several of this species toward extinction. Recently, a "cod war" flared up between Iceland and the English who fish in the Icelandic area. The pressure of population upon food is thus very much in evidence even for many developed nations.

In the realm of conjecture, the food problem has been solved many times over. Science fiction merges with food technology to put an end to the pressure of population upon food. For example, Robert Katz contends that by 2030 the Sahara Desert will be "in the process of becoming a single tropical garden" and could feed the world's 15 billion

[23] Ehrlich and Ehrlich, *Population Resources Environment*, p. 133.
[24] Borgstrom, *Hungry Planet*, p. 68.

people all by itself.[25] Others envision a controlled nuclear fusion process creating food out of water, air, and energy. More down-to-earth schemes see food from culturing single-celled organisms on petroleum to produce single cell proteins (SCP), a process already accomplished. The cultivation of yeast as a highly efficient means of producing protein is also possible. Getting protein out of alfalfa leaves has also been suggested as a method of increasing the world's human food supply. Foods from plankton is another idea. Converting the cellulose from municipal trash and garbage to glucose and then to SCPs has been suggested, a conversion process which would purportedly yield 35 million tons of SCP from U.S. municipal waste alone. Expanding farmland by billions of acres from atomic powered seawater irrigation is considered a future possibility by some.

Food scientists such as Borgstrom and Paddock, however, see no panacea for the food crisis in such technological schemes. In some instances, such as that of food from plankton, the conversion process would consume more energy than would be derived from the food. In other instances, such as SCP from petroleum, one is confronted with a limited and finite resource which has thousands of other demands being placed upon it. In still other instances, the required technology is nowhere in sight and decades of intensive research would be required for its development. This is not to say that the food supply could not be greatly expanded through synthetic and manufactured foods. But as in other situations of resources and production, there are environmental limitations to such a new foods industry. Further, what conceivable justification could be given for mankind to resort to such "foods" as those derived from waste paper, oil, and algae? In order to support ten or 20 more billion people? Is the mission of the human species to see how many of them can survive on earth? Such would seem to be the case the way things are now going.

Given the fact that much additional food is needed to keep the population alive that is inevitably scheduled to arrive on earth, it would seem much saner and safer to rely on traditional foods in the effort to struggle through. It would make much more sense to reduce the world's livestock and thereby increase the amount of plant food available for

---

[25] Robert Katz, *A Giant in the Earth* (New York: Stein and Day Publishers, 1973), p. 50.

human consumption in the ratio of at least five to one than to devise SCP schemes. If soybeans are deemed an undesirable human food, what would people think of eating their municipal waste? If we were to rely on municipal waste for food, wasting would become an even more patriotic act than it already has become. Would it not be much simpler to try to eliminate waste and uitlize the more ordinary agricultural solutions combined with more rational diet, food distribution, and land use strategy? For a closer look at this more ordinary agriculture we turn next.

Agriculture and underdevelopment

Throughout much of the Third World, food production falls considerably short of the potential. There are major interrelated problems in connection with this inefficient land usage. The first has to do with the agricultural uses of the land and the second with the distribution of the land. These two problems are interrelated insofar as the use to which the land is put is decided by only a few powerful people. Let us begin with distribution and see then how this affects usage. We shall focus on Latin America, but the facts apply to greater or lesser extent elsewhere in the underdeveloped world.

The exact statistics of land distribution in Latin America may vary, but the message is always the same: a miniscule proportion of the rural population hold large amounts of land, whereas the great mass of people hold little or none. One set of data for 20 Latin American countries reveals that a mere 1 percent of the rural population owns fully 60 percent of the agricultural land, whereas 72 percent of the population own little or none.[26] A set of figures for Brazil has approximately 0.5 percent of the rural population with almost one half of the land and 57 percent owning no land.[27] In both cases, the remaining category of population own small to medium farms. Even in this middle category, however, the tendency is for a great discrepancy in holdings, since it is estimated that overall only 5 percent of the rural population hold

---

[26] Ernest Feder, *The Rape of the Peasantry* (New York: Anchor Books, 1971), pp. 30–59.

[27] Joao Quartim, *Dictatorship and Armed Struggle in Brazil* (New York: Monthly Review Press, 1971), pp. 126–27.

95 percent of the land; thus, those who do own land tend to own very little indeed.

The simple fact that land is grossly maldistributed does not by itself tell us anything about how efficiently the land is used. Yet those who have studied the agriculture of the Third World know that maldistribution almost always means inefficient use of land. In Latin America, the large estates or latifundios occupy the majority of the agricultural land but account for only a small minority of the actual cultivated land, whereas the miniature plots or minifundios account for a small minority of the total land area but for a majority of the cultivated area. In Brazil, for example, holdings of 500 hectares or more occupied 58 percent of the agricultural area but only 18 percent of the cultivated area, in contrast to holdings of under 100 hectares accounting for only 20 percent of total agricultural area but 59 percent of cultivated area.[28] The latifundios and plantations leave much of the land to lie fallow or put it into pasture for cattle herds, whereas the small holder works most or all of the land owned.

Not only do the minifundios account for a disportionate amount of cultivated area, but they are also much more productive per unit of land because of the intensity with which soil is worked. This is true even though the large holders own the richest bottom lands, while the peasant works the more marginal land. All the while there is the push against the small holder by the latifundios who expand their property at the expense of the powerless peasant. And all the while there is the continual exploitation of the landless laborer who must work for a pittance on the large estates. The result of this land system is that 86 million out of a total 114 million of Latin America's rural population in 1970 were impoverished.

The inefficient use of land on the latifundios does not end with holding much of it out of production. The land which is in production is used extensively for growing export crops, almost exclusively so on the huge coffee, sugar, and banana plantations. This is the monoculture which has rendered economies dependent upon a single agricultural commodity and which has cost the underdeveloped countries dearly in terms of soil fertility and food for domestic consumption. Much of this export agriculture is conducted in conjunction with foreign own-

---

[28] Ibid.

ership. It has been a prime consideration in the interventionist role the United States has played in Latin America, especially Central America and the Caribbean. The underdevelopment of agriculture in Latin America is profitable to the few but costly to the many. The landed aristocracy holds together their structure of power by preserving the agricultural status quo while foreigners take home most of the produce and much of the profit. Reinvestment is minimal, since productivity is of little concern with so much cheap labor available. Latin America devotes only about 10 percent of total investment to agriculture; this compares to one half of the state budget going to agriculture in China.

Would land reform, the breaking up of the large holdings into small enough farms for everyone to own, end hunger and poverty in rural Latin America and elsewhere in the Third World? Many would argue that land reform is a solution, and they point to cases where redistribution has resulted in agricultural growth. Proponents of land reform are especially optimistic with regard to Latin America, where the man-land ratio is still quite favorable, in contradistinction to densely populated Asia. Even in Asia, land reformers direct attention to Japan with its many working farms of only several acres. The skeptical contend that small plot farming cannot effectively utilize the inputs of modern agricultural technology and science, nor pool the necessary financial resources to purchase them. Labor power, too, can be more effectively pooled when applied to larger production units, according to the land reform skeptics. Moreover, there is the important concern about population growth continuing within the context of a completely individualized, peasant agricultural society. Gains in agricultural output could be nullified by the family size increase the small holder brings about in his interest to provide for labor needs and future security. Those doubtful about the practicality of land reform cannot envisage the great mass of Third World peasantry and landless laborers becoming efficient capitalist farmers. They see the need for a different kind of approach to raising the necessary food and establishing the necessary social order to bring an end to debilitating population growth. This approach is that of cooperative or collective farming, which has as its goal the fullest possible utilization of land, water resources, capital, and labor on a national basis. This approach gives top priority to agriculture in the developmental struggle, and seeks to establish as rapidly as possible an adequate diet for every person.

This is not to say that capitalist agriculture has not proven highly successful in productivity terms in the Western world. On the contrary, its surplus has often been an embarrassingly costly financial and political problem. However, the structure of rural society in the underdeveloped countries is hardly conducive to the development of Midwest-type commercial farming. The latter has itself ceased to be a family farm in the traditional sense; modern farming, where it is not outright agribusiness in the corporate form, is a business or industry with heavy capital investment in machinery and land. It is collectivized by private individuals and groups, and all the time becoming more so. It is backed by government, banks, insurance companies, and mortgage companies. Where could the Third World peasantry fit into such a structure? They could not fit at all, and if this type of farming were somehow thrust upon the Third World, it would result in an unimaginable flood of people into the cities where they would have nothing to do but beg, as hundreds of millions already do. No, it is too late for the Third World to follow a Western course of private agricultural industrialization, even if it had the finances to do it—which it does not.

It is informative, nevertheless, to look at what endeavors have been made by the developed countries to upgrade Third World agriculture. In particular, we need to examine the nature and status of the Third World's "Green Revolution."

THE GREEN REVOLUTION

The Green Revolution raised high hopes among all those seeking a solution to the world food crisis within the existing political and economic system. The Green Revolution signified the possibility of the underdeveloped countries becoming agriculturally self-sufficient and adequately fed without recourse to a social revolution. During the 60s, significant increases in wheat and rice yields in places such as India, Pakistan, Taiwan, and Mexico provided considerable support to the new optimism. Yet within another few years, most of this optimism had faded. Per capita food production even in areas where the Green Revolution received considerable fanfare, such as India and Pakistan, had not lived up to expectations and proved unable to significantly alter the critical food situation. By now the panacea of the Green Revolution has all but died. The effort to increase crop yield and productivity goes on, but it is done more as if on a treadmill than a revolutionary stairway to freedom from hunger and want.

What was the Green Revolution and why has it failed to live up to expectations? The productivity of land is determined by its fertility in combination with climatic conditions. Soil fertility is based on the amount of plant nutrients which the soil contains. Soils rich in nutrients give heavy crop yields; thin soils yield light crops. Only a relatively small area of the globe has been blessed with highly fertile soil, and even this must be arduously maintained through conservation practices, mainly the application of fertilizer. The more fertilizer applied the more the plant growth, provided an additional amount of water is also made available to the plant. However, applying large amounts of fertilizer and water to traditional tall-standing grains results in top-heavy heads which fall over. The crux of the Green Revolution was the production of dwarf strains of rice and wheat through crossbreeding of traditional varieties until a straw short and sturdy enough to hold up a heavy head of grain was isolated. With the new seeds able to accommodate large amounts of fertilizer and water, crop yields could rise dramatically. Several times the usual amount of fertilizer and water could be applied to the new seeds, which could reach maturity in four months instead of five or six and thus allow for double- or triple-cropping. The new hybrids could also get by on shorter days.

The results of the Green Revolution were at first impressive. In the late 60s, Green Revolution acres in India were made to produce 50 to 100 percent higher wheat yields. Mexico, an early site of wheat experimentation, tripled production on the affected wheat acreage from 1950 to 1967. Taiwan tripled its rice crop in a similar period of time.[29]

What brought the high hopes of the Green Revolution down as fast as they went up? Two broad problems have undercut the goals of the Green Revolution. The first concerns financial and resource obstacles and the second involves social and political ones. The financial requirements of instituting a Green Revolution are four times those of raising a traditional strain. Chemical fertilizers from petroleum are expensive and have recently become prohibitively expensive for the already debt-ridden underdeveloped world. There is no way India, for example, could possibly pay the fertilizer costs required for the Green Revolution save for a small amount of total acreage. Other major cap-

---

[29] On the Green Revolution, see Lester R. Brown, *Seeds of Change* (New York: Praeger Publishers, 1970).

ital costs to conduct a successful agricultural revolution around the new strains include tubewells, tractors, pesticides, chaffing machines, and storage and transport facilities. It is not surprising given such costs that the Third World has had only 17 percent of its wheat acreage and 9 percent of its rice acreage planted in the new seeds. The costs of bringing in the necessary water can also come high, since irrigation must be the primary means of new supply. Water per se is a scarce resource in much of the world and stands as a major limitation in many potential Green Revolution areas.

In connection with the water resource limits to the Green Revolution, we might mention related environmental problems. Irrigation systems present the problems of intestinal parasites which already debilitate some 200 million people. Dams, as discussed earlier, present problems of upstream flooding and downstream soil changes; dams silt over and irrigated lands may waterlog and salinate. Fertilizer runoff from the fields raise serious pollution problems, as does the heavy pesticide use required by the new strains. The monoculture created by growing the new hybrids on a wide scale at the cost of the older varieties increases the prospects of crop disease, as the cases of corn blight in the United States demonstrate. More pesticides are required to protect the new strains than the old native species which had been naturally selected to meet the adversities of the local environment.

As to the second major problem, the sociopolitical one, the Green Revolution requires and sets in motion greater social inequality than even existed before. Landholders with acreage and capital large enough to support the new techniques earn accordingly larger revenues from grain sales. They are able, in turn, to expand further by taking over failing smaller farmers in the area. A new class of rich farmers arises alongside the old large landholders. The price of both land and grain greatly increases. Existing high seasonal unemployment rises further with the introduction of machinery. Social cleavages between rich and poor widen. The entire structure of rural society is threatened by the new economic forces put into motion by capitalist farming operations.[30] The rural to urban flow is intensified by what amounts to a new enclosure movement. The traditional large landholders who do not enter the

---

[30] See Harry M. Cleaver, Jr. "The Contradictions of the Green Revolution," *American Economic Review* 62(May 1972):177–86; and Cynthia Hewitt de Alcantara, "The 'Green Revolution' as History: The Mexican Experience," *Development and Change* 2(1973–74):25–44.

capitalist drive for expansion end up at odds with the rising class of new rural rich, and resist the modernization process. In short, the old social order is placed in jeopardy by what amounts to the extension of capitalist economic relations into the countryside. The Green Revolution becomes something of a greed revolution as market forces tear into the fabric of peasant society.

A capitalist revolution in the gigantic countryside of the Third World is precisely what the developed countries are seeking to foment, especially the multinational corporations which supply the technology for the Green Revolution. In Ernest Feder's words, "The Green Revolution is in reality aimed at ever-increasing economic, hence political, control by the industrial nations over the agricultures of the developing world well beyond the plantation sector."[31] The leading role played by the Rockefeller and Ford Foundations in implementing the Green Revolution is no accident. Lester Brown points out that "the multinational corporation promises to institutionalize the transfer of [agricultural] technology on a global scale."[32] Wherever the growth society is able to take root, so much the better for the interests of those already far along the path. However, as much of the foregoing analysis has attempted to show, the social structure of the underdeveloped world contains enormous obstacles to the implementation of rural capitalism as imported from the advanced countries. Even the kind of capitalism found in the major cities is an unbalanced and distorted version of that found in Europe or America. Such is, in fact, the nature of underdevelopment.

The conclusion to be drawn from the history of the Green Revolution is that, technology in isolation from socioeconomic reality can only raise false hopes of an end to world hunger. The principles of the Green Revolution cannot be extended much further without major socioeconomic change in the Third World. The environment could not tolerate a Green Revolution on all the agricultural lands of the earth, but it could and must be carried out to some degree on a larger percentage of the land than can be accomplished within the structure of underdevelopment if the ongoing world food crisis is ever to be overcome.

---

[31] Ernest Feder, "Six Plausible Theses about the Peasants' Perspectives in the Developing World," *Development and Change* 2(1973-74):14-15.

[32] Brown, *Seeds of Change*, p. 55.

A social revolution could, in fact, result in yield increases at least equal to those affected by a technological revolution. A combination of the two could put an end to hunger and starvation in the Third World as it has already in China.

American agriculture

We have previously alluded to the fact that in the United States, agriculture is one of the most capital-intensive sectors of the economy. Agriculture is more heavily capitalized than metal mining, iron and steel production, chemicals, and transport; only electric power, petroleum products, and coal rank ahead of agriculture. The extensive capitalization of agriculture over recent decades has greatly centralized food production. Between 1959 and 1964, for example, 300,000 farm enterprises folded; between 1935 and 1965 the farm population of America dropped by some 20 million people. Agricultural employment is down to around four million out of a labor force of 100 million. Since 1960, output per man-hour in agriculture has more than doubled, as have farm assets. The overall picture is one of dwindling agricultural population, increasing farm size and assets, and increasing labor productivity; but in combination with 25 million fewer acres under cultivation than in 1930 and only slightly increased per capita food production. Far fewer people are producing more food on less acreage with more technology.

Still, the major problem in American agriculture has been surplus production which has placed downward pressure on farm prices and incomes in a sector which has retained considerable market competition. Farm productivity has over the years increased much faster than have farm incomes; farmers' purchasing power has not kept pace with that of most other income groups. This has been a major reason in the displacement of much of the rural population to the cities, often as among the poorest and most destitute of the newcomers. Surplus production brought on government intervention on a large scale, mainly in the form of subsidies paid to farmers for not growing food. The farm subsidy has come to around $5 billion a year. However, because land ownership is unequally distributed, so are the subsidies; in one year in the late 60s 264 large commercial farmers received as much in federal subsidies as the 540,000 smallest, or an average of nearly $200,000 for the big operators and $96 for the smallest.[33]

Agribusiness is increasingly a more appropriate term for American agriculture than is farming, with its implication of the small, mixed, family farm. Grain production is carried on over massive spreads of land with expensive machinery. Incorporation, family and non-family, plays an increasingly prominent role in both ownership and production. Fruit and vegetable production is even much more incorporated and tied in with some of the nation's leading companies. Meat production is dominated by the big feedlots and a few big packers. The dairy industry is precisely that, with even most farmers that remain buying their milk, butter, and eggs in town from an ever more concentrated group of corporations.

Overseeing America's agricultural operations from the federal government in the Ford administration is Earl Butz, ex-dean of the Purdue agricultural school and member of the board of directors at Ralston-Purina Company, J. I. Case Company, International Minerals and Chemicals Corporation, and Stokely-Van Camp Company.[34] Butz's predecessor as Secretary of Agriculture, Clifford Hardin, was former chancellor at the University of Nebraska and became vice chairman of Ralston-Purina after leaving the cabinet. It all points to an agricultural power elite of food producers, chemical suppliers, feed and seed suppliers, farm machinery manufacturers, big growers and cattle feeders, and land grant colleges. Power in agricultural production is also more and more linked into power in industrial production. The growth society centralizes and concentrates all power, whether it has to do with lettuce or jet airplanes, hogs or life insurance.

The centralization of agricultural production has undermined the viability of rural America. Farmsteads stand in decay and small towns wilt away. All of the remaining vitality is being sapped by the pull of the closest metropolitan area. Housing in small towns can hardly be given away; the same housing in the city is greatly inflated. Rural institutions wither and rural people are cast adrift in the impersonal and congested city, adding to the breakdown of urban integration and social control. The decline and decay of farm and small town life is thus

---

[33] Richard Parker, The Myth of the Middle Class (New York: Harper & Row, Publishers, 1972), p. 107.

[34] Lauren Soth, "Politics and Agribiz: The Operations of Dr. Butz," The Nation, October 26, 1974, pp. 396–98.

to an important degree a factor in the decline and decay of urban life. If the town to city flow had been halted in decades past, today's cities would have had much more breathing room to make adjustments to their own demographic, technological, and social changes. Instead they have been inundated by the countryside, both directly and then indirectly in the form of offspring of the rural migrants.

This is not an appeal for a nation populated by small farmers, although our urban problems would be nowhere near what they are today if this were, in fact, the case. It is an appeal for a more rational population distribution and utilization of land areas, for the viability of smaller cities and towns within which people can be more readily integrated and communalized, and for the resurrection of the city as the focal point of civilized society. It is a call for cooperative and collective farm enterprise where agricultural producers and workers own their own means of production and make decisions on the basis of the real food needs of the people rather than on the basis of profit and growth. Perhaps then it would not be found that in a random sample of 12,000 persons from low-income areas in four states, including New York, 17 percent had serious protein deficiencies, one third of those under six years old were anemic, and one third to one half of the total exhibited signs of serious nutritional deficiencies.[35]

John Deere's first sod-busting steel plow and Cyrus McCormick's mechanical reaper were not devised for the benefit of corporate executives and stockholders; they were intended to increase food production and meet food needs. If only John Deere and International Harvester could have those ends in mind today, there would be far fewer hungry people in the world. But they cannot, for first and foremost, they must have in mind the interests of executives and stockholders, and this means growth irrespective of hunger and want elsewhere in the country. Food shortages and deficiencies anywhere in America are clearly absurd and inexcusable; but they are as much the expected results of the growth society as the daily smorgasbord of the rich.

Agriculture and the environment

"All progress in capitalistic agriculture," wrote Marx, "is a progress in the art, not only of robbing the laborer, but of robbing the soil. Cap-

---

[35] Ehrlich and Ehrlich, *Population Resources and Environment*, p. 94.

italist production . . . develops technology . . . only by sapping the original sources of all wealth—the soil and the laborer."[36] About a century later, Barry Commoner wrote that "the new [agricultural] technology is an economic success—but only because it is an ecological failure." "Some of the most serious environmental failures can be traced to the technological transformation of the United States farm."[37] Behind the technological development and environmental failure is the incessant push for growth. The harder soil resources are pushed to produce, the more rapidly will they deteriorate; the more rapidly they deteriorate, the less food will they produce. However, both economic and population growth apply the pressures which drive the society toward further exploitation of land. Food production can be increased greatly, but only at higher costs to the environment—unless that increase is accomplished with entirely conservationist principles overriding those of profit and economic growth.

The ecological problems in agriculture arise chiefly from the excessive usage of chemicals. Agriculture is also highly energy consumptive as is any capital-intensive operation. In the United States, one calorie of food production requires one and a half calories of fossil fuel energy, including that expended on the manufacture and operation of machinery, chemical fertilizer, and transport. One ton of fertilizer requires the energy equivalent of five tons of coal, and 80 gallons of gasoline are burned in raising an acre of corn yielding 80 bushels.

Chemical fertilizer poses the biggest and most immediate environmental threat, as discussed previously in connection with water pollution. The world production of over 25 million metric tons is responsible for feeding one fourth of the world's people. Projections run as high as three fourths for the year 2000. This would require doubling the current output of nitrogen fertilizer. If fertilizer application were used more efficiently, that is, spread out on the world's farmland evenly instead of being highly concentrated in particular areas, enough of it is already produced to feed one half the world's population.[38] Diminishing returns have long been reached in the developed countries. This is illustrated by data from Illinois, which produced 50 bushels of corn per acre in the 1940s with less than 10,000 tons of fertilizer, 70 bushels in

---

[36] Karl Marx, *Capital*, vol. 1 (Chicago: Kerr & Company, 1906), pp. 555–56.

[37] Barry Commoner, *The Closing Circle* (New York: Alfred A. Knopf, 1971), pp. 152–53, 146.

[38] Borgstrom, *Hungry Planet*, p. 71.

1958 with 100,000 tons, and 90 bushels with 500,000 tons in 1965. The last extra 20 bushels have come at an extraordinarily high financial, resource, and environmental price. If these 400,000 tons used to produce 20 extra bushels in Illinois had been applied to poorly fertilized lands in the Third World, the total per acre increase in corn output would be four times what it actually was in Illinois. Yet other developed countries may use even more fertilizer per acre than the United States; the Netherlands uses ten times the amount and England three times.

Despite the scale of fertilization, the original nitrogen content of Midwestern soils has been depleted by one half. The use of inorganic nitrogen, without plowing back the crop residues after harvesting, destroys soil humus which prevents leaching of nitrogen. The natural population of nitrogen-fixing bacteria is also reduced. Besides the pure waste of fertilizer involved, the leaching process lies at the center of the nitrate pollution of water. Soil abuse through excessive chemical fertilization is partially responsible for the fact that 60 percent of United States cropland is in need of conservation treatment. The profit margin required by today's heavily capitalized farm operation, not rational agriculture or world food needs, commits growers to that extra few bushels extracted by ever larger doses of fertilizer.

A second major chemical threat to the environment is that of pesticides, and increasingly, herbicides. Used in limited quantities pesticides have substantially increased crop yields, but diminishing returns soon set in with overuse. In fact, declining yields have occurred in instances where immunities to pesticides have evolved and predators have already been reduced or eliminated by the pesticides. In addition to the interruption of the normal structure of biological controls, most pesticides are long-lived and tend to accumulate in all forms of life which come in contact with it. DDT, for example, is by now well-known for its far-flung distribution in a variety of bird and animal species almost from pole to pole. Altogether, around 1,000 chemicals are used to formulate some 60,000 different pesticide preparations in the United States, producing an approximately 15 percent annual growth in pesticide use.

The latest available figures from the Department of Agriculture indicate that 1.2 billion pounds of synthetic organic pesticides were purchased in 1973. Pesticide sales yielded $1.3 billion in revenues for the petrochemical industries, which obviously have a strong interest in increased application. USDA figures disclose that in 1966 36 percent of all cropland was treated with pesticides, but the figure jumped to 52 percent by 1971. Another major increase is likely for the 1976 report. For certain crops, the figures are much higher: 90 percent expected for corn in 1976 and 80 percent for soybeans.

Behind the sales pitch of growth-oriented chemical firms, pesticides are heaped on crops in far greater amounts than actually needed. Estimations are that a 70 to 80 percent reduction in pesticide use could be offset by only a 10 percent increase in cropland.[39] (Or, by the same token, a 10 percent reduction in the amount of food produced.) Erhlich and associates believe that "the procedures in use in the 1950s and 1960s will eventually be seen as one of mankind's most tragic blunders, and that when the total accounting is done, it will be found that other methods of control would have provided higher yields at less direct cost and with fewer deleterious consequences for mankind."[40] However, profits are too big and important to the petrochemical industry to turn off the pesticide flow in the least. Much more discretion needs to be used with pesticides, less damaging and pest specific ones need to be developed, and more biological controls should be tried—that is, introducing predators and breeding more pest resistent crop strains.

As it is with other environmental crises, the agricultural one has been largely set in motion by the pressures of growth—demographic and economic. Fertilizer and pesticide may at first glance seem far removed from the structure of society, but the linkages are very much in evidence upon closer examination.

---

[39] Sterling Brubaker, *To Live on Earth* (Baltimore: Johns Hopkins Press, 1972), p. 27.

[40] Ehrlich and Ehrlich, *Population Resources and Environment*, p. 173.

11

Growth and socialism

Socialism as survivalism

Our work thus far has largely dealt with the problems of growth as they have been manifest under established capitalism. To some extent, growth and survival problems facing underdeveloped areas of the world have also been examined, as in connection with population and food. The thrust of our discussion has been that the problems associated with growth tend to intensify under a capitalist regime, and that capitalism as a total way of life is incompatible with an environmentally permanent and economically stable society. Capitalism's problems are rapidly accumulating and compounding, and the result is in all likelihood to become increasingly unpleasant from a variety of perspectives. The present chapter concerns socialism and growth. As socialism is conceived and defined here, not necessarily as it has been variously practiced or thought of to date, it is an environmentally and economically viable society. We shall argue that the Soviet Union is not now, or evidently becoming, such a viable socialist society, but that China presents us with the beginnings of socialism, at least within the context of early development. We have no models of socialism in an advanced economic and technological context.

If capitalism as a system lacks the requisites of survival, indeed is paving the road for multifaceted disaster, there must be an alternative for humans to hold up and pursue as being a hope for social permanence and self-development. While particulars must by definition be worked out "on the spot," the broad requisites of both survival and quality in life—as to equality, democracy, environment, population, resources, peace, material needs, food, employment, an integrated life —are fairly evident. The rational specification and attainment of these broad ends are in large part what socialism is striving for. Socialism is, therefore, another way of looking at a society not only capable of survival in all of the senses we have discussed, but of leading on toward new challenges of social and individual growth.

Paradoxically, while developed socialism means economic stability and an end to economic growth as we know it today, socialism also holds out the greatest promise for the now underdeveloped countries of the world *to* develop economically in a balanced and long-term way (see Chapter 12). Socialism is thus an effective means, perhaps the only effective means, for getting underdeveloped countries started on the road to full economic independence and security *and* the effective means for bringing growth to a halt and channeling human energies from narrow economic to broad cultural endeavors. Socialism holds the key to survival and liberation.

The socialist transition

Prior to our discussion of contemporary socialism and growth, we shall spell out what is meant by the concept of socialism and its relationship to growth. As should become evident from our discussion of Soviet socialism, socialism as conceived by Marx has only superficial resemblance to the Soviet system. Marxist socialism, however, has much more in common with socialism as it is pursued in contemporary China. The difference between Soviet and Chinese socialism will be drawn out in the ensuing discussion.

Theoretically speaking, socialism as conceived by Marx is a transitionary form of society. It is an intermediary system bridging capitalism and communism, the final goal of socialist development. Socialism bears many of the marks of the old capitalist order which cannot be brushed aside in a short period.[1] A transitional period is required dur-

---

[1] Karl Marx, "Critique of the Gotha Programme," in Karl Marx and Frederick Engels, *Selected Writings*, vol. 2 (Moscow: Progress Publishers, 1970).

ing which time the material relations of production are altered from private to communal ownership and the cultural norms and values are transformed from bourgeois individualism to social collectivism. The change of material or property relations from capitalist to socialist can transpire in much shorter time than that required for the cultural change to take place. The former involves an objective, legalistic change of ownership and administration of production, whereas the latter involves a change of subjective, valuational aspects of human interrelationships.

The two facets of the socialist transition are interrelated insofar as the acceptance and success of collective ownership and administration implies psychological change toward equalitarian and libertarian values. If movement along the psychological front is lacking, the collectivization of property and production will inevitably encounter difficulties which require extensive intervention by the state—the antithesis of Marxist socialism calling for the withering of the state.

If there is advance of socialist culture, however, the democratic and equalitarian relationships required for genuine collectivist ownership and administration of production are allowed to develop, and the command role of the state recedes.

The Soviet Union exemplifies insufficient psychological movement toward communism. State ownership of the means of production is largely accepted by the people, but because the cultural aspect of the socialist transition has failed to develop, the state apparatus has become a new ruling class which is confronted with many of the same motivational and social control problems capitalist ruling classes confront in their societies. Socialist ideals take on a platitudinous form, much as democratic ideals have done in the parliamentary states. The achievement of Marxist socialism is demoted to rhetorical status, a distant goal which must be postponed until further economic development is achieved. Day to day realities are increasingly those of the old bourgeois order, with state bureaucrats substituting for private capitalists.

Chinese socialism, after early years of conflicting intentions, has now decisively set forth on a course toward Marxist socialism as conceived both in objective property and subjective cultural terms. Socialist ideology in China is no mere rhetoric; it is the substance of everyday life. The bourgeois tendencies in the Soviet Union are among the principal reasons for the Sino-Soviet rift. China has itself struggled with "revisionist" factions who sought to change the society according to the Soviet model. Only with the influence of the Cultural Revolution, beginning in 1966, have the anti-revisionist, Marxist-Maoist principles of the socialist transition prevailed.

What specifically makes the Soviet model a "revisionist" form of socialist development and, according to some critics, not a form of socialism at all? What characterizes a genuinely transitional socialist society which is moving or growing toward full socialism or communism?

Within the context of the present study, socialism might be most simply viewed as a society which places equality and democracy above economic growth. Economic growth, at least within a transitional socialist society, is seriously pursued, but only to an extent and in a manner which promotes greater equality and fuller democracy. Indeed, only the kind of economic growth which contributes to equality and democracy is considered as socialist growth. If growth merely enhances the wealth of the powerful, it is not growth in the socialist sense but in the bourgeois sense.

Socialist economic growth may or may not be recorded in traditional economic indicators, since growth which contributes to equality and democracy may have a high social content as in educational, medical, child care, dietary, cultural, or recreational services. The building of social resources does not reflect nearly as strongly in the objective economic growth measurements as does heavy industry, or consumer sales.

Socialist growth is growth of equal opportunity, equal rewards, and equal social participation. So long as there is oppression, material hardship, and powerlessness, or any one of the three, there can be no successful socialist transition. Giving priority to equality and democracy means the cultivation of the kind of economic growth which will in the longer run provide a foundation for the establishment of genuine communism. To countries yet to develop economically, the primacy of equality and democracy may be the only route left to the achievement of balanced growth. Unless every individual now oppressed, wanting, and powerless is given the opportunity to lift himself or herself above a degraded condition, the pursuit of economic growth can only flounder into a morass of social contradictions between foreigners and nationals, rich and poor, educated elites and illiterate masses, employed and unemployed, city and countryside. The lifting task in the underdeveloped world is so enormous as to require collective commitment of all the people, and this can be had only through an ideology of socialism.

To *developed* societies, the struggle of socialism becomes even more a struggle for equality and democracy since the economic foundations are already available.

Equality and democracy in the socialist context imply many things. The struggle for equality implies the gradual movement away from necessary wage labor with markedly unequal material rewards and individual incentives toward voluntary labor with more equal material reward and social incentives. Equality implies the eradication of work hierarchies in which bosses lead and others passively follow. Equality implies a process of women's and minority liberation which progressively eliminates sex-typed and ethnic-typed subserviant roles. Equality implies opportunity for the individual to pursue his or her social aspirations and talents to the fullest. To accomplish these ends of equality, democracy must be at work. A working democracy draws the individual out of the isolated act of casting a ballot in an annual election into the daily activity of decision-making in areas of life which affect the individual the most: as a worker, a farmer, a housewife, a student, a citizen. An effective democracy means direct participation in decisions governing the distribution of material rewards, the organization of work, the quality and kind of things produced, the kinds of services to be performed and for whom, and who shall represent the group in outside relations. A working democracy has no permanent bureaucratic, professional politicians or career executives. There are only temporary and elected representatives directly responsible to cooperatives, collectives, communes, and other work groups and civic groups.

Central to the socialist transition is the decentralization of power, production, and population. The ideal is a network of interrelated but functionally autonomous political units structured around industry and agriculture or a combination of both. These units are small enough to permit the individual to actively participate in a variety of decisions and grasp the larger purposes of the group's policies. Production occurs on a scale understandable by workers, and technology has a complexity amenable to worker repair and innovation. This suggests the importance of light industry within socialist society. Production on a smaller organizational and technological scale renders the goals of equality and democracy more reachable. It permits the active intervention of the human mind and hand in the production process, and recognizes the importance of human skill and craftsmanship in industry.

The giant industrial complex has a limited role to play in socialism, just as does the giant bureaucracy and the giant urban complex. Giganticism is not compatible with either socialism or ecological survival.

Life is directed toward the local scene in terms of both production and consumption; this is much of what is meant by autonomy. Certainly exchange of resources and goods are required in socialism, but the major emphasis is placed upon local and regional self-sufficiency and independence. There is no great center which overshadows the rest of the country; there are numerous centers each with their own identity and integrity. Existence is focused upon regional resources and environmental adaptation, making for a much broader variety of cultural manifestations in the society at large. There is no mass media, mass production, mass consumption, and mass culture, unless it is the general culture of socialism.

Socialist production is production for use. The standards of excellence are those of utility, durability, workmanship, and safety. Profit has no role in socialist economy, except perhaps for administrative or accounting purposes. Money itself assumes only a transitional role in socialist economy; money is used as a means of distribution of goods and services which are not yet freely available to everyone. In the early stages of socialist development, only such things as education, medicine, housing, and school lunches may be freely available, but gradually other needs are met through the growing social surplus.

In socialist economy, no need exists to search for profitable reinvestment of surplus, or to be concerned about overproduction, unemployment, and depression. Social needs of all kinds can receive the surplus without concern for profitability. If material needs are satisfactorily being met, work can be reduced in favor of leisure. Work and leisure begin to fuse, as people pursue their interests and self-development with the increasing free time. These interests and self-productions contribute, in their own diverse ways, to material sustenance, and the notion of voluntary labor gains further clarity. The craft, artistic, horticultural, technological, scientific, and literary productions of individuals in their free time become the highest quality productions of the society, and the drudgery and colorlessness of standardized production and consumption recedes in favor of the satisfaction and variegation of individualized skill. Socialism places even more weight on the act of creation than upon that of consumption, for it is the act of creation that marks off the liberated individual.

The socialist society in its transitional period is an economically growing society, even though the kind of growth is markedly different from that characterizing a capitalist society. But as rational and real material needs are satisfied, the production machine can slow down, as it must if a society is to be environmentally viable. An economically stationary state is approached as population levels off and the stock of goods, including agricultural, is stabilized. Waste is held to the absolute minimum and the life of goods extended to the absolute maximum. Consumption of all sorts becomes increasingly measured and cultural and decreasingly excessive and material. The relevance of these kinds of changes for ecological survival is very evident.

The communist society is a stationary-state society, at least from an economic standpoint. Technological innovation goes on as an expression of free time and voluntary labor, much as does cultural and social innovations. Growth becomes what it must become: social growth. Thus, communism is far from being a no-growth society in the broad sense; a no-growth society can only be a stagnating capitalist one, or a state-directed socialist one which has failed to make any progress along the transition to communism. True socialism is a growth society *par excellence,* the beginning of growth on a human scale unimagined in the past. True socialism provides the conditions for growth in knowledge, art and literature, music, science and technology, ties with nature, sociality, individuality, bodily activity and spiritual appreciation —available for all and pursued with everyone's well-being and personal dignity in mind.

Socialism and survival are, in effect, synonymous. A developed socialist order is not compelled to push growth in the relentless manner of capitalism, and is thereby enabled to establish a permanent relationship with environmental support systems. Socialist values promote longstanding and harmonious ties with the material and natural world and utilize this world in a measured and moderate degree. Restoration, longevity, reuse, and practicality in material living guarantees a harmonious relationship to the rest of the biological and physical environment. The individual's activity is geared toward rational production of the material means of existence and is thus imbued with creative content. Life rewards and satisfactions arise out of this cooperative, creative production of the means of living rather than the vain pursuit of happiness through unlimited material consumption. This by no means implies a Spartan way of life, although more of this is involved than the other extreme of bourgeois forms of hedonism which have no place in socialism.

The collective rationality of socialist society presupposes a stationary population, or one suited to the available resources and to the goals of individual self-development. Measured consumption, stationary population, and cooperative production combine to yield all necessary food supplies, and in a manner which minimizes environmental degradation. Collective discipline in population, food production and consumption, and environmental preservation are part and parcel of a viable society and of personal freedom and security.

With such goals for socialism, the necessity of a transitional period is easy to understand. The full transition may well require centuries rather than decades; centuries have been required to develop bourgeois culture to its present form, and it will take no less time to eliminate this culture and construct a new socialist one in its place. Those living today must make a worldwide start on the socialist transition, or their descendants will not have the material means to make the try, let alone complete it. Life will instead literally be a struggle for daily survival in an environmental wasteland.

Soviet socialism

Among a wide variety of Western observers, there is considerable agreement that the Soviet Union is becoming more like capitalist society than it is moving toward a new social order. The most fundamental similarity between the Soviet system and capitalism is the primacy each places upon economic growth. Subsumed under the primacy of economic growth in the Soviet Union as in the West are most of the bourgeois psychological and behavioral principles which we are now familiar with: bureaucratic elitism, centralism, significant amounts of social inequality, hierarchical organization, specialization, material incentives and wage labor, consumerist values, quantitative thinking, technologism, giganticism, and political apathy. The socialist rhetoric beclouds the underlying reality of what is in fact a state-run capitalist society, or state-run socialist society—if one is willing to use the term socialism interchangeably with state ownership and control.

The shallowness with which socialist principles are held is suggested by research in Poland among university and polytechnical students.

Only about 15 percent considered themselves Marxists or egalitarians.[2] The technical students were especially devoid of these ideologies, including those coming from the working class. What else might be expected in a society where the state promulgates an ideology of economic growth and technological development, while setting itself up as an elite in positions of power and privilege? A class stratified society based on significant differences in income, education, power, and prestige not only exists in Soviet society, but displays no clear signs of weakening.[3] In fact, some observers are of the opinion that the social class structure of the Soviet Union is hardening, particularly the class consisting of party bureaucratic and technical elites. (In strictly *economic* terms, though, this view is highly debatable.) The reward system encourages specialization, professionalism, and careerism, and these are the values which the large majority of students will adopt.

The economic growth record of Soviet socialism has been excellent by world capitalist standards.[4] There is ample proof here that private individuals need not be responsible for economic development; many in the underdeveloped countries even see proof that development is most rapidly achieved through full state direction. Growth may be pursued purely as an end in itself, without regard to profit interests and unhindered by the cycles of boom and bust which a privately incorporated economy classically engenders. The Soviet Union has achieved remarkable progress in economic development by combining noncapitalist investment and production principles with capitalist technological, organizational, and incentive principles. Collectivist ownership in the abstract is wedded with private individualism in the concrete. Managers and workers alike strive for bonuses paid out for growth performance, and they are motivated by the consumer goods which can be purchased with such salaries and wages. The same cycle of wage incentives and consumerism is developing throughout the Soviet and Eastern European systems as hold sway in the capitalist societies. The higher goals of the socialist transition are pushed aside for those of

---

[2] Dennis Pirages, *Modernization and Political-Tension Management: A Socialist Society in Perspective* (New York: Praeger Publishers, 1972), pp. 93–97.

[3] See, for example, Mervyn Matthews, *Class and Society in Soviet Russia* (London: The Penguin Press, 1972); and Sten Tellenback, "Patterns of Stratification in Socialist Poland," *Acta Sociologica*, 17, 1, 1974, pp. 25–47.

[4] J. Wilczynski, *Socialist Economic Development and Reforms* (London: Macmillan Press Ltd., 1972).

capitalist development directed by the state. The Soviet culture of to-day draws ever closer to that of yesterday's capitalism. There is slight evidence of any serious effort to create the foundations of a genuinely new kind of society and person.

The Soviet system is in the material sense very close to that of so-cial democracy found in Western Europe, in Sweden for example. Heavy investment is made in social welfare and security systems; op-portunities for the underprivileged are extended beyond those of un-modified capitalism; the state plays a prominent role in economic plan-ning; and the degree of income inequality is lessened by state taxation and subsidy. Important differences may also be stressed, in particular the role of private initiative in capital formation, property ownership, and transmission of wealth. However, the future emergence of these capitalist cornerstones in the Soviet-type system cannot be ruled out.

The very success of Soviet economic planning is forcing a move toward decentralization of decision-making within the overall national plan. As planning shifts from that involving the heavy industrial core to lighter consumer goods manufacturing, more control must be ex-tended to production units themselves. This does not imply the emer-gence of workers' control and local participatory democracy, although Yugoslavia has established a form of workers' and citizens' participa-tion which surpasses anything in Eastern or Western Europe.[5] The Yugoslav case represents a unique combination of decentralized capi-talist incentive schemes and centralist state planning. The drift in Yugoslavia is more toward social democracy than Marxist socialism. Social democracy, it has been said, is a capitalist society with a humane face.

In the Soviet economic growth drive, agricultural development has posed major problems. Given the primacy of heavy industry over light industry and agriculture, state investment emphasized the former over the latter. In this strategy, agricultural development is viewed as a means of urban industrial growth rather than as a cornerstone of so-cialist development. The secondary status of agriculture resulted in a history of political and productivity problems in rural society, which only later on received the emphasis required for more balanced growth.

---

[5] See Howard M. Wachtel, *Workers' Management and Workers' Wages in Yugoslavia* (Ithaca: Cornell University Press, 1973); and Gerry Hunnius, "Work-ers' Self-Management in Yugoslavia," in Gerry Hunnius, G. David Garson, and John Case, eds., *Workers' Control* (New York: Random House, Inc., 1973), pp. 268–321.

The agricultural surplus was originally squeezed from the peasantry to pay the costs of heavy industry, and the resistance of the peasants led to the bloodiest internal episode of the Soviet experience. In order to gain control over the agricultural product, the Soviet state in the 1930s instituted collective agriculture. The forced manner in which this was accomplished further alienated much of the peasantry, and agricultural production has never lived up to the expectations of state planners.

Nevertheless, the steady industrialization of Soviet agriculture has achieved respectable gains in productivity, particularly over the past two decades. Private plots still account for 20 percent of the Soviet agricultural product, and in vegetables, fruits, dairy, egg, and poultry production from 40 to 70 percent. Agriculture in Poland remains largely in private peasant hands, and while agricultural growth has been slightly slower there than in the Soviet Union, the rural population is relatively better off compared to industrial workers than they are in Soviet society. It is a matter of the private producer asking higher prices and holding more of the product out for personal consumption. Past riots by Polish urban workers over food prices and availability attests to the conflict of interests between workers and peasants in a state socialist society.

Soviet growth has sparked an urbanization process much like growth under capitalism. A steady flow of agricultural population into the cities has reduced by one half the percentage of population in agriculture throughout the Soviet Union and Eastern Europe over the past 25 years. The city remains the mecca of opportunity for what has always been a second-class agricultural population. Wages, educational opportunities, cultural outlets, and modern conveniences draw people into the major cities, despite some government effort to limit the flow and better distribute the benefits of growth throughout the country. While rural society is far from the state of decline which economic growth has produced in America, neither would it appear that Soviet society is progressing toward the socialist ideal of equality and integration between agriculture and industry.

As in any society which places economic growth above all else, the Soviet Union is beset with pollution problems.[6] However, owing in part to the fact that the country is not as economically advanced as the

---

[6] See Marshall I. Goldman, *The Spoils of Progress* (Cambridge, Mass.: MIT Press, 1972).

United States, the Soviet Union's environmental problems are not nearly as bad or as costly to deal with. Indeed, the Soviet Union is considerably ahead of most industrialized countries in the area of environmental control policies. Perhaps the Soviet's greatest advantage is their scarcity of automobiles, although their numbers are steadily increasing. Nearly as many cars are abandoned on the streets of New York each year as operate on Moscow streets. The Soviets have placed emphasis upon urban transit and subway development, suggesting that there is an awareness of the dangers of automobilization. Further, there are no special oil or auto interests to promote the private gasoline motor. Nor does the Soviet economy require the stimulus of auto sales. It is doubtful, then, that the Soviet landscape, urban or rural, will be so hopelessly scarred by private autos and their support system as has Western Europe, Japan, and North America—or for that matter, the major cities of the Third World. The battle to save the environment in the Soviet Union is thus one long step ahead of the West.

The major Soviet environmental problem is water pollution, which the government already spends $6.5 billion a year to combat.[7] Major Soviet rivers such as the Volga have been seriously polluted, as have major water bodies such as the Caspian and Aral Seas. The latter have been greatly reduced in size as well because of the dams and irrigation drain made upon their supporting rivers. The Caspian will soon be as eutrophied as Lake Erie if the water loss and pollution are not reversed. Water shortages and the lowering seas have raised schemes of reversing Siberian and even Arctic rivers to flow back toward the agricultural and industrial heartlands. Such are, needless to say, highly dangerous undertakings from an ecological standpoint.

The symbol of environmental welfare in the Soviet Union has been the Siberian Lake Baikel, one mile deep and 400 by 50 miles in surface area. Eighteen hundred plant and animal species found nowhere else in the world inhabit the Lake Baikel ecosystem, making it one of nature's most spectacular creations. However, untreated sewage being released into the lake from the city of Ulan and careless cutting of shoreline forest cover causing soil erosion have made the first environmental assaults. The prospects of deterioration of such an unparalleled lake disturbed enough people to bring about anti-pollution measures, and it appears the future of the lake is secure for the time being.

---

[7] Bill Bleyer, "The Environmental Economics of the Soviet Union," *The American Economist* 18(Spring 1974):124–27.

Agricultural pollution problems do not approach those found in Western Europe or America, owing chiefly to the fact that the Soviets use only 33 kilos of chemical fertilizer per hectare compared to 183 for Western Europe. The same holds true for the use of pesticides and herbicides. Nor does the Soviet Union have anything to compare with the environmental dangers posed by American feedlots. Whether the lower chemical input into the rural environment is due to ecological concerns or simply the "lower level" of agricultural development is difficult to assay. It may be a combination of both limitations. With the Soviets going abroad for grain purchases in dry years, we may expect increased use of chemical fertilizers, which in the Soviet context could probably still be expanded without diminishing returns.

Other major rural environmental problems include reckless cutting of timber and subsequent erosion. The country's vast forests have been reduced by some 60 to 70 percent from the original content. Strip mining has also been practiced because of lower costs.

The nature of growth in the Soviet economy is two-sided when it comes to its relationship to the environment. On the one hand, Soviet growth is not decided by profit and thus one might expect a clear path to environmental controls despite the costs. If stockholders are not going to be out any money and executives are not going to experience a salary or bonus cut when funds go to pollution controls instead of to profits, what stands in the way of environmental cleanup? In point of fact, nothing, except the demands of growth per se. If factory performance and management reward is measured by quantity of output or filling a quota, directors may go all out to achieve their ends regardless of environmental impacts. This, in fact, has been a tendency within Soviet industry. Quite aside from directors' personal interests, which as in the capitalist firm plays a prominent role in production decisions, an economy which is characterized by capital scarcity is led to neglect environmental costs. A growth priority system in intermediate stages of development as in the Soviet Union can always be said to have a capital shortage or competition for scarce capital. Even an overdeveloped stagnating growth society such as the United States is reluctant to give up funds for the environment.

In balance, however, the Soviet growth system can more readily turn to environmental conservation than can the American version. Growth in the Soviet system is not necessary to its survival. Growth is a desired end of the Soviet system, not the margin between life and death. If the public sees the necessity for strong environmental action within the economy, or if the state elite itself perceives the need of decisive action, nothing stands in the way. The choice between autos and mass transit can present itself in an objective manner, and the decision to greatly expand the subway system in the growing cities of the Soviet Union is not made at the cost of any vested oil or auto interests. Given official responsiveness, popular preferences can be pursued without any hindrance from the property-owning upper class whose existence depends upon the continuation of certain narrow kinds of growth. State bureaucrats will receive the same salary whether they administer the production of trains or cars, and there are no members of the public which have heavy financial stakes in one or the other. The danger in this case is that the bourgeois culture tendencies in Soviet life will promote the expansion of autos as the ultimate material incentive. Then it will make little difference whether or not there are vested interests in oil and private motor traffic.

An environmental awareness and movement has been growing in the Soviet Union, as it has in the West. Government, university, press, and general citizenry have all variously evinced active concern with environmental problems. Given the planned nature of the economy and this growing public concern, there is reason to believe that the Soviet Union can reverse further environmental breakdown and preserve a livable ecological habitat. Time will provide the answers as to whether or not the logical course of action will be followed.

Chinese socialism

Socialism as practiced in China is, from everything that can be gathered from the now quite large body of descriptive literature available, Marxist socialism in the mainstream sense. Marxist socialism, as theoretically understood, concerns an advanced industrial society, which China is not now and not likely ever to be in the sense we know an advanced industrial society today. China is a developing nation, but it is developing socialism at the same time it is developing its industrial, agricultural, and technological spheres. China did not embark upon socialist construction from advanced capitalism, but from the throes of underdevelopment as set by the longstanding oppression of the masses by landlords, money lenders, capitalists, and imperialists.

A predominantly rural society at the outset of the new regime in

1949, China remains a predominantly rural society today, declining only from 90 to 85 percent rural population. What is more, this rural balance will in all likelihood continue, for socialism calls for a well-distributed population and the linkage of agriculture with industry.

China, of course, has many great cities out of sheer dint of numbers. But there has been no uncontrolled, rampant urbanization which has turned so many other Third World cities into urban disaster areas. In an important way, China has taken advantage of the original rural nature of the society by bringing development directly to the countryside and doing so in the manner of a socialist transition. In effect, China has not only skipped over capitalist development, it also has not had to deal with an advanced rural-urban population and economic imbalance. This does not mean that China had nothing or has nothing to do about the rural-urban cleavage. The pressures toward urban privilege and dominance were and have remained strong, and they have been resisted only through such major counterattacks as the Cultural Revolution. The development of rural society on an equal basis with cities continues to receive the full efforts of government and party.

If the Soviet Union represents socialism which places primacy of economy over the politics of equality and democracy, China represents socialism which reverses this relationship. In China, politics is said to be in command.[8] By politics in command is meant that the ideological values of the socialist transition predominate over the unmodified ends of economic and technological development. To the Maoist, not only is this the only way to socialism, but also the surest road to economic development in an underdeveloped society. Politics in command means that full employment is more important than efficiency calculations; but it also means that full employment in an overpopulated underdeveloped society is likely to give more material output than are a few capital-intensive factories and an army of idle people. Politics in command means that production and distribution is decided as far as possible by those directly involved; it implies the extension of collective decision-making to every factory, neighborhood, school, hospital, village, and farm.[9] Equality of participation has not been achieved, but the important point is that China is making major efforts to move the

---

[8] Jack Gray, "Politics in Command: The Maoist Theory of Social Change and Economic Growth," *Political Quarterly* 45(January–March 1974).

[9] Barbara Ehrenreich, "Democracy in China," *Monthly Review* 26(September 1974):17–22.

society in this direction and has moved further than any other society in this regard.

The very nature of technology and industrial organization which is being developed in China reflects the concern for individual participation and understanding of the production process. This is a technology and organization which cultivates simplicity, alterability, lightness, smaller scale, worker knowledge and involvement, local resources, and self-reliance.[10] It is a technology and organization which avoids giganticism, complexity, foreign modeling, specialization, worker alienation, dependency, and external control. Early developmental efforts were patterned more upon the Soviet model, but after the Soviet pullout in 1960 the trend has been toward distinctly Chinese socialist planning and organization, markedly so since the impact of the Cultural Revolution. The supremacy of productivity and efficiency has been reduced to secondary consideration in the pursuit of equality and democracy. The result has been greater popular participation in productive labor. Students, party officials, soldiers, and government workers must all engage in material production along with their primary activities.

Despite work by a mixed assortment of people, or perhaps because of, per capita income and well-being has been steadily rising for everyone. Since 1960 there has been a shift of economic gains to the rural population and less-privileged urban sector,[11] in stark contrast to what we find most everywhere else in the world.

A genuine democracy must have a more profound meaning than even an active popular participation in social and economic affairs. Felix Greene, an Englishman who has spent many years closely observing events in China, writes that:

> A democracy means that there exists between individuals a thousand invisible threads, threads of trust, and mutual respect and liking— everything that makes us feel at one with each other and not on guard with each other, creating an atmosphere that does not call for us to be tough or competitive.

Greene goes on to characterize China:

> You feel in China the extraordinary inter-relatedness of people, so that in one sense no one is a stranger to anybody else. . . . A co-operative

---

[10] E. L. Wheelwright and Bruce McFarlane, *The Chinese Road to Socialism* (New York: Monthly Review Press, 1970), pp. 163–64.

[11] Derek J. Walker, "Revolutionary Intellectuals or Managerial Modernizers?" *Political Quarterly* 45(January–March 1974):5–12.

society develops an entirely different kind of ethic, a wholly different concept of freedom, and this is what I learned in China.[12]

The ideology of politics in command has given a strong emphasis to the development of socialist culture and personality which we previously mentioned as the crucial component of the socialist transition. Socialist economic organization requires the support of socialist culture and personality, which is open to voluntarily associated labor, social incentives, direct participation, and material equality. Derek Bryan observes that:

> This vision may sound utopian, but what repeatedly impresses visitors is the way in which a new type of human being, able and creative, but open and unsophisticated, very much an individual, but also a member of a strong and wise community, is in fact beginning to be typical of people, especially young people, in China.[13]

Economic growth in China thus takes place within a revolutionary social and political context. To the economic rationalist, an economy working within such a social and political milieu could not possibly survive. Yet the Chinese economy is not only surviving but growing in a steady and balanced fashion, despite periods of adversity over the past quarter century. Growth statistics cannot reveal the extent of material improvements in China, since a large part of socialist growth occurs in social welfare areas such as education, housing, food supplements, medicine, family planning, and cultural programs. Indicators of economic growth rely on monetary measurements and socialism uses money purely as a control and accounting mechanism. Prices are raised or lowered depending upon the importance of the product to socialist development; many things are free or nearly so. Thus, economic values are quite impossible to accurately assess in quantitative terms. After all, the goal of socialism is to eliminate money not only as capital, but as a means of transaction as well. There can be no such thing as a gross national product under developed socialism; there can only be gross national well-being and social growth, phenomena not subject to customary quantification.

Agriculture has always received the highest priority in Chinese development. After the initial expropriation of large holdings, Chinese

---

[12] Cited in Derek Bryan, "Changing Social Ethics in Contemporary China," *Political Quarterly* 45(January–March 1974):57.

[13] Ibid., p. 56.

agriculture went through a period of independent small plot cultivation. From about 1955 to 1958 collectivization moved through progressively more comprehensive stages beginning with mutual aid teams (40 percent of the rural population had joined into such teams consisting of several households *before* the national government launched the collectivization drive), then to cooperatives, and finally to the larger commune. Maoist strategy of laying the political and material foundations for collectivization prior to the act itself is largely responsible for the relatively smooth transition from peasant to collective agriculture. Allowing the richer peasants to hold their land after the revolutionary victory, and then giving them leadership responsibilities in the collectivization drive, helped avoid disruptions in production and subversive resistance.

The commune is the pivotal social, political, and economic unit in China, and serves both as the framework for smaller units within it and as the focal point of national planning. As much as is possible, a commune endeavors to be a society unto itself, developing its own economic self-sufficiency and political autonomy. A salient aspect of rural China is the manner in which communes are developing their own industrial base to support the agricultural economy. This is done on a small-scale and local basis, but such light industry is invaluable to effective manpower and resource utilization. It also assists in attaining the goal of integrating industry and agriculture, and bridging the gap between agricultural and industrial workers. The field worker comes to know the industrial needs of agriculture, while the worker in the shop also understands the nature of agricultural production. The two become interchangeable, both in technical understanding and labor force.

Even after collectivization, privately-worked land in China still accounted for one half of the total as late as 1962. Difficult climatic conditions from 1959–61 led to a loosening of collective production and an increasing return to market forces. Household production for private gain did not take long to spread, since the commune had not been in existence long enough to become firmly established as a superior mode of production. One of the thrusts of the Cultural Revolution beginning in 1966 was to return agricultural production to socialist principles and reduce the prominence of the peasant plot and pricing, and in this it has been successful. Individual peasant agriculture is disappearing from the Chinese landscape as the superiority and advantages of communal organization and utilization of manpower, resources, and industry become evident.

Two thirds of China's huge population is employed in agriculture, which accounts for only one fourth of the country's economic product. This in itself suggests the low level of mechanization found in China's fields. Production remains highly labor-intensive, meaning that tractors are still in short supply. Roughly one fifth of the land is plowed by tractor. In irrigated sectors, the majority of the land is still watered by foot-driven wheels, although pumps are gradually becoming more plentiful. One third of Chinese cropland is irrigated, and the non-irrigated lands are not known for their great fertility after millennia of cultivation. China relies upon chemical fertilizer for approximately 30 percent of crop nutrients, has 20 percent of the rice crop in high yield new seed varieties, and rates about 20 percent of its agricultural land as being under modernized farming techniques.[14] The emphasis is upon the productivity of the land rather than that of labor, since the latter is in ample supply while the former is not. Agronomy ranks high among the sciences, and agricultural conservation and experimentation is a constant activity in rural China. The tremendous agricultural effort has made China basically self-sufficient in food, although it remains a small net importer of agricultural products. With the magnitude of such an accomplishment, China becomes the hope and the model for the rest of the Third World to overcome the menace of hunger, malnutrition, and starvation—all daily realities to prerevolutionary China.

Economic growth in China has turned on its head the customary widening of class differences within a population. Instead, class differences have moderated as a result of significant reductions in income inequality and the steady expansion of free social services.[15] Prestige evaluations bear little correspondence to those elsewhere in the world, as social contribution and labor productivity replace conspicuous consumption, family inheritance, and occupational elitism. In contradistinction to almost every other country in the world, class differences between rural and urban populations have been markedly reduced and in many aspects completely eliminated. This has been possible through the work of urban educated cadres willing to spend their lives working among the agricultural population as teachers, medics, technicians, and other trained workers who typically congregate in urban centers for better pay, mobility, and prestige.

---

[14] Ben Stavis, "China's Green Revolution," *Monthly Review* 26(October 1974): 18–29.

[15] *China! Inside the People's Republic* (New York: Bantam Books, 1972).

China is unique in diminishing the size of government in the 20th century, an event which follows the Marxist prescription for politics. Recently, China has also reduced the size of its military budget, another remarkable development in view of great power diplomacy in the 20th century. The Chinese model of development will not be made to succeed elsewhere in the world by the Chinese military. There are no Chinese troops on foreign soil. Revolution can only be won when the people themselves are prepared for the struggle. Then no power on earth can stop them.

Given a prominent role in the socialist transition is education. In the Western growth society, and the Soviet Union, education performs an important stratifying function by distributing the population into various hierarchical categories according to educational certifications. Education in the West underlies the manual-mental occupational dichotomy, the social prestige ladder, and the ascendancy of urban opportunities over rural. In brief, education reinforces class inequality. In China, the Cultural Revolution has had as one of its central goals the democratization of education, endeavoring to render education as a means of attaining socialism rather than preserving social hierarchy. The magnitude of the task to alter the impact of education from that of an unequalizer to an equalizer is great indeed, for the entire history of education has been the reinforcement of elitism.

China has attempted to integrate education into the socialist transition through a number of reforms.[16] The traditional examination system has been abolished; the curricula have been shortened at all levels by dropping "useless subjects"; the age range has been widened for advanced schooling; part-work and part-study programs have been increased; political education is emphasized; educational facilities have been dispersed to all small villages to assist work-study integration; finances have been reallocated to rural areas and from more affluent areas designated as self-sufficient in funding; secondary and higher education combines productive labor with study in order to finance themselves; schooling is placed on a flexible timetable to accommodate needs of the various communities. The overall goal is to combine knowledge and production, mental and manual labor. The result is the diminution of social class differences.

---

[16] Rudiger Machetzki, "China's Education Since the Cultural Revolution," *Political Quarterly* 45(January–March 1974):58–74.

Given the orientation of Chinese technology toward the smaller scale and production toward the more labor-intensive form, we may anticipate less environmental problems than in the heavily capitalized, highly energy-consumptive productive machine. Add to this a strict ethic of frugality and an abhorrence of waste, and the possibility of over 800 million people living in an economically developing society without ruining the environment becomes a distinct reality.[17] Can anyone imagine 90,000 people digging out over 400,000 tons of organic mire from a river to use as fertilizer? It happened in Shanghai. As another instance of frugality over economic cost, sulfuric acid gas and ammonia are converted to fertilizers instead of smoke in Chinese factories. As to desecration of landscape, there are no nonreturnable containers, very few plastics, and virtually no junked automobiles. Since the Chinese are in no hurry to become industrial giants, they are able to place environmental considerations above those of cost accounting wherever they see fit to do so. And since capital and resources must by definition always be treated as scarce in a country with China's population situation, it is unlikely that waste is a prime condition of existence as it is to the capitalist growth society. As waste is viewed, so goes the environment.

We have previously commented upon China's population growth. Therefore we shall only point out here that China's collective security system provides important structured support for an official family planning policy. With the household no longer the key production unit, and the commune assuming extensive social welfare responsibility, the incentive for large families as security for income and old age is reduced. Furthermore, the proliferation of education and medical teams into the countryside provides the literacy and technical assistance to implement family limitation. We may well anticipate further significant declines in China's population growth rate.

The Chinese family becomes smaller but without weakening internal ties and commitments. Marriage comes later than in the rest of the Third World and even most of the West, but the strength of the family unit as an emotional support system has not faded. The major change within the family is the improved position of women. While much remains to be accomplished in the way of equality between the sexes, the

---

[17] Leo A. Orleans and Richard P. Suttmeier, "The Mao Ethic and Environmental Quality," *Science* 11(December 1970):1173–76.

Chinese female occupies a revolutionary status compared to her predecessors.

A final word must be said regarding the nature of the Cultural Revolution. We have stressed previously that the transition to socialism involves two major developments, one economic and the other cultural. China scholar William Hinton observes that "the socialist transformation of an economy is only the first step in a socialist revolution. In order to consolidate socialism the working class must not only transform the economic base of society but also the whole superstructure."[18] The superstructure includes the entire realm of culture, including ideology, values, customs, and institutions. We have noted how the Soviet Union has not thus far succeeded in moving very far beyond the basic economic changes and on toward the cultural transformation. Instead, it has institutionalized a capitalist mode of social organization and cultural values on top of state ownership of the means of production. This situation cannot long persist, since the two realms, the economic and the cultural, are in conflict and are only being held together by state power—an untenable long-run situation.

The Cultural Revolution came at a time when Chinese revisionists, those who would follow the Soviet pattern of economic policies, were making their bid for ascendancy over the Maoists, those who sought to continue the socialist transition by means of "permanent revolution." Hinton sums up the meaning of the Cultural Revolution succinctly:

> It has been a class struggle to determine whether individuals representing the working class or individuals representing the bourgeoisie will hold state power. It has been a struggle to determine whether China will continue to take the socialist road and carry the socialist revolution through to the end, or whether China will abandon the socialist road for the capitalist road.[19]

To speak of the existence of a bourgeoisie in China after over 20 years of socialist power would seem to be a contradiction in terms. Yet as long as there are those in powerful positions who see economic and technological development in basically Western or Soviet terms and adhere to politics of elitism and bureaucracy, one may still speak of a bourgeoisie, a state bourgeoisie more precisely. And so long as there is

[18] William Hinton, *Turning Point In China* (New York: Monthly Review, 1972), pp. 19, 46–47.
[19] Ibid., p. 17.

a state bourgeoisie, the potential for a return to privately incorporated capitalism, and this is not such a drastic move at all considering that the social organization and administration of production are already akin to that of capitalism, remains great. The Cultural Revolution was designed to turn the historical tables against the possibility of such a return ever happening in China. There have been further cultural or ideological movements since the Cultural Revolution, and there will in all likelihood be many more for decades to come, or as long as the legacy of the old order must be resisted. New historical epochs and modes of production are not established in a matter of years or even decades. It is more plausible to think in terms of centuries.

China as a nation is practicing the sociology of survival. In China, we may see how socialism and survival are closely paired. The rest of the Third World is bound to see this crucial connection. Indeed, the rest of the world, developed or underdeveloped, must see the connection if it is ever to meet the mounting challenges facing it.

12

Growth and underdevelopment

The roots of underdevelopment

Growth in the advanced capitalist countries has had an impact far beyond these countries themselves. The unlimited growth drive has pushed capitalist enterprise far from its own borders and across those of, at one time or another, virtually every country in the world. Only nations which have nationalized the means of production are now without direct investment by private foreign interests, and even some of these may court foreign capital. As alluded to previously, states which have nationalized production are *not necessarily* engaged in a socialist transition. Nationalization provides a kind of blank slate upon which new forms of power can be erected. In the Soviet Union, nationalization has evolved into rule by a state bourgeoisie; in China, nationalization has evolved into rule by the proletariat and peasantry. In the former, the socialist transition occupies a questionable status, whereas in the latter definite socialist growth is taking place.

However, despite its lack of socialist growth today, the Soviet Union has achieved remarkably rapid economic and technological development once it had broken away from the aristocratic, backward, and dependent order. Its Revolution enabled the Soviet Union to escape the confines of economic backwardness and become an independent industrial state. No country which has failed to make a break from the old aristocratic order and the colonial (or "neocolonial") system has succeeded in the task of development.

The condition of underdevelopment simply deepens the longer a country remains as a backward cog in the world capitalist system. The elite-mass cleavage widens. Rural-urban inequities increase. City slums grow. Unemployment increases. Illiteracy abounds. Agricultural production stagnates. Malnutrition spreads. Diseases debilitate millions. Birth rates remain high. Death rates begin to rise in some areas. Imported luxuries drain foreign exchange. Foreign debt and balance of payments deficits mount. Inflation runs rampant. Military spending for army and police repression increases. Foreign corporations drain huge amounts of raw materials and profits from the country. Such are some of the hallmarks of an underdeveloped society. Economic growth in the underdeveloped society means unbalanced growth which neglects the most urgent social needs of the people while catering to the consumption whims of the national bourgeoisie and the tax and profit concerns of foreign investors.

There is no debating the fact that, in terms of raw economic growth rates, countries having the heaviest foreign investment have "prospered" in a very narrow sense. For example, Taiwan has experienced an enormous influx of American investment capital relative to its gross domestic product, and increases in the latter have outstripped most other underdeveloped nations. In Taipei, Taiwan, 75 foreign firms operate, paying about $1.80 a day to, for example, young girls for painting in assembly-line style thousands of plastic dolls a day.[1] In addition to this basic industrial blessing, Taipei is a sea of squatter shacks, experiencing an uncontrolled crush of 1.5 million population growth in 15 years. The city's water must be boiled for 20 minutes, raw sewage and industrial wastes flow freely, the city sinks four inches a year, the air is heavily polluted, traffic accidents and death are high, and flooding is common. However, firms such as Admiral, Bendix, Zenith, RCA, Arrow, Mattel Toys, Dow Chemical, Singer, and DuPont enjoy the open investment context and the consequent wide profit margins.

The growth of the developed economies results in the further growth of underdevelopment. Development and underdevelopment are two

---

[1] Edmund Ames and Mariel Ames, "Taiwan's Development Typhoon," *The Nation*, March 20, 1972.

sides of the same world capitalist system. By now it should be clear that underdevelopment does not refer to a traditional rural society living an independent subsistence agricultural way of life, nor to an isolated tribal society following a pastoral way of life. Such are precapitalist, *un*developed societies. An underdeveloped society has been brought within the orbit of world capitalist economy. The social structure of the society is altered from the traditional form of integration it once had and set on a course of deepening class cleavage, economic imbalance, and political dependency.

Underdevelopment may begin with colonialism. Or it may begin with foreign cultural, military, or economic intervention, and become "neocolonialism." Whatever the initial roots, the impetus behind underdevelopment is the growth drive of the developed economies, their systematic pursuit of economic gain through control of raw materials, cheap labor, export markets, tax concessions, prices, and a variety of financial gains. The early history of underdevelopment was dominated by forceful exploitation of natural resources and existing wealth; contemporarily, underdevelopment deepens through a more sophisticated economic investment structure.

The energizing force of world capitalism is the multinational corporation. It is multinational only in the sense that a given capitalist firm with headquarters in a specific country operates subsidiaries scattered around the "free world." The firm originates and is headquartered in a particular country, and the government of this country and the firm have a host of common interests. To a large extent, governmental foreign policy has as its chief concern the promotion of a political climate favorable to the operation of its own foreign investors. Clearly, the most powerful group of multinational corporations is located in the most powerful bastion of world capitalism, the United States.

It is important to understand that the multinational corporation is an extension of some particular national economy and interests and not some universal agency bereft of national obligations and commitments. An English authority on the subject, Christopher Tugendhat, summarizes the focus of the multinationals:

> A characteristic feature of multinational companies is that their subsidiaries operate under the discipline and framework of a common global strategy, and common global control. The head office is their brain and nerve centre. It evolves the corporate strategy, decides where new investment should be located, allocates export markets and re-

search programmes to the various subsidiaries, and determines the prices that should be charged in inter-affiliate exchanges.[2]

The multinational corporation is thus an extension of the competition between advanced capitalist states for control of raw materials, labor, markets, prices, and profits. At the same time developed countries are establishing the conditions for underdevelopment in the Third World, they are pushing each other toward further growth and expansion in an arena of international competition. The Third World is caught in a crunch between the growth drives of different advanced capitalist states and between those of different corporations from the same foreign power.

Why do corporations become multinational? It is a matter of survival in a system demanding growth. Just as corporations cannot long tolerate stagnation within the domestic context, neither can they do so internationally. In fact, it is the tendency toward domestic stagnation which drives them out into the international arena. As the magnitude of domestic profits increases, additional profitable outlets must soon be found. Or, as profits are squeezed, cheaper means of production must be sought. The latter might be illustrated by the fact that General Electric pays 30 cents an hour for labor in Singapore compared to $3.20 for the same work in the United States.[3] It is not surprising, therefore, that 80 of the country's largest 200 corporations have one fourth of employees, sales, earnings, and assets in foreign countries. The American economy as a whole has one fifth of its financial assets in foreign operations.

Without going into extensive statistical detail of foreign investment,[4] it may be pointed out that U.S. foreign economic activity alone is the third largest economic unit in the world, ranking behind the American and Soviet domestic economies. In 1972, American multinationals invested $7.9 billion abroad, over one half of which was reinvested earnings taken from foreign operations themselves. Retained profits for 1972 amounted to $10.4 billion, despite an intrafirm pricing system

---

[2] Christopher Tugendhat, *The Multinationals* (London: Eyre & Spottiswoode, 1971), p. 95.

[3] Steve Babson, "The Multinational Corporation and Labor," *Review of Radical Political Economics* 5(Fall 1973):22.

[4] Paul M. Sweezy and Harry Magdoff, "Growing Wealth, Declining Power," *Monthly Review* 25(March 1974):1–11.

which grossly underestimates true profits.[5] Profit increases on foreign investment for 1973 were 30 to 50 percent higher than in 1972. These profits are largely taken by a relative handful of the corporate giants. These giants are so large as to dwarf many of the national economies within which they operate. Combining the world's largest economies and multinationals, approximately three fifths of the largest 100 economic units are multinationals.[6] For example, General Motors is outstripped in size only by the large advanced industrial economies and by China, India, Brazil, Mexico, and Argentina among the Third World economies. Smaller developed countries such as Switzerland, Denmark, Austria, and Norway are outranked by a host of multinationals, mainly American. Few Third World economies can compare in size with the major multinational firms.

Profits from Third World investments are markedly higher than those made in the developed economies. Labor costs are much lower, tax holidays and concessions are numerous, and raw material extraction yields higher gains than manufacturing. Whereas profits may not greatly exceed investment in developed countries, though much of the investment capital is reinvested profits and loans from local money markets, profits from Third World operations have averaged three times the amount of funds exported into the Third World. Underdeveloped societies serve mainly as a source of raw materials, tropical agricultural products, sites for assembly operations for imported parts, and increasingly as markets for consumer durables. Although the relative number of affluent people in the Third World is small, they constitute a sizable market nevertheless. For example, if only 10 percent of the Brazilian population is able to purchase manufactured goods, this is still a market with a size potential to that of several smaller European countries.

Meanwhile, the per capita income gap between the developed and underdeveloped economies continues to widen. Back in 1850 the per capita income gap between the rich and poor countries was only two to one. By 1950 the ratio had jumped to ten to one, by 1960 15 to one, and by 2000 it would reach 30 to one if trends continue. Part of this

---

[5] Sanjaya Lall's analysis of the multinational's pricing system concludes that "In many cases it is likely that declared profits are but a minor proportion of the total real value of profits remitted abroad by use of transfer prices." *Monthly Review* 26(December 1974):39.

[6] Lester R. Brown, *World Without Borders* (New York: Random House, Inc., 1972), pp. 214–15.

deterioration is due to more rapid population growth in the Third World which eats away at any economic gains; part of it is due to the greater rate of economic growth in the developed world. Population growth has outstripped economic growth in a long list of Third World nations, whereas in all developed countries economic growth has easily surpassed population growth.[7]

The best indigenous growth years for the Third World as a whole were when the developed nations were occupied with Depression and war. Since 1960 and the rapid increase in foreign investment, per capita economic growth in the Third World has been sharply reduced.[8] Even the growth paragon of Brazil had a 1970 foreign debt of $5.2 billion, with debt interest payments alone consuming one third of the country's foreign exchange earnings. To a large extent this poor international financial position is due to the fact that foreign capital controls three fourths of Brazilian heavy industry and consumer durable production.[9] There are other factors, such as a big military equipment import bill. The drain of Latin American capital overall is such that two thirds of the continent's foreign exchange earnings must be turned around for payment to foreigners for profit on investments, debt servicing, royalties and managerial fees, transportation and travel, and other financial demands. With little foreign exchange left to pay for goods imports, which the wealthy desire very much, the balance of payments situation worsens and the debt mounts further. The financial noose with which the rich hold the poor in abeyance can be again tightened. The national bourgeoisie become all the more dependent and subservient to foreign financial and political power.

Despite the wealth of evidence to the contrary, there remain those who contend that the multinational corporation is a force for progressive change in the Third World. Political philosopher Peter Drucker argues that "the multinational of today is—or at least should be—a most effective means to constructive nationhood for the developing world."[10] Drucker holds that the multinational corporations are the crucial entity in the emergence of a world economy, the only real hope

[7] Bill Warren, "Imperialism and Capitalist Industrialization," *New Left Review* 81(September–October 1973):3–44.

[8] Andre Gunder Frank, *Lumpen-Bourgeoisie and Lumpen Development* (New York: Monthly Review Press, 1972), p. 93.

[9] Marcio Moreira Alves, "The Political Economy of the Brazilian Technocracy," *Berkeley Journal of Sociology* 19(1974–75):113.

[10] Peter Drucker, "Multinationals and Developing Countries: Myths and Realities," *Foreign Affairs* 53(October 1974):134.

for most developing countries. A world economy is necessary for the full development of most of the small Third World countries, but clearly not an economy dominated by multinational corporations. There can be no doubt that the multinational corporations are fast spreading the framework of world capitalism and capitalist technology as well. The multinational corporation is the prime instrument for the dissemination of such technology. However, as we shall note presently, the role and impact of advanced technology upon the host country's economy and society heightens rather than diminishes underdevelopment. Technological exchange between advanced capitalist states, such as between the United States and Japan, is quite another thing than the imposition of the latest Western technology upon an underdeveloped country.

Before turning to a closer examination of the underdeveloped economy, it should be mentioned that even critics of world capitalist expansion may view it as a means of Third World development.[11] Marx's early analysis of capitalist development may even be cited as proof of the eventual development of countries where capital is now increasing its hold. However, Lenin's later and more firsthand view of the impact of imperialism suggests that the body of Marxist thought is more correctly interpreted as leading to an interpretation of underdevelopment as a permanent and deepening phenomenon rather than a stage in the transition to developed capitalism. Most Western Marxists hold to the latter interpretation, as do the Chinese. The Soviets, on the other hand, prefer to interpret world bourgeois development as a necessary stage of world history. This explains in part why the Soviet Union is highly opportunistic rather than ideological in its relationships with the Third World. The nonrevolutionary posture of Soviet foreign policy, though arms assistance to the Vietnamese was substantial enough as a commitment to an inevitable winner, is in contradiction to 30 years of Western propaganda on the subject.

The road to balanced growth

The critique of growth as applied to the advanced capitalist states should in no manner be interpreted as a flat rejection of growth per se.

---

[11] Warren, "Imperialism and Capitalist Industrialization."

Our rejection of growth is restricted to superfluous and destructive growth for its own sake. Such misplaced growth costs opportunities to develop much needed growth elsewhere in the world. Growth, then, is desperately needed elsewhere in the world, namely the Third World. The future of mankind hinges extensively upon the nature and extent of economic and technological growth in the underdeveloped regions of the globe. For the nature of this development will determine whether nations and peoples will be able to create cooperative and viable relationships among themselves and between themselves and the environment. Failure on either count will greatly damage survival chances. Growth as is occurring in the advanced countries cannot be repeated on a similar scale in the rest of the world; for that matter it cannot long continue in the advanced countries themselves. The earth's environment and resources have so decreed.

In any event, development after a European or American pattern is in all likelihood impossible. The further growth and development of the advanced regions simply deepens the dependency and underdevelopment of the backward regions. This fact alone will preclude the creation of cooperative international relations. Rather, it will increasingly heighten international tensions, severely destabilize the world economy, and dash any hopes of security and peace. The alternative is growth which is both environmentally tolerable and internationally equalitarian. Neither kind of growth can be achieved within the logic of capitalism which is by definition environmentally blind and internationally unequal. The eradication of underdevelopment with all of its destructive tendencies can only be accomplished through a cooperative worldwide economy oriented directly toward meeting people's needs rather than toward class profit. This eradication may begin within the individual underdeveloped countries themselves, but can be concluded only with the assistance of international development agencies which serve to redistribute power and wealth in a just, humane, and democratic fashion. We have seen how this redistribution has begun to happen in the world's largest nation. A redistribution of power and wealth sets in motion the full productive potential of the population, and the benefits of growth begin to accrue to all equally.

As previously stated, the first step toward balanced growth is economic independence from the constricting tentacles of world capitalism. This was proven first in the Soviet Union, and is again being proven in China. On a smaller scale, Cuba and North Vietnam are other cases in point where major forward strides in development—economic, technological, agricultural, educational, medical, and social equality—have been taken following the ouster of foreign power and its local political allies who cooperated in holding the masses in a condition of subjugation. In any case of development, large or small, the most urgent requirement is that the people's own needs and the country's resources are matched up with economic production and technology.[12] This is so obvious a prescription that it seems redundant to state it. Yet this is precisely what is *not* happening in an underdeveloped society. Investment, production, and technology are geared to meet the financial interests of the national bourgeoisie and foreign companies.

Thus, expensive capital-intensive machinery is imported to produce consumer durables for the small middle and upper classes. In Latin America the top 5 percent of the population takes almost all of the expanded manufacturing of autos, appliances, television, and similar durables. The upper income groups have most of the money to spend for profitable luxury items, and they would rather consume than invest in long-term industrial growth. The host country becomes a mere assemblying ground for foreign-made parts in foreign-owned plants. It lacks its own heavy industry and its own scientific and technological stratum required in the research and development of capital-intensive production. It even lacks a growing industrial working class despite expansion in manufacturing, since this expansion is largely achieved by importing advanced technology. Although industrial production accounted for twice the share of Latin American economic output in 1967 as it did in 1925, the percentage of the labor force employed in industry remained at 14.[13] As a corollary of this pattern of imported capital-intensive technology, unemployment is estimated to be around one fourth of the labor force, and hidden underemployment is much higher, especially among persons not in the formal labor market.[14]

---

[12] Clive Y. Thomas, *Dependence and Transformation: The Economics of the Transition to Socialism* (New York: Monthly Review Press, 1974). This study clarifies the divergence between an underdeveloped society's needs, domestic demand, and economic production, and is important to a full understanding of why economic as well as political independence is necessary for development.

[13] Frank, *Lumpen-Bourgeoisie and Lumpen Development*, p. 112.

[14] See the studies by Sheldon G. Weeks, "Where are all the Jobs? The Informal Sector in Bugisu, Uganda," *The African Review* 3(1), 1973, pp. 111–32; and Tina Wallace, "Working in Rural Buganda: A Study of the Occupational Activities of Young People in Rural Villages," *The African Review* 3(1), 1973, pp. 133–78.

Economic activity in an underdeveloped country is largely undertaken to satisfy the profit requirements and raw material needs of the developed countries and to support the life styles of the Westernized elites in the host country. The elemental housing, food, clothing, sanitary, medical, educational, and occupational needs of the large majority of people are neglected. Balanced development requires that domestic resources be applied to national purposes by way of a technology adapted to local needs and abilities. This means the growth of food as much as possible for domestic consumption instead of plantation crops for export, though some such exports would be required to earn the foreign exchange necessary for essential trade. It means the utilization of mineral wealth to build up domestic industry rather than exporting it for processing into finished products elsewhere. It means an industrial sector which produces enough machinery to manufacture sufficient basic commodities to meet the living and working needs of all the people, including those in the traditional and agricultural sectors. It means a technological level suited to the skills of the labor force, and a means of production which takes advantage of unskilled workers, that is, a more labor-intensive and lightweight production apparatus.

Given these kinds of changes, a developing country could redress the drastic imbalance in foreign trade, which is now one of largely importing expensive finished products and exporting cheaper raw materials. Their lower-priced manufactured goods could compete successfully on the world market, especially in trade with other developing nations. Their balance of payments deficits could be reduced by the elimination of the heavy financial drain made by foreign corporations. Their military imports could be cut as the need for domestic repression would subside, and instead of spending from one third to one half of state budgets on the military, as Brazil, India, and Pakistan do, most of this could go toward education or technical training programs. A military force large enough to protect against foreign interventionists would have to be maintained, but as nationalist revolutions spread, the prospects for international cooperation would increase and hostilities diminish. A nation enmeshed in lifting itself out of the mire of underdevelopment is too occupied domestically to be undertaking foreign military interventions. Of course, it must remain defense conscious, but civilian militia can assume a prominent role in this regard.

The balanced road today means a socialist road, for the national bourgeoisie of the Third World cannot lead an independent economic revolution; they are both too subservient to foreign powers and wedded to the preservation of the political status quo to venture into egalitarian social change. From the Soviet experience, we learn that the socialist road is no automatic consequence of national revolutionary activity, which may lead to the creation of an independent but bureaucratic state. From the Chinese experience we learn that the socialist road requires permanent struggle on the part of the people against the hierarchical and elitist tendencies inherited from the old order. These actual historical models are invaluable to those seeking growth on a social and environmental scale both in the developed and underdeveloped societies.

The choice is between deepening underdevelopment and socialism. The latter choice is itself a hard one and fraught with many difficulties, especially for the smaller nations caught in a vice of international power politics. Both North Vietnam and Cuba have demonstrated that it is possible to deal successfully with these international obstacles and launch socialism in smaller countries. Yet full development, particularly for smaller states, cannot hope to be achieved outside an international network of mutual assistance and cooperation. This fact will continue to loom large for those smaller nations seeking balanced economic development which accrues to the benefit of all the people.

Cuba and underdevelopment

The Cuban case is an informative one from the standpoint of the concept of underdevelopment. Cuba has been carrying on the developmental struggle via socialism for over 15 years, during which time it has experienced both setback and marked advance. The important thing is that substantial developmental gains have been achieved and the road is open for the struggle to overcome the many remaining challenges.

Just off the mainland of the United States, Cuba had long been a rich colony of American corporations. In land, minerals, and natural resources, Cuba has had everything needed for successful economic development. Yet the vast majority of its people subsisted in the misery and poverty of underdevelopment. The chief function of pre-Revolutionary government was to see to the protection and interests of American corporations through tax privileges, favorable tariff controls, cheap labor, and the general political status quo. Cuba served as an off-shore United States corporate plantation and mine, and a whorehouse, casino, and luxury hotel for the vacationing rich. A rural proletariat labored on plantations for the profits of export agrobusinesses, while at the same time facing food shortages and frequent hunger themselves. Miners worked for American nickel, copper, and aluminum interests, while themselves living in a condition of technological backwardness. Urban factory workers assembled finished products for export to the United States, being too poor to purchase or have any use for them themselves. The unemployed masses in the cities and rural slums looked on from their hovels as the rich lavishly spent their portion of the spoils at luxury resorts; even their own beaches had become inaccessible to the underlying population. The Cuban rich lived high with expensive imported goods and thus consumed what domestic wealth might be available for investment and imports for the mass needs. Isolated enclaves of industrial development were matched by a sea of backwardness surrounding them. Unemployment was so extensive that less than two fifths of the labor force was employed all year. Fully 51 percent held jobs for less than ten weeks! A U.S.-supported dictatorship maintained police surveillance. All of the trappings of underdevelopment were present, including racism.[15]

Given the iron-clad dictatorship of the Batista regime, no liberal political advance was possible, even though a considerable amount of radical and reform feeling existed in mines, fields, and factories. Armed insurrection could be the only way to throw off the shackles of underdevelopment. It was in this context that Fidel Castro, an Havana University-educated lawyer, began the Cuban Revolution. Active as a radical lawyer, leader of a 1953 armed assault against the regime and imprisoned, Castro overthrew the Batista regime in 1959 after leading a small but growing army of guerrillas—largely peasants—out of the mountains to a takeover of key military and communications centers. Mass popular demonstrations, a general strike, and the arming of workers and peasants all contributed to the breakdown of bourgeois and army resistance.

Making pre-Revolutionary statements which had liberal reform commitments and avoided socialist overtones, Castro originally stressed

---

[15] Edward Boorstein, *The Economic Transformation of Cuba* (New York: Monthly Review Press, 1968), Chapter 1.

nationalism over socialism, though recognizing socialism as the only solution to Cuba's backwardness. Castro's initial openness to relations with the United States indicated a willingness to move slowly or at least avoid a hard-line confrontation. With the Cuban economy so overwhelmingly oriented to American trade and technology, the achievement of a smooth transition to development could not possibly be accomplished without at best a cooperative and at worst a neutral government in Washington. That Castro was not initially a national villain in the United States, as he soon was to become following a propaganda offensive against him, is symbolized by his ticker tape New York reception shortly after his victory in Havana.

The U.S. oligarchy had previously displayed its intentions to crush national reform movements in the Third World, and it soon launched a massive economic attack against Cuba. A revolutionary success model in Cuba would spell added trouble throughout an already restive Latin America. Given the popularity of the revolution, the U.S. ruling class was well aware of the high military cost of a full-scale invasion of the island. It had hoped for the easy way out by bringing the country to a state of economic collapse. (This strategy of economic disruption was later successful in Chile, where socialism was being pursued within the traditional parliamentary political context.) The Cubans responded to the economic blockade with determination and ingenuity, and with assistance from the Soviet Union and Eastern Europe overcame the initial disruptive impact of trade and technological isolation. Given hindsight on the Cuban case, the American ruling class militarily crushed a democratic reform movement in the Dominican Republic in 1965. Military aid to Latin American military dictatorships increased greatly following the Cuban Revolution.

The task of restructuring an underdeveloped economy and society was an imposing one. The formal plans offered by advanced state-controlled systems, such as Czechoslovakia, were ill-suited to the concrete realities of the Cuban context, and many costly mistakes in production and distribution were made. Nationalization of industry moved slowly but steadily, so that by the end of 1960 80 percent was state-controlled. Nationalization included all of the major industries, transportation, utilities, exporting, and finance. Entertainment and recreation facilities were also expropriated and opened to the Cuban public. As 15 years later in South Vietnam, the Revolution moved against corruption, gangsterism, vice, gambling, and prostitution—at the whole underbelly of the old bourgeois culture. The import of luxury items was stopped and foreign exchange deployed for the essentials of building an independent economy, such as for industrial and agricultural equipment instead of expensive automobiles and gourmet foods. Most of the good farmland was expropriated and collectivized, and an agricultural labor force accustomed to large-scale plantation capitalism were largely supportive of the process. A system of absentee landlordism had dissolved rural loyalties to the past order, not to mention the forces of hunger, disease, and illiteracy.

The Revolution was faced with an enormous backlog of social problems in medical care, literacy, education, housing, diet, employment, sanitation, and poverty in general. Regardless of the inroads such social needs make upon economic investment, they are of utmost importance in the overall developmental process. Indeed, they are what a socialist revolution is all about. Thus, social expenditures must share importantly in what wealth is available to a developing society, even though industrial and technical needs are also urgent. The two sides must be mutually reinforcing of one another; industrial advance promotes greater social security, while social improvement lends the necessary background to technological and industrial development. This interaction has been at work in Cuba. Cuba's achievements in health care, education, employment, housing, nutrition, and recreation have been significant.[16]

Agricultural production had been largely collectivized in the early years of the Revolution; approximately one fourth remains in private hands. An immediate policy of agricultural diversification brought on a serious trade deficit inasmuch as the new economy was not yet prepared to operate efficiently from a position of diversification after a long history of sugar monoculture.[17] The strategy returned to that of pushing sugar production to ever higher levels in order to obtain the foreign exchange necessary to purchase the tools and machines of agriculture and industry, which could then lay the foundation for full diversification. Friendly critics of Cuba have observed the dangers in too great a preoccupation with sugar production and the distortion it produces within the economy and society. However, legacies of the old

---

[16] See "Cuba: Ten Years After," *Trans-action*, April, 1968; also available as I. L. Horowitz, ed., *Cuban Communism* (Chicago: Aldine-Atherton, 1970).

[17] Leo Huberman and Paul M. Sweezy, *Socialism in Cuba* (New York: Monthly Review Press, 1970), pp. 65–85.

order take time to overcome. Productivity in agriculture has been significantly increased. Animal husbandry has been developed and emphasized. Milk production has been greatly increased and rationed to the country's children.

Work brigades consisting of government officials and students do tours of duty in agriculture, particularly at harvest time, while farm workers attend schools and educational classes. An official government statement reads, "Bureaucracy is a legacy from the capitalist system. Its complete and radical elimination is fundamental in achieving the complete triumph of the Revolution."[18] There has been, then, an attempt to break down the sharp cleavage between city and country, industrial and agricultural labor. Sexual inequality has also been under attack in a traditional masculine culture, and major gains have been recorded for women, though many inequities remain to be erased.[19] In race relations, the Cuban black has traveled an especially long route from inequality and degradation to equal treatment and status.

Wealth has been fundamentally redistributed. Income disparities are easily the smallest in Latin America and employment rates approach the full level, albeit there remain shortcomings in the efficient application of labor time and resources. Like China, Cuba has placed considerable emphasis upon nonmaterial or moral incentives in work. Empirical research by Wisconsin sociologist Maurice Zeitlin indicates a prevalence of positive attitudes toward work and a refurbished interest in the process of production following the change of regimes.[20]

Although the Cuban Revolution has advanced a great distance and overcome major obstacles in its path, the transition to full socialism has only just begun and its completion is, of course, by no means guaranteed. Success depends upon the ability of leadership to avoid the deadly sterility of rigidly centralized, authoritarian, and hierarchic self-perpetuating bureaucracy and to cultivate the full participation of the people in the organization and planning of new and emerging social, political, and economic institutions. In this manner, too, another class stratified re-creation of the old society upon a new state-administered base may be averted.

---

[18] "Bureaucracy and Revolution," in Rolando E. Bonachea and Nelson P. Valdes, eds., *Cuba in Revolution* (New York: Doubleday & Company, Inc., 1972), p. 176.

[19] Petur Gudjonsson, "Women in Castro's Cuba," *The Progressive*, August, 1972, pp. 25–29.

[20] Maurice Zeitlin, *Revolutionary Politics and the Cuban Working Class* (Princeton: Princeton University Press, 1967), p. 295.

The Cuban people have obtained a new lease on life with the Revolution. Daily survival is no longer the pressing concern for the masses it had previously been. Living standards have been continually improved. A level of economic security is afforded everyone and the real promise of a better future is available to all. With today's high level of literacy, and the presence of medical clinics throughout the countryside, the Cuban birth rate has declined to among the lowest in all of Latin America, significantly below its Caribbean and Central American neighbors. Thus, there are strong indications that there is a gradual alleviation of demographic pressures taking place within Cuba as well. The survival of socialism in Cuba, difficult as the beginnings were and as challenging as the future might be, has assured higher levels of human survival for the great majority of people on this small island nation.

"Affluent underdevelopment"

As the Cuban case demonstrated, selling one's fate to the multinational corporation as a means of development is an ill-chosen path to follow. The promise of instant industry and financing may prove irresistibly tempting, but the long-range outcome is very costly. Even such a rich and privileged country as Canada has come to understand the penalties of selling out to foreign capital. Kari Levitt, McGill University economist, argues that "present-day Canada may be described as the world's richest underdeveloped country."[21] Foreign corporations, mostly American, account for three fourths of Canada's economic output, while foreigners control approximately two thirds of all Canadian natural resources.[22] Canada has only one fifth of its labor force in manufacturing, less than every Western nation except Greece and Ireland. As a result, Canada is the world's leading importer of manufactured goods, $463 per capita compared to $239 for the European Economic Community, $116 for the United States, and $41 for Japan.[23] In true underdeveloped fashion, 70 percent of exports to the United States consists of raw materials.

---

[21] Kari Levitt, *Silent Surrender* (Toronto: Macmillan, 1971), p. 25.

[22] See Robert M. Laxer, *Canada Ltd.: The Political Economy of Dependency* (Toronto: McClelland and Stewart Limited, 1973).

[23] James Laxer, *Canada's Energy Crisis* (Toronto: James Lewis & Samuel, Publishers, 1974), p. 117.

Canada has nearly all of the minerals and raw materials for an independent industrial sector, yet even what industry the country does have depends extensively upon fabrication, assembly, and primary processing. The crucial heavy industrial, scientific, and technological core of Canadian society is determined largely by foreign interests.[24] Canadian scientists and engineers go jobless or underemployed as the head office consigns research and development to American-based operations. Canadian workers rely extensively upon the service and government sectors to provide employment, and Canadian taxpayers pay the cost of operating a top heavy white-collar and service sector. Canadian tax burdens are as large or larger than those of Americans, despite Canada's small military outlays and comparable welfare spending. Canadian taxes shore up a tertiary employment sector to offset the loss of industrial jobs to the United States. The areas of the country outside the focus of American investment, which is largely concentrated in southern Ontario, may have unemployment and poverty rates three times the Ontario rate.[25] Canadian provinces are rich or poor depending upon what interests American capital might have in their labor force, markets, and raw materials.

American multinational firms in Canada operate inefficiently owing to the fact that several firms in the same production line serve a population of only 23 million, with resulting duplication, under-utilization, and high prices. Worst of all, Canadians do not have control over their own economic fate, since whenever the times dictate, American owners can shut down plants and transfer operations out of the country. Canadians cannot govern the most crucial investment decisions affecting their country's future; these decisions are made in the board rooms of the United States. Indeed, Canadian investment capital cannot find adequate outlets within its own country, inasmuch as American-owned subsidiaries preclude Canadian stock ownership. Thus, we have the ironic situation of Canadian investors having to enter the American market for want of local outlets. Even such a critical area as energy finds Canadians dependent upon the actions of foreign oil monopolies, which are always able to keep Canadian governments in tow. The better part of Canada's oil and gas production has been siphoned off across

[24] Abraham Rotstein and Gary Lax, *Getting It Back* (Toronto: Clarke, Irwin & Company, Ltd., 1974).

[25] Ian Adams et al., *The Real Poverty Report* (Edmonton: M. G. Hurtig Limited, 1971), p. 63.

the border by American oil companies, leaving Canadians with their long, cold winters looking at shrinking reserves in southern fields and costly, environmentally hazardous, northern development.

Beyond the economic dependence of Canada, and its highly vulnerable political situation vis-a-vis the U.S. corporate state, its subservient position in the American empire has all but crushed anything that could be considered Canadian culture and identity—save for a few pockets of European-influenced subcultures. Canada has been unable to generate a national culture and identity; even the will to do so is largely lacking. The Canadian bourgeoisie are satisfied with their comfortable dependence and affiliation with the American superpower, while the rank and file passively adjust to whatever standards of culture and economy happen to prevail to the south. Canada, or any other country, cannot import American economic and technological modes without getting with them most of the social and cultural superstructure which rides along. Canada is among the rich, but its destiny lies at the feet of the American corporate state. This is not a position to be envied.

The Canadian road to independent and full economic development would be, of course, much shorter than that which the poor underdeveloped countries face. Yet as the stability of the American economic empire is eroded, the cost of being a subsidiary to the heartland is going to be high. Those who have struggled forward on an independent road to development will reap far greater rewards in the future as a result of their independence than will those countries which sold out their resources, environment, and people to the profit-minded schemes of powerful foreign investors.

13

Toward survivalism

Guidelines

Where do we go from here? This is a question that has been raised
in response to this study several times. It is a question frequently
raised by students in discussions of these topics. If our society is moving in an untenable direction, digging itself deeper and deeper into its
own grave, what is to be done to reverse the process and set social
change onto a constructive course?

Throughout the book we have made scattered but frequent allusions
to what should be done. Economic growth as an end in itself should
be slowed and placed on a course which has largely social and environmental ends in mind. There is no point in being dragged down by the
demands of an impersonal economic system which has only its own
survival requisites as guidelines. The salvage operations for capitalism
are becoming more costly in both human and environmental terms. Its
survival is endangering societal survival. The broad course of action is
evident here: reconstruct the economic system so as to meet human
survival needs and set aside the antiquated assumptions of profit and
growth. Call this new economic system socialism if you will; call it
something else, such as survivalism, if socialism has come to mean
monolithic state power. What it is called is not especially important.
What its aims and aspirations are to be is important, as is how these
goals are to be achieved. Beyond saying that both ends and means

270

should be democratically achieved, do not ask how to go about creating an economy subjected to human and environmental requirements. If a detailed blueprint could be worked out, and no single individual could obviously accomplish such a task, it would merely be dismissed as "utopian" by the skeptics. They would smugly put the question, "Where has it ever happened? Answer: nowhere. What evidence is there it *can* happen? Answer: none." Where would human civilization have ever come if members of the status quo had been shackled with such fatalism? Answer: nowhere. Never let skeptics obstruct your visions with the defeatism of "it has never existed before." Obviously the future has never existed before. It is up to human beings to create and carve out that future. Those with positions of power and privilege in the status quo will surely attempt to dim and discourage creative social imagination. When they succeed in this, then the sociology of survival is finished.

So if you are working at a mind-dulling task, a wasteful task, an environmentally destructive task, or if you have no task to work at at all, think of what you might do to develop yourself as an individual, to enhance the well-being of others, to conserve the delicate life of the ecosphere, and to fully occupy your life in an integrated work and leisure. When entire groups of individuals begin to think, and then act, in such a fashion, then the rudiments of a new economy will begin to emerge. Human social psychology is not so diverse as to send everyone in different directions in their search for a viable life. Human social psychology is remarkably uniform in its desire for material security, a sense of personal satisfaction, a need to be engaged in worthwhile activity, and the desire for sociality. Surely this psychology has been convoluted and distorted by existing institutions in many ways. However, these distortions can be modified, even eliminated in the act of social reconstruction.

Entire groups of individuals have already broken from the existing economic order and are working toward communal economy, mostly in isolated rural settings. These are very small, but not insignificant, beginnings. The problems involved are so much larger than meets the eye of an agricultural commune. Yet it is this same spirit of radical reorientation of values and production which must be instituted on a vastly larger "social structural" scale within the urban-industrial context. The breakdown of narrow specialization as a lifetime routine can be made to give way to the broadening experiences of a mixed work experience within which producers work directly to meet socially defined needs within the group. In this way, people produce what they need rather than needing to consume what someone else has produced in order to keep an ownership class in business. The environment is greatly spared in the process, as is waste of time and resources. Time may be wasted, but freely rather than as a slave of massive machinery owned by someone else.

What shall we do with all our newly acquired time once wasteful work and production has been left behind? In the first place, there is so much worthwhile and necessary work to be done in meeting the simple rudiments of life that no one need to be concerned about idleness. Environmental, conservational, agricultural, housing, educational, medical, transportation, energy, recreational, and social needs cry out on an enormous scale for solutions. Reorienting the production system from goods for profit to goods for use would itself require the time and talents of large numbers of workers. In the second place, if people so liberated to pursue their social and economic ends cannot conceive of how to use their time, there would seem to be little justification for human life itself. Turn the earth back over to species which do have something to do within the realm of evolutionary life other than ravish and consume.

Need it be further stressed that the human species must limit its population if it is to live with any dignity or even in the long run survive? A stationary population is mandatory if the other problems of survival are to be met. This means no more than approximately two children per female as an average. If individual restraint is not sufficient, social controls will have to be worked out and firmly carried through. Each society must at first be its own demographic caretaker, and the careless ones will endure their own demographic problems. Yet the overflow of irresponsible population growth is felt around the world, as for example in heavy demands upon the soils of countries with surplus agricultural potential. Thus, international organizations could conceivably be required to act politically and economically (that is, sharply reduce food shipments to irresponsible governments and countries, making them face the reality of self-sufficiency in a shrinking world).

By the same token, levels of consumption among the overdeveloped countries must commensurately be cut back in the name of global survival. Irresponsibility in economic life is no more tolerable than it is in demographic areas. But now we may be accused of preaching to sinners, another pitfall of trying to chart new directions.

The new environmentalism must be much more than doing away with litterbugs and cutting down billboards. Environmental survival chances are much enhanced by the aforesaid reduction of consumption. But the nature of consumption must itself be transformed: the manner in which we eat, dress, furnish our homes, transport ourselves, use leisure. Questions which must be asked: What pollution effects are produced by the products we consume? What are the energy sources used in their production? How long will the products last? Can they be reused or recycled? What are their environmental impacts in raw material extraction, use, and disposal? In every case, products must be sought out which have positive evaluations on these questions, and it must be done at the point of production rather than at that of individual consumption where the individual may be forced by the structure of things to act wrongly in environmental terms. Insofar as possible, production should be based on local and regional resources, and self-sufficiency should be held out as an ideal maxim. In the production process itself, environmental concerns must be given full weight rather than sacrificed as necessary byproducts of human life in technological society. This is not to say that all pollution be eliminated, an impossible task. It is to say that environmental costs be reckoned directly into the current accounting books and the debts be paid on an ongoing basis. It is to say that waste byproducts be turned into reusable materials even if it is not "profitable." Environmental research and the development of environmentally conservative technology need to replace the current emphasis on marketing what the public does not need and developing endless military sophistication.

Tying into population and environment is the problem of food supply. A stationary population is clearly going to be better able to feed itself and an environmentally conservative population is going to attain greater long-term soil productivity. More labor-intensive production might well be advised for a viable society insofar as in many instances human labor is less resource-consumptive and environmentally destructive than costly advanced agricultural techniques. Might not an army of bureaucrats and office workers sitting at fluorescent-lit desks in hermetically sealed air conditioned buildings be more useful weeding a field of crops twice a week than devising more efficient ways to handle paper and people; the use of herbicides could be commensurately reduced and the biosphere and environment, not to mention food quality, could be better preserved. In the meantime, all the energy used to keep the skyscrapers going could be saved. The costs of medicine in treating sedentary related illnesses could be reduced. These office workers turned manual workers might also find their way into the production of cotton and wool, materials created basically from solar energy, and thus alleviate the pressures upon synthetic fibers and their energy-intensive production. If given the choice, how many people would go on preferring to wear polyester clothes eight hours a day in an office built of unidentifiable synthetics while arranging meaningless columns of figures if they could wear cotton or wool they themselves had a hand in producing or processing when and how they wished to do so? Producers can be brought so much closer to producing the things they themselves need and use, and in the process gain a greater understanding of the technical and environmental aspects of production. This holds true for industrial as well as agricultural goods.

It is intriguing that so many people enjoy their pastimes much more than their work, and that they plan their lives around these pastimes, many of them productive or potentially productive, rather than around their work. Many men are much more content working in their gardens than in their office or factory. Why must they squeeze garden work in between their eight-hour wage days? Why could they not be full-time gardeners and part-time office workers? They could in an economic order they devised to so parcel their time. The same holds true for every other leisure interest with productive content. Even no content at all would be better than much of the consumptive make-work known today as employment. Such employment serves to distribute income (unequally) and as a sociality milieu, but these functions could be handled better in alternative ways, not the least important of which would be aforesaid neglected areas of social need.

Urbanization cannot continue as it has in the past without raising the costs of survival. The giant megapolis has no place in the survival society. Cities there certainly should be; unwieldy conglomerates of many millions pose severe environmental, technological, and economic problems. A giant city of millions can be made to work in a fairly balanced fashion, but not under the weight of heavy consumption and expanding technology. It becomes a social system beyond the safe control of its human members. The threat of disruption and breakdown mounts and the quality of life for the large majority diminishes. The ongoing flight from the central city to suburbs reflects in part the un-acceptability of urban living in the growth society. The urban-suburban imbalance has only added to the woes of metropolitan regions, financially, racially, and for general social integration. Smaller population units enable people to get a better grip on the forces affecting their lives and a better possibility of taking a hand in shaping these forces. This is not to say that such is the case in today's society; the potential for greater democracy, however, is present.

A society ordered by and for participating individuals will not re-quire the mountainous government bureaucracies which encumber the growth society and endeavor to hold it together with debt and regula-tion. A viable society holds itself together voluntarily and self-reli-antly; there is no necessity for professional politicians and government administrators. There are organizations with elected representatives directly responsible to their groups, but most of the crucial decision-making is done right within work and community units and not at a distance by careerists and experts. Here again, decentralization is basic to the achievement of political aims.

We have previously stressed the importance of equality to survival. Given the current economic and technological realities, the continua-tion of the marked inequalities within and between societies cannot persist without the intensification of conflict. This conflict may be the prerequisite to the establishment of substantial social equality, since the powerful and privileged are not likely to engineer their own demise to positions of equality. This is not equality in any literal and rigid sense where everybody is rationed identical amounts of goods and services. It is a flexible equality within which everybody is entitled to access to what the economy and culture has to offer in the way of values. Some of these values would in all likelihood have to be rationed or awarded by group decision to different individuals. Other values could be made available to everyone without restriction. Again this implies the exis-tence of group consciousness and responsibility on the part of the in-dividual; a sense of what is needed and due must be developed to re-place the current stockpiling, hoarding, and insecurity. This requires the restoration of trust between people and groups, the building of confidence in the future of one's society and way of life. The growth society can never instill this trust and confidence. It can no longer even sell financial stakes in its most important and largest city, the very center of its own financial existence. Only a society building upon a foundation of equality can hope to begin working for social trust and confidence.

Withering of bureaucracy and the state? Social equality? Decentralization of people and power? Fusion of work and leisure? Integration of manual and mental labor? And end to economic growth? Environmental priorities over profit? Agricultural investment over military spending? An end of population growth? The spread of social trust and confidence? An impossible heaven on earth say the proponents of growth and capitalism. Utter utopianism say many observers of human history and society. A great many other people have seen the human condition in different terms and envision the possibility of building toward a world which holds the kinds of values and priorities alluded to above.

Time and survivalism

Basic to the construction of a viable society is a new conception of time. This fact has been implied in much of the preceding discussion. So much of what is wrong within the present system is linked with its preoccupation with time. To capitalism, or any growth society, time is money. The amount of time required to produce something is relentlessly pushed lower and lower. We analyzed the economic forces behind such a push in the early chapters. Here it is stressed only that time must be liberated from the restrictions the growth society places upon it. When this happens, when time is freed from the mandates of profit and growth, then time can be used on behalf of survival. There will be no pressing need to reduce the time it takes to produce something, thereby, all importantly, reducing the heavy drain on energy, resources, and environment.

The liberation of time thus goes hand in hand with the liberation of labor from capital. It also goes hand in hand with decentralization and small-scale production, even to the level of individual physical labor—an act which has come to be degraded by growth advocates who can flourish only by selling the latest "labor-saving" devices. (May it be noted that such labor-saving devices very often require far more time and energy in their production, servicing and replacement than more simple and direct, but "outdated," methods.)

When time is freed from the demands of profit and growth, that

which is produced can be produced with the kind of care and delibera-
tion which yields the quality of traditional craftsmanship. Indeed, a
survivalist society should proceed with a combination of artistic and
scientific motivations. Science, like craft and art, cannot be rushed, programmed, and operated by a timeclock—at least not a survivalist science. The social and psychological satisfaction of engaging in meaning-
ful and productive activities, conceived, planned, and implemented by
individuals in cooperating groups, can become a widespread reality.
Think of the time and resource savings in medicine and mental health
alone by such an event. Further, that which is produced is then produced to last, truly durable goods that acquire a character and permanence of their own. The implications for energy, resources, and environment are obvious.

This all does not imply a return to "back-breaking" hand labor and
the elimination of power machinery, although it could well involve
considerably more physical work than most people are accustomed to
in the growth society. (Imagine the impact of an activist society upon
mass spectatorship businesses such as television, Hollywood movies,
and professional sports when people do not have "free time" to sit idly
in front of screens.) It does imply a new view of machinery and technology in general, a view which promotes balance in human activity
and in nature instead of pursuing a robot world. Such balance can become a reality only within a time-flexible society.

There exists a profound contradiction regarding time within the
present society. While the time required to produce something has
been unceasingly compressed, the obverse consequence has been an
increasing amount of "non-work" or "free time," at least for large
numbers of people. As alluded to above, this free time is heavily absorbed by passive consumption. Add together the number of hours
people spend in essentially aimless traveling about in motorized vehicles with those spent as spectators and a sizeable chunk of free time
may be accounted for. Much of this sort of time usage is crucial for
growth through consumption. In effect, people perform vital functions
for profit and growth both in work and free time; some people perform
more of one than the other.

It is evident that free time as time spent not working as a wage
earner is fundamentally different from the meaning of the liberation
of time from the mandates of capital. Free time under capitalism serves
functions vital to growth, whereas liberated time is the servant of noth-

ing except for its human users who arrange its use according to entirely social and environmental needs. This means a substantial fusion of work and leisure and an inability to proceed with the whole system of hourly wages. Growth advocates will uniformly oppose the breakdown of the work-leisure dichotomy, for it is at the heart of the growth system.

Individual behavior and social change

The foregoing discussion of the move toward survivalism should in no way be interpreted in solely individual or moralistic terms, though as individuals there is much that can be done to enhance the prospects of survivalism. If as individuals, consumers refused to purchase or use spray cans, for example, they could not be profitably marketed and the atmospheric damages to the ozone layer could be thereby reduced. The boycott remains effective weapon, and its success depends upon individual motivation and moral decision. Such private actions, however, cannot change the structure of the economy and society, which must be done if survivalism is to triumph. Structural change, change in the formal patterns of economic and social relationships, is indeed initiated by individuals acting in groups. But the consequences of these groups' actions add up to society-wide changes which are capable of sweeping aside old institutions and replacing them with new ones. The new institutions evolve as a process within the revolutionary social context. These new patterns of action enable everyone to freely act positively in survivalist terms rather than channeling their behavior toward a negative collective impact upon survivalist concerns. This is the meaning of structural change. Such change not only permits the individual to behave in survivalist fashion, it makes such behavior a societal rule or norm.

We have still said nothing as to how the process of structural change is set off, other than that individuals working in groups are the pivotal instruments. Nor have we specified how long it might take to build a viable society, or whether those people living today will be willing to make the changes and sacrifices necessary for the well-being of generations not yet born. These are large and difficult questions, perhaps unanswerable in advance of any given case. We have seen other societies launch upon a path of radical structural change, knowing that the course is long and the benefits often delayed. We thus know it *can* happen and will in all likelihood happen again and again. *How* it happens is less well known, and the dynamics may differ substantially from one case to the next. Certainly the dynamics of structural change in advanced industrial society would differ drastically from those involved in underdeveloped society. Since revolutionary change has not overtaken an advanced industrial society, we have not even a case history of one such event to study and learn from. If the dynamics of setting off structural change in mature capitalism were known, the process would probably already be underway. This *is* the problem. Societies do not undergo structural changes by themselves; in fact, there is an enormous built-in resistance and inertia. It is this resistance which change-oriented groups always meet, and it can be overcome only when these groups are large and strong enough to do so.

The move toward survivalism thus need not wait upon total societal transformation, though its success certainly does depend upon such structural change. Scattered individuals and groups may perform crucial experimental and prototypal functions, while the institutionalization of survivalism awaits profound social reconstruction. The concrete nature of these institutions and how they come into being can only be understood within the actual change situation, where ideas and practice interact to form the new social reality. Whatever the diverse specifics of the new order, it is mandatory that their individual and combined impact is supportive of the several survivalist concerns. This implies arduous and lengthy innovation and experimentation.

Clearly there will be costs, but there also must be invoked a new cost calculus, one that does not have the profits of an ownership class at the fore of concern as today. If such private profit concerns are set aside, a whole variety of new action opportunities are possible in areas relevant to economic production, use of labor, use of resources, energy, food production, and environment. For example, without profit drives, labor does not have to be subjected to ever increasing intensive energy consumption; labor time would not represent money and profit and could be applied with, for example, conservation and environmental impacts in mind. By the same token, smaller-scale production blends with "less efficient" use of labor time, while decentralization of people and power also harmonizes with such a noncapitalist cost calculus for labor. Unemployment could become both unnecessary and unlikely, while social needs could be met on a much broader scale than is possible in today's debt-ridden economy.

Advanced industrial societies are fortunate in that they have so many of the scientific and technological resources necessary to lay the foundations of a survivalist society; these societies are unfortunate in that their sophisticated science and technology has been all too frequently applied in such wasteful and destructive ways. The time has come for a reversal in the military and profit logic of scientific and technological application. This will be necessary for the survivalist society, both because the continuation of the present logic is suicidal and a survivalist science and technology will be crucial to successful social reconstruction.

It is perhaps much easier to drift along with the currents of the present society, trying to make it here and there as individuals and legislate a variety of ameliorative policies and programs in hopes of staving off an open defeat of the system. The results of such a course will become increasingly ineffective, costly, and irreversible in damages done. It is perhaps much harder to forge a new economy and society which have the conditions for permanence and viability. Yet time is running out on the possibilities for a successful move toward a survivalist society. What an agronomist had to say about the aspect of survival which most concerned him, feeding the world's people, applies in a large way to the other survival challenges dealt with in this study: the time is already five minutes past 12.

Name index

Leibnitz, 120
Lekachman, Robert, 82 n, 83, 96 n
Lenin, 258
Levitt, Kari, 267
Lewis, Russell, 62 n
Linder, Staffan, B., 16, 166 n
Lipset, S. M., 32 n
Loraine, John A., 121 n, 191 n

M

McCormick, Cyrus, 225
MacEwan, Arthur, 48 n, 158 n
McFarlane, Bruce, 244 n
McHale, John, 93 n, 127 n, 137 n, 149 n, 154 n, 205 n
Machetzki, Rudiger, 248 n
McKean, Roland N., 26 n
Maddison, Angus, 37 n
Magdoff, Harry, 27 n, 48, 73 n, 111, 255 n
Malthus, Thomas, 54, 200–201
Mamdani, Mahmood, 182
Mandel, Ernest, 46 n, 74, 168, 197
Marglin, Stephen A., 106
Marx, Karl, 9, 29, 45–46, 49, 57, 61, 121, 140, 164, 172, 198, 200, 225, 226 n, 230, 258
Matthews, Mervyn, 237 n
Meadows, Donella H., 90
Meek, Ronald L., 173 n
Miles, Michael W., 99 n, 102 n
Mill, J. S., 25–26, 34 n, 39–40, 54–55, 57–58, 61, 89, 168, 172
Mills, C. Wright, 16
Mishan, E. J., 15, 20, 27, 165–68
Miyamoto, Ken'ichi, 39
Morgan, J. P., 83
Morris, Jacob, 16 n
Murray, Martin, 160 n

N

Nagel, Stuart S., 146 n
Nicolaus, Martin, 72 n
Nordhaus, 143

O

O'Connor, James, 78 n
Orleans, Leo A., 77, 178 n, 249 n

P

Packard, Vance, 15–16, 58
Paddock, Paul, 207, 215
Paddock, William, 207, 215
Parker, Richard, 17 n, 29 n, 224 n
Perelman, Michael, 140 n
Pincus, Fred, 99 n
Pirages, Dennis, 237 n

Q–R

Quartim, Joao, 126 n, 188
Reilly, William K., 137 n, 189
Revelle, Roger, 192 n
Ricardo, 54
Ridgeway, James, 71 n, 161 n
Rockefeller, Laurence, 137–39
Rockefeller, Nelson, 62
Roelofs, Robert T., 119 n, 120 n
Rosenberg, Nathan, 93
Roszak, Theodore, 35
Rotstein, Abraham, 268 n
Rowland, Wade, 130 n, 136 n
Ruff, Larry E., 143 n
Rusk, Dean, 159–60

S

Salgo, Harvey, 33 n, 58 n
Schenk, Hans, 182
Schmookler, Jacob, 94
Schumacher, E. F., 27 n, 35 n
Schurr, Sam H., 25 n, 30 n, 60 n, 132 n, 143 n, 148 n, 153 n
Scitovsky, Tibor, 169 n
Segal, Ronald, 80 n
Sharma, Hari P., 37 n
Singer, Fred, 150 n
Slonim, Gilven, 165
Smith, Adam, 112
Smith, Desmond, 161 n
Socolow, Robert H., 57 n
Sorokin, Pitirim, 61
Soth, Lauren, 224 n
Spengler, Joseph J., 192 n
Stavis, Ben, 247 n
Stone, Katherine, 107
Sundquist, James, 189 n
Suttmeier, Richard P., 249 n
Sweezy, Paul M., 27 n, 44 n, 73 n, 78, 116, 255 n, 265 n
Sykes, Philip, 156 n

T

Tanzer, Michael, 37–38, 154 n, 156 n, 158
Teitelbaum, Michael, 184
Tellenbeck, Sten, 237 n
Thomas, Clive Y., 211 n, 260 n
Tien, H. Yuan, 178 n
Tobin, 143
Toynbee, Arnold, 55, 90 n
Trimberger, Ellen Kay, 100 n
Tugendhat, Christopher, 254–55
Turner, James S., 19 n

U–V

Ulmer, Melville J., 164 n

Subject index

285

New York State, 137
  abortion law, 184
Newsweek, 16
No-growth society, 26 n, 28, 32, 46, 57,
    60, 101
Noise, 15
Nonaffluent classes, 79–80
  loans to, 72
  redistribution of income of, 74
Noncapitalist society, 46
Nonconsumptive services, 64
North America, 240
  agricultural surpluses, 202
  cropland, 205
North Vietnam, 259, 262
Norway, 256
Nuclear energy, 162
Nuclear fission, 130
Nuclear fusion, 130, 162–63
  food created by, 215
Nuclear holocaust, threat of, 6
Nuclear power, 130
  proliferation of, 6

O

Obsolescence; *see specific type*
Occupational specialization and hier-
    archy, 103–8
Oil
  consumption, 153–54
  energy source, 156–59
  expansion in demand for, 158–59
  giganticism, 160
  glut, 157
  power, 159–64
  price revolution, 160
  production, 38, 134
  tax position, 160–61
Oil companies, 157–58
  nuclear field, 162
  power of, 159
  tax favors to, 160–61
Oil shale deposits, 156–57, 161–62
  in situ extraction of oil, 161–62
OPEC, 157–58
Open space, loss of, 15
Oppression, 232
Organizational growth, 24
Overcultivation, 121
Overdeveloped societies, 3
Overeducation for job requirements, 99
Overgrazing, 121, 203
Overpopulation, 16, 152–53, 170–74
  capital development in relation to,
    172–73
Overproduction, 58

P

Pakistan, 37, 219, 261
Paper money, 73
Paper waste, 123
Participatory democracy, 3, 32
Particulate matter, emission of, 125–26
Past decade, highlights of, 1
Pauperism, 29
Payroll taxes, 77–78
Peasant agricultural society, 181–83
  elimination of, 198–99, 201
Pep pills, 165
Per capita income, 193
Permanence, value of, 58
Personal development, 3
Personal property taxes, 78
Pessimism, areas of, 22
Pesticides, threat of, 227–28, 241
Petroleum; *see* Oil
Petroleum Engineer, 160
Philippines, 192
Physical survival, 14–15
Physical threat, 15
Pill, the, 185
Planned reorganization of society, 54
Point of no return in major life-giving
    systems, 12–13
Poland, 184
Political democracy, 32
Political equality, 32
Political oppression, 32
Political organization, 5
  importance of, 6
Political revolution, 201
Politics and food supply, 201–2
Politics of liberation, 108
Pollution, 2, 10, 15; *see also specific
    types and* Environment
  costs of, 30–31, 141
  Soviet socialism, 239–40
  technological solution to, 130–31
Pollution tax, 145
Population, 5, 10
  control of, 90–91
  food supply and, 202–6
  limitation of, 272
  Malthusian positive checks on, 177
  optimal level of, 56
  resources and, 151–53
  socialism, 236
  stationary-state society, 56–57
  substantial number, 151–53
  technology and, 88–93
Population explosion, 2, 6, 10, 34
Population growth, 4, 9, 11, 24, 170–96,
    257

This book has been set in 10 point Palatino leaded 3 points, and 9 point Palatino leaded 2 points. Chapter numbers are 30 point Palatino roman, and chapter titles are 24 point Palatino italic. The size of the type page is 26 × 44 picas.